THE GREAT LOCK-OUT
OF 1926

By the same author
Princess Alice

Gerard Noel

THE GREAT LOCK-OUT
OF 1926

Constable London

First published in Great Britain 1976
by Constable and Company Ltd
10 Orange Street London WC2H 7EG
Copyright © 1976 Gerard Noel

ISBN 0 09 461160 2

Set in Monotype Bembo
Printed in Great Britain by
The Anchor Press Ltd
and bound by
Wm Brendon & Son Ltd
both of Tiptree, Essex

To
P, R, & E

Contents

Illustrations

ILLUSTRATIONS

Preface

This book tells the story of the period from just before the General Strike of 1926 until nearly seven months later, during which Britain's million miners were locked out of work through the worst industrial dispute of its kind we have ever experienced.

Apart from the fact that the book's main stress lies elsewhere than on the well-known nine days of the actual Strike, it differs in two principal respects from other studies of the period. It is an informal sketch rather than a detailed chronicle based on heavy documentation from written sources. I have used the latter primarily to build a framework within which to tell the story as I myself heard it from veteran miners and others with vivid memories of 1926. The tale is thus told very largely from their point of view.

This does not mean that the mineowners have automatically become the villains of the piece. Herein lies part of the second differentiating factor. For I have devoted what may seem, at first sight, a somewhat disproportionately large share of space to the 'build-up', mostly political, to the actual Lock-Out (as I have throughout described what some others have referred to as a 'strike'). I have done this in order to highlight the connection between the shrewdly long-term speculations of Stanley Baldwin – as the 'man for the Establishment' – and the definitive domestic conflict of the inter-war period, namely the long struggle over the status of the mining industry and those who worked in it.

I have, finally, resisted the temptation to attempt anything approaching a final judgement on the 'legacy' of the Lock-Out. It seemed more appropriate, in a book so largely built on oral testimony, to end with selected quotations of the remarks made by some of the numerous men and women who have been so enormously helpful in the preparation of the book. To the large amount of people I have met and listened to, whether in cottages in County Durham, Working Men's Clubs in Rhondda Valley, one thousand feet underground at Hem Heath Colliery, Stafford-shire, or many unexpected places in between, I am, in consequence, deeply indebted.

There are certain people for whose help and kindness I am particularly grateful, and these include: Mr Sidney Powell, and Mr and Mrs Selwyn Jones of Tonypandy, and Mr Henry Edwards of Trealaw, Rhondda, Glamorgan; Dr and Mrs David Rosenberg and Miss Ann Ford of Leicester; Sr Mary Henry, O.P., and Mr Victor Ankrett of Stoke-on-Trent; Mr Michael Rooney of Leeds; Mgr Philip Loftus of Ushaw College, Durham; Mr and Mrs Thomas Goundry of Ushaw and Mr Aloysius Goundry of Langley Park, County Durham; Mrs Gina Vianney, Mr James Dollan and Mr Eric Forster of Newcastle-upon-Tyne; and Mr John O'Keeffe of London.

The written records I consulted covered some rare and now almost unobtainable leaflets, newspapers and other relatively obscure sources. In tracing many of these I am most grateful to Mr Ronald Gray of Hammersmith Books, London SW13, who also, very kindly, lent me his file of the *Sunday Worker* for 1926-7, and his bound copies of the *New Leader* for the year 1926.

PART I

THE BUILD-UP

I

The miners

Fifty years ago Britain's coal industry was still 'the spoiled favourite of fortune' with 'wealth washed to its shores by the mere tide of economic expansion.'[1] Just enough of the relative prosperity flowing from such expansion had worked down the line – as far, even, as the miners themselves – to be able to put off the evil hour of thoroughgoing reforms and reorganisation. Successive crises had been averted at the last moment by stop-gap concessions. Hence Trotsky's judgement that 'the shocks of the European revolutions have always found a clear reflection in Britain's social development; they led to reforms as long as the British bourgeoisie, through their world position, retained in their own hands gigantic resources for manoeuvre'.[2]

Everything, however, was changed by the First World War. Thereafter 'partly because of its rapid growth and partly because of technological innovations in other countries, the British coal industry failed to fit into the new setting of the third decade of the twentieth century'.[3] Despite the epic heroism of 1914–1918, Britain's post-war unfitness for heroes has become one of the great social scandals of her history. Few, if any, groups were hit harder than the mining community. No other industry was in so great a need of change if standards of living and safety at work were to mean anything; yet no other industry resisted change with such fierce intensity. At the same time the key position of coal, and the vastness of its industrial ramifications, made it a greater source of profit and power for one section of the population than any other commodity.

This section was spread throughout the Establishment of the

day which quickly closed its ranks after the war. It lacked the leavening quality of that rich cream of young Britain slaughtered in the conflict. It was thus all the more determined to preserve its ascendancy. If some domestic showdown were needed to show who was boss, so much the better. The hardest of the 'hard-faced men' – whom the moderates would have to follow in an emergency whether they liked it or not – were ready for a conflict if it came. They knew that social grievances abounded, nowhere more conspicuously than among the nation's colliers. But if any 'damn Bolshie' wanted trouble – with such grievances as a mere excuse – so be it. Meanwhile the lid must be kept on tight.

There was, of course, another side to the coin, a side often neglected. The tradition of Britain's mineowners was among the country's most valiant and vaunted. The fact that its prosperity and profit-making potential was so stupendous just before the First World War, and had thus involved it inextricably in the morass of 'big business', could not detract from the original spirit that had inspired the makers and owners of Britain's collieries. Such spirit lived on among those coalowners – the majority – who wanted fair profit to walk hand in hand with fair play. By the mid-1920s, however, they were faced with a cruel dilemma. Bit by bit, as the crisis deepened, they found themselves being 'represented' by men in London and elsewhere who put profits first and industrial relations nowhere. This marked a dramatic change in the old spirit as coal became more and more entwined with other industrial interests. Could the old spirit, encouraged by the temporary glow of classless, war-time solidarity, survive the new pressures? The answer would surely depend to a large extent on whether human communications had improved since the Great War, particularly as between the mining communities on the one hand, and, on the other, the owners and their new friends in society, industry and government.

There was one great obstacle, and it would now be more difficult than ever to remove it after the drift of a century or more. And this was the curious isolation of the miners by virtue of their alien and mysterious craft. 'Miners were always a peculiar people. Toiling below our workaday world, in compact and numerous bodies, trained to mutual loyalty by peril, passing on from father to son the traditions of their hereditary calling, they have developed a group mind, which has made them, as it were, a distinct race among us.'[4] Such isolation has always had a deep effect on their outlook, making them suspicious of outsiders. This in turn had inevitably set up a vicious circle of mutual misunderstanding and lack of sympathy. There are strong traces of it even today; in the 1920s, however, lack of communication between miners and the middle-class world outside was almost total.

Without actually going down a coalmine for oneself, in fact, it is impossible to imagine what the working life of the miner is like. An underground visit to a colliery in 1976, moreover, can give but the barest inkling of conditions in the pits of the twenties, let alone in those of the nineteenth century. It is, indeed, almost an impertinence to try to describe such conditions when armed with anything less than first-hand knowledge. There are too many obvious dangers, ranging from failure, despite scrupulous application, to get at the inner core of the reality, to that of distorting the picture by romanticising. So vivid, however, is the oral testimony of most ex-miners that it cries out for combination with written evidence to form part of recorded history. And however often this source is tapped, it seems always to yield further fruit.

The early twenties, of course, are still well within living memory. The wages and conditions of that period, themselves the legacy of a grim but, paradoxically, not always unhappy past, are, even today, looked back upon with a curious blend of revulsion and nostalgia. The ex-miner's love-hate type of relationship with his past is well known. It is perhaps understandable in the case of those who knew no other working life than that of the colliery from their early teens onwards. Some, however, moved from the mines into other jobs and have a very different story to tell. One North-Easterner interviewed started work at the colliery surface at the age of thirteen, a year younger than the normal starting age at that time. He got to know enough about conditions below ground to realise what life seemed, inexorably, to have in store for him. His nights became heavy with foreboding. He lived in dread of the day when he would have to go down the pit. It was as if he were going to be swallowed up for ever.

The premature start brought home the nightmarish quality (as it seemed to him then) of the mining world of the early twenties. He was saved only by pure chance when he became, instead, apprenticed to the cobbler's trade. But his case was unusual, as most boys brought up in mining villages had nothing to look forward to but a life below ground, and many looked forward to it with excitement. For such boys, nevertheless, the early teens were as traumatic as for any other boys. Though everything is relative, anxiety is no respecter of class, even the boy starting life at his public school is often equally prone to sleepless nights and secret agonies. His parents will be no less worried on his behalf. This common human element becomes inhuman only when imagination fails to take in the other person's plight.

In the twenties, at all events, it was an advantage for the son of a mining family to be thrown in, literally, at the deep end. He might, after a stint at pony-driving or 'trapping',* be put to work cutting alongside his father or one of his brothers, and the initial shock would be cushioned. He was too busy by day and too tired at night to have much opportunity to reflect on his fortune. Few boys, when they first started work, did not fall asleep over their tea. They would wake up only to find it was then time to go to bed. Many resented that there never seemed time for anything like 'play' or wakeful relaxation. But they got used to it; and they knew there was nothing worse than being 'out of work' – the fate of two million people in 1921.

Mining was indeed a way of life all of its own; a world apart. Such a world produced its own brand of solidarity and sense of self-sufficiency. The family was particularly strong as a unit, and families were large. Advantage could be and was taken of a quirk of the system operated in many areas. The management would indicate to an individual collier that he wanted a certain job done on a certain coal face. It was to take so long and to be paid for at such and such a rate. This virtual 'sub-contracting' left the collier

*Shutting the ventilation doors after the trams had passed through.

free to choose his mates; and the father of a family would naturally choose his sons. If one or more of them might otherwise have been unemployed at that time, no one would be happier than the woman of the house, even if it added to her work. This was already so prodigious that the extra burden was barely noticeable. She would have to be up at four in the morning anyway to feed the menfolk – perhaps seven of them – before they went off to the pit. Even if there were only two rooms, she was intensely house-proud.

She smiles now – if she is still alive – at the ritual that took place every evening when the men came home. In the days before pit-head baths, they all had to strip off and wash in front of the fire, one by one in the same round tub. The coal dirt was already almost congealed into their bodies; only the whites of the eyes relieved the blackness. The quasi-subcutaneous grime finally yielded to vigorous scrubbing. They washed all over except on their backs, which were often too tender even to touch. Much of the day had been spent bending or crawling, and your back was constantly hitting the planks placed crossways at the top of the low tunnels. The whole spine could become a string of scabs. The most painful part was when the scabs got knocked off by yet another collision with the overhead planks. This happened all too frequently. Instead of scrubbing, a man's wife or mother would dab his back as clean as possible and put some iodine on the scabs. The washing process, for a large family, was naturally lengthy, and there was a rush to be first in the tub. The last one sometimes came out little cleaner than when he had gone in.

The independence, through isolation, of British mining communities is a natural part of their earlier history. Mining villages existed for the sole purpose of housing the men and boys working in the pits around which the villages had grown up. The houses as well as the pits belonged to the mineowners, as tenants of the local landlord. The workers felt they belonged to the mineowners as well, even after 'bonding' had disappeared. But the mining industry prospered as time went on. The early twentieth century saw the best years for miners as well as owners. Though the miners were to suffer a more crippling setback in the early twenties than any other group of workers, their position just before the Great War gave hope of better things to come.

None of this, however, ended the sense and fact of 'isolation'; and public opinion was many years behind, even as late as the thirties, in grasping what the life of the average miner was all about. Thus many a collier from South Wales had some strange experiences between the wars when travelling to, say, Birmingham or London. The statement 'I'm a coalminer' was known to bring astonished and embarrassed looks from strangers, even from the working class. A picture of mining life as it had once been was the one that still came to the minds of those who met a miner face to face for the first time. It was the picture of half-naked women and children, as well as men, practically living underground and doing the work of animals: crawling on all fours draped in harness to drag the wagons through the tunnels; wallowing in filthy water and eventually emerging pitch black from head to toe. To see a man from this phantasmagoric world, once a reality, sitting, with clean white face, on a train with ordinary folk, was a sight that seemed incredible to some. The embarrassment caused was akin to that experienced in the presence of coloured people when they were still a rarity in Britain or, even now, when people try to act naturally in the presence of blind people, spastics or cripples. Miners were made to feel like some sort of leper or 'cave-man'. The impression was not intentionally given, but it was clearly received and painfully assimilated. Some miners, to this day, equate misunderstanding of their problems with a subconscious continuation of former contempt: with the attitudes that once classified them – like slaves of a century earlier – as little more than savages whose primitive requirements could easily be met by the barest of subsistence wages.

The very appearance of miners returning from work in the twenties somehow contributed to the lack of esteem in which they were held even by themselves, as well as others. Unable to wash before leaving the pit, an unrelieved coating of grime made them a sorry sight. The pit-head showers envisaged but not enforced by the legislation of 1911 and 1926 were slow to arrive, though an important transformation had come about by the early thirties. James Robson, a veteran campaigner for his fellow miners and ultimately Chairman of the Durham District Welfare Committee, claimed in 1932 that pit-head baths had revolutionised village life in his part of the world: 'To observe the men returning from their work in their ordinary garb has changed the whole of our outlook and given a social standing to the miners never previously dreamed of.'[5] For a decade and more Robson had been arguing for the desirability of such baths, and the obvious extent to which their provision would relieve the womenfolk of much of the almost intolerable drudgery their incessant work at home entailed.

An interesting example of one kind of person who did not share this view was that of Joseph Pease, first Lord Gainford of Headlam and Vice-Chairman of the family firm of Pease and Partners, who were extensive mineowners in Durham. A Quaker, Liberal and sometime Cabinet Minister, he deserved the description 'enlightened coalowner'. He was not opposed to the provision of showers and lockers within the pit-head area, but doubted whether the miners themselves actually wanted them. As part of his evidence to the 1919 Sankey Commission on the coal industry he recorded his opinion that 'Where men are exposed to all kinds of inclement weather they would much sooner go home than they would walk long distances in their dry clothes, which they have had put on at the pit-head, and then walk home in rain and sleet and snow, and reach home in their ordinary clothes, and leave their pit clothes behind them.'[6]

This view of Lord Gainford's exemplifies the wide gulf between the thinking of workers themselves and the thinking of others, even when the latter were benevolent and reasonably in touch with the mining rank and file. It also prompts a reflection on the qualifications needed for trying to evoke a fair picture of the social conflicts and tensions of this whole period. It is invariably, and quite rightly, assumed that the observer must have sufficient knowledge of working-class life. It is no less important – though this is far less frequently assumed – that there should be equal familiarity with upper- and upper-middle-class life. For it was this section of society that dominated the whole pattern of events; and the chasm between this section and the working classes was immense – almost incredible to the onlooker of fifty years later.

Side by side with many a rich estate throughout the England and Wales of the twenties stood the rows and rows of tiny houses inhabited by the miners and their families. 'The size of such houses varied depending on the scale or criterion taken by the individual colliery who built them. Houses with two rooms – "one-up-and-one-down" – were very common. Two upstairs rooms were quite a luxury. The kitchen of such houses was a dining room, drawing-room, bathroom, wash-house and bakery. Sometimes the new-baked bread made it fragrant, but more often it smelled of sweaty pit clothes – sour and something more. When the clothes were not heaped in a corner beside sweat-sodden shoes, they were hanging up beside the fire to get ready for the next day.'[7]

As already implied, the stringent barriers that divided the two very different worlds in question did not, of themselves, mean that one set of people was happy and the other was not. Nor can the fact that such barriers existed support any generalisations about who was generous and who was selfish, or who were heroes and who were villains. It was merely that such barriers, in themselves, were so unnatural as to make possible at any time a particularly unpleasant type of confrontation or attempted showdown. The time for the latter's occurrence would be dictated by the moment at which the long but slow-burning political fuse finally reached the inflammatory elements now being described.

An avoidance of this catastrophe – a de-fusing of the explosive economic situation – could only be achieved by the right kind of remedial action. But such action, on any really decisive scale, was the last thing anyone could reasonably expect in the mid-twenties; and the reason for this was bound up, in the final analysis, with the human ingredients of the mineowning world and its many ramifications. A solution to the situation of seething unrest in the mining industry was thus the supreme test-case for industrial – and, indeed, general civilised – human relations between the wars. Mining, employing more men than any other industry and embracing a uniquely high proportion of injustice and unwarranted hardship, would determine the whole course of the embryonic confrontation.

The important question of whether the hardship of the miners themselves in the early twenties was real or alleged does not merely depend on whose statistics and conclusions are followed. It is far from being just a matter of 'right' versus 'left' propaganda; and 'average' figures and generalised findings can be misleading. The same applies, as we shall see, to the question of whether or not the mineowners, *as a whole*, were a predominantly selfish group. Conditions varied almost infinitely in different areas. While, in the Midlands, some owners lived comparatively modestly and the miners in relative comfort, it was no less true that some almost feudal landlords, owning lucrative mineral rights, luxuriated within a few miles of the miners, who eked out a barely human existence and lived in disgraceful hovels, while enormous profits accrued to the operators of the actual collieries.

Shortage of good-quality housing, in fact, was the greatest hardship suffered by Britain's miners in the early twenties, apart from low wages and long-term unemployment[8] which are discussed among the economic ingredients of conflict. The Durham Coalfield 'has remained to this day [1919] in some respects among the worst as regards the housing of the people. The bad housing, the insanitation, the ugliness, and generally the "uncivilisation", of the typical mining village – together with the terrible overwork of the miner's wife which the bad housing intensifies – seem to me to constitute the most grievous blot upon the county.'[9] The author of this observation asks if 'this unhappy distinction' had anything to do with the fact that this was the only coalfield in England and Wales in which the coalowners provided the miners with 'free' houses. The provision of free colliery housing or a rent allowance to those miners in private houses were both long-established customs in Durham. The miners had long claimed that such customs had helped to perpetuate the worst evils of the housing problem by reducing the local authorities' sense of responsibility for providing and maintaining more houses. Thus Durham had a larger number of local authorities than any other coal county in England, and this in areas where the population averaged more than five to a dwelling.[10]

What it amounted to was that, with wages almost impossibly low, miners were forced to look hard at every penny; and the saving of a whole shilling was a major achievement. So if any part of the wages could be diverted from paying rent by occupying a 'free' house, this option was invariably taken. In one colliery area visited by a Health Officer in 1921, liquid excreta ran from the doors of ash-closets into the back street. 'Outside one house,' his report noted, 'is a miniature cesspool round which young people play. The houses are intended for two tenants, but there are three or four in most of them, and in one house there are eighteen people.'[11]

Had such conditions existed even in this area only – in fact they existed in many – there would have been cause for grave anxiety among those able constructively to affect the situation. But no such general anxiety existed, and there was no hope whatever that the only group of people able to provide real remedies would in fact do so. For though the coal industry cried out, as will be seen, for proper reorganisation on a national scale, no such re-organisation was at all likely to occur in the socio-economic climate of the early twenties.

This period, apart from anything else, was one during which the most influential people in Britain were looking firmly toward the past. The Great War had shattered so many dreams that such retrospection was natural and inevitable. The sadness and horrors which all classes had shared could be expected to produce reactions of nostalgia and sentimentality. There was even a hope that the new solidarity between the classes could usher in a sort of golden age. Had there been no particular black spot (i.e. the mining areas) on the post-war socio-economic map of Britain, such an age could have commenced.

The question of bringing the miners into the mainstream of ordinary social and industrial life proved, however, to be as difficult as had been the abolition of slavery in the previous century. For slavery had been so integral a part of an accepted system that its discontinuance seemed inconceivable. Decent and honourable men were convinced that, given certain safeguards, the concept of slavery was morally justified and economically indispensable. Even as late as 1926, the year of the great lock-out, the League of Nations felt impelled to take up the question of slavery 'in all its forms'. It drew up a special Convention whose first article defined slavery as 'the status or condition of a person over whom any or all the powers attaching to the right of owner-ship are exercised'. Such a definition was not meant to include coalminers even though *some* of the powers attaching to the right of ownership undoubtedly still governed their status.

The practicalities of the situation as far as Great Britain was concerned were that the peculiar hardship of the miner's life and the piling up over a century of consequent injustice in the con-ditions under which he was forced to work had produced, by the nineteen-twenties, a well-nigh insoluble dilemma. The miners, in order to meet the elementary demands of natural justice, had either to be treated as a special case, thus necessitating politically radical and socially unacceptable alterations to the country's economic structure; or their special problems had to be tackled piecemeal by conventional methods of bargaining and negotiation, thus rendering unavoidable a head-on, and possibly violent, showdown between strong rival camps. For it was inevitable that the coalowners would be joined by such natural allies as a right-wing government, the press, the City and other sections of in-dustry. It was thus no ordinary struggle between socialism and conservatism that loomed ahead.

The respective merits of these two particular political philo-sophies, taken in the widest possible sense, have far less relevance to the unique miners' struggle than certain elements of human nature that happen to have been intimately involved in the 'world-apart' of the miners and their bosses. 'Socialism' and 'conservatism' ultimately became involved when the struggle widened to embrace economic realities affecting practically all parts of British life. But this book is emphatically not a defence or an indictment of any particular political 'ism'. For such 'isms' become involved only indirectly, and if, in general, socialism often does as much harm as good, the same can no doubt be said, again

in general, of conservatism. The uniqueness of the drama involving, via the 'general strike', a prolonged civil war as between the
mining and certain other communities, cannot be too strongly
stressed. When this 'war', or siege – the 1926 Lock-Out – was
finally over, the country returned gradually to a more conventional type of co-existence. Orthodox 'right' and 'left', to a great
extent, sank their differences. The miners were largely forgotten
in the general depression and then later on, in the atmosphere of
foreboding about a possible Second World War.

To understand the long struggle of the miners for their own
kind of 'emancipation', it is necessary to make much sharper
political judgements about the conduct of interested groups than
is usually done. Such groups had produced, and were hoping to
perpetuate, the great 'scrambled egg' of a national industrial
system, not to say a whole civilisation, based on coal; and the coal
industry was so heavily labour-intensive at this time as to make
any substantial sharing of this civilisation with the miners themselves impossible without unscrambling the egg. This, the coalowners claimed, was impossible. And given the correctness of the
owners' very narrow terms of reference, they were right in their
contention.

The only hope lay in the imposing or devising from outside of
some entirely different kind of solution. For once, and for a very
short time, the more extreme sort of socialist happened to be
right in pressing for such a solution when it finally became apparent that no government or other capable body was willing to
grasp the nettle of drastic reorganisation of the whole coal industry
from top to bottom. Had this nettle been grasped after the First
World War – as the latest possible moment for it to be successful
– the inter-war years, with the sequel of bitterness, would have
been shorn of their worst domestic troubles. The mining problem, however, remained unsolved, and was thus dragged into
factional politics in a manner that turned normal British standards
on their head, and sent decent men and women reeling in different
directions in the resultant confusion and bewilderment.

The threat to Britain's domestic tranquillity posed by seething discontent among the 'other-world' of the miners did not of course come to sudden birth only in the nineteen-twenties. Even in the eighteen-twenties that dark and mysterious 'other-world' was beginning to receive attention, though very little at first. Thanks almost entirely to the prodigious work of R. Page Arnot,[12] the miners' long road to 'emancipation' has been summarised and documented with brilliance. The nineteenth-century period, up to 1888, was concerned largely with a prolonged attempt to eliminate two things: the working conditions describable as not merely unjust but inhuman; and extreme danger. That certain men, women and children toiled underground under circumstances rendering their plight as pitiable as that of West Indian slaves was a fact unknown to the elegant world which greeted Queen Victoria's accession to the throne in 1837. An attempt to bring the horrors to public attention was made in this very year by the Chartists. Their proclamation, however, was ignored by the ruling class who ridiculed the Charter's exaggerated and emotive language. Not realising they had dangerously provoked worse agitation to follow, society breathed again, for the time being, in the romantic atmosphere engendered by the country's new and gracious young sovereign, and under the soothing premiership of her mentor, Lord Melbourne. Any suggestion that a form of slavery was flourishing underground and stunting the lives of many thousands of Britain's sons and daughters would have been greeted as hysterical. No one in fact was considered more hysterical than the aristocratic, Tory son-in-law of Lord Palmerston. So well-connected an advocate of reform as this man, Lord Ashley – better known by his title of Earl of Shaftesbury – could not, however, be ignored for ever. Melbourne was forced by Shaftesbury's persistence to set up, in 1840, a commission to report on the conditions under which children and young people were employed in the coalmines.

The results – published in 1842 – stunned a complacent and unsuspecting country. It was revealed that the employment of children of seven was general rather than exceptional. Some started work in the pits younger; one case of a child of three was discovered. The first job – then as in the twenties – was usually that of a 'trapper', shutting the ventilation doors, on which miners' safety depended, after the coal tubs had gone through. The slaves of the sugar plantations at least worked together in the open air. The child trappers of England's coalmines in the eighteen-forties crouched alone for about fourteen hours each day in the solitary darkness of small black holes. Yet they were luckier than the children who were picked out to move the trucks, and, 'harnessed like dogs in a go-cart', crawled through passages often less than two feet high as they pulled or pushed the coal trucks along the pit tunnels. Still others were put to work at the pumps which necessitated standing in several inches of water for up to twelve hours each day in the under-bottom of the pits. The brutality which often accompanied this unspeakable existence made incredible reading in the commission's report.

Victorian England reeled in horror, not least at the revelations that girls as well as boys were undertaking such tasks, and becoming, in consequence, cripples by the time they were thirty. Shaftesbury was no longer considered hysterical but could now count on wide sympathy for his campaign. As soon as possible he introduced a Bill in Parliament excluding from the pits all women and girls and all boys under thirteen. 'We have listened to the cries of the slave afar off,' was the comment of one leading newspaper of the day, 'but we have shut our ears to the moaning of the slave at our feet.' In practice, however, the road to thorough-going reform was found to be impassable. Adam Smith and Jeremy Bentham had set up a great signpost indicating a very different road: the road to riches which was paved by economic rather than natural law. Its driving force was 'freedom': the freedom to exploit every factor that might lie to hand in order to feed the appetite of enlightened self-interest. This was, indeed, the new 'enlightenment', inherited from the 'age of reason'.

That some – in practice many – should go to the wall was an unavoidable concomitant of this doctrine of *laissez faire*, the only response humane and philanthropic men could find to the gargantuan demands and intoxicating potentialities of the industrial revolution. So the rich got richer and the poor got poorer. There was nothing to be done about it – so educated people thought –

except to stop men from actually dying from hunger. Philanthropy thus came to the rescue in the form, as of 1834, of the Poor Law; and the horror of the workhouse became a familiar part of everyday life. Progress – in getting rich – had proceeded with such speed that the essentials for a definition of slavery existed in all parts of our isles. Labour became, and was long to remain, a mere commodity, divorced almost entirely from the men and women who supplied it with their lives. Nowhere was this truer than in the mining industry, where men were expendable but coal was infinitely precious.

It was thus that the road to reform was impassable for the time being. Very gradually, however, the pioneers began to open it up. Shaftesbury's Bill became an Act, though falling far short of his full demands. No females could henceforth be employed underground, and no males under the age of ten. The colliery owners greeted the measure with aversion. Their response that year (1842) was the lowering of wages and the discharge of as many miners as possible. Few crumbs were to be allowed to fall from rich men's tables. Yet these were the hungry forties, getting more desperate by the hour. Chartism, though ridiculed by legislators, was far from dead; the demand for cheap bread and repeal of the Corn Laws was rising to a clamour. The whole population was on the move. The employers of Bayley's Mill, at Stalybridge, decided to take action in accordance with prevailing philosophy. On 4 August they gave notice of a further reduction in wages. It was all that was needed to set a general insurrection in motion. The great 'Turn Out' being threatened came to pass. The radical Quaker, William Benbow, prophetic advocate of the 'general strike' theory, seemed to be witnessing the realisation of his dreams. It almost happened, but not quite, though work stopped completely throughout the great industrial north. Miners, sickened by years of slave labour – now, it appeared, to be rewarded only by starvation – led the insurrection in some areas. In the Potteries their march on Burslem Town Hall gave them the appearance of an 'invading army'.[13] There were shades of 1926 as the yeomanry were called out in force and 'farmers' sons sharpened sabres on the grindstone at the village smithy before riding off to patrol the grimy streets of a world they did not understand. Tall-hatted magistrates rode beside them ready to mumble through the Riot Act and loose the forces that had triumphed at Peterloo over the urban savagery their own neglect had created.'[14]

The insurrection and near-general strike of 1842 was duly crushed, but nothing was ever quite the same again. For miners, the fact of isolation from the rest of the community increased as the subsequent years dragged by. Strangely, unnaturally, cut off from both ordinary urban and rural life, their work took them, like the monks of old, to the remotest of valleys. There they lived in villages, but not the sort of villages associated with picture postcards. A new type of village – the 'mining village' – grew up wherever there was more coal to be dug. And such villages consisted less of houses than tightly packed terraces of grim barrack-like containers for the basic commodity of mining, human labour. Such was the setting for the dramas and struggles of the last quarter of the nineteenth century, and the first quarter of the twentieth.

Inevitably a main preoccupation, as mentioned, was for safety to life and limb in what became a more and more dangerous existence. The death toll mounted in proportion to expansion of the industry; but life was cheap. Producers and consumers, not inhumane people, were too dazzled by the prizes or blinkered by sheer lack of information to be concerned. But the housewife of the mining world, from that period onwards, saw off every morning, for every shift, be it two, four, six or eight o'clock, every man in her family. She knew she might never see him again; it was as if, every day, he were going off to war. The habit and the thought behind it stayed with the wives and mothers of colliers well into the twenties and thirties of the next century.

Meanwhile the terrible underground explosions continued and the tunnels went on collapsing. Underground inspection, irksome to owners, was ludicrously inadequate. More and more colliery disasters caused a Select Committee to report to Parliament in 1852. Inspection was tightened, and safety measures nominally improved. But the greatest enemies to the miners' safety were apathy and ignorance, even on the part of the colliery officers, let alone of the ultimate owners. With hundreds of men being killed every year, and thousands seriously injured, it was little wonder that of all British industries none produced so intense an atmosphere of bitterness on the part of employees against employers. Even in the nineteen-twenties the average death toll was as high as five per working day. In the longest of all the miners' stoppages, the Great '26 Lock-Out, a factor favouring a hold-out to the very last was that even hunger was at least preferable to death.

Successive legislation and select committees failed to stop the disasters. The seventies and eighties were years of cruel carnage. Names like Swaith Main (Yorkshire), Blantyre (Lanarkshire), Haydock Wood (Lancashire), Abercar (Monmouth), Risca (Monmouth), Seaham (Durham), Clifton Hall (Lancaster), were among the many that became household words to miners of future generations, as bloody battles are for soldiers.

1888, however, saw the greatest of all landmarks in the miners' history, with the formation of the Miners' Federation of Great Britain.* Unrelenting pressure finally forced the convening of a major Royal Commission on Mines in the year 1906. It resulted, though not until 1911, in a Coal Mines Act which was 'at the time the most advanced ameliorative mining law in Europe or America'.[15]

If the elaborate provisions of the Act were properly administered, as it was thought at the time, a new golden age of safety for miners could confidently be anticipated. It was not to be. Within only a few months of the Act's coming into full operation, there occurred (on 13 October 1913) at Senghenydd, Glamorgan, the worst disaster in the history of British mining. The people in the coalfields erupted with fury when it became clear that this terrible tragedy, claiming 439 lives, was caused by the culpable negligence of the owners and their agent. But even greater fury was to come when those guilty of little short of murder were, though prosecuted by the Home Office, let off with fines so small as to be an insult to the whole mining community. Only in Britain, perhaps, would the public, though widely roused to

*See Chapter 4.

disgust, feel restrained from taking the law into their own hands in such circumstances.

*   *   *

Soon another kind of carnage, that of World War, had come to dominate the nation's imagination. The mines eventually came under Government control, and so remained until 31 March 1921, when they were handed back to private owners with great wage reductions. 'The next day over one million miners were idle, locked out, standing in the village streets, gazing at the gaunt and silent machinery on their pithead.'[16]

A new phase in the life of the miners opened on that date. All the bitterness of a century of isolation, strife and frustration had finally reached boiling point. A new struggle, proclaimed by the mineowners, was in embryo and was to germinate with lulls until the final prolonged showdown of total war in 1926. Who were these mineowners and what sort of world did they inhabit?

Coal Strike 1921

Children gathering coal

2

The mineowners

As an emblem of well-informed *locus standi* on the breakfast tables of the nineteen-twenties, there was nothing quite like a copy of the *Morning Post*. The proprietor of this newspaper was 'the pro-fascist, coal-owning Duke of Northumberland'.[1] Not all his friends would have agreed with this particular description, even allowing for the fact that it was not necessarily considered taboo to be 'pro-fascist' in the twenties and thirties. People who remember the Duke today content themselves with saying he was 'very right wing'. His receipts from coal – over £80,000 a year – were only part of his not inconsiderable income, and he was a man of substantial influence. He was an arch bogey man of even the moderate left who bitterly resented, even if often affecting not to read, the anti-working-class homilies which appeared regularly in the *Morning Post*. Many of these, as was well known, were directly inspired by the paper's proprietor, whose overall image was, and is, a somewhat forbidding one. But what was he like as an individual?

It so happened that a young Labour M.P., Andrew McLaren, was waiting one day in the early twenties to meet the 'pro-fascist' Duke in the lobby of the House of Commons. McLaren was a member of the Independent Labour Party, the Party founded by Keir Hardie himself and thus the cradle of the Labour movement in Parliament. Its members, who came to be called 'the Clyde-siders', were 'neither the red iconoclasts depicted by the more sensational or conservative papers' (such as the *Morning Post*) 'nor the socialist purists of the new revolution'.[2] But they were well to the left of the main body of the Parliamentary Labour Party, occupying a position not unlike the Tribune Group of today. McLaren, a fiery and outspoken backbencher, was also a warm advocate of the principle of taxing land values and a disciple of Henry George.[3] As such he had little in common with a man who not only possessed land of vast untaxed value but was also prepared to defend his inalienable right thereto against all comers.

It was thus with some trepidation that McLaren waited for his Ducal fellow Parliamentarian from the Upper House. In the event he found him absolutely charming. They got on extremely well; and though they agreed on little, they parted the best of friends after a constructive and interesting conversation.

The Duke of Northumberland was far from untypical of his class, even if more right wing than many of its members. So many of these, however, from that particular period, are known and judged almost entirely by what has been written of them in a general sense. And of those in particular who were involved with coal and mineowning, there is a great paucity of detailed knowledge. 'Though they naturally played a decisive role in the coal crisis, very little has been written about them. Even their names are not easy to discover. A good deal is known about the miners' side of the dispute; virtually nothing about the owners' case.'[4] Most of the pre-nationalisation records were lost or destroyed, and many colliery operations were complicated and largely undiscoverable, often because of intentional camouflage. Much, however, is discernible by examining the lists of directors of leading colliery companies – with special reference to other directorships held by the same men.

One may also rely on personal knowledge of and first-hand stories about some of the principal landowners who enjoyed large incomes from coal royalties. Among examples of the latter may be mentioned the Lord Bute of the day,[5] than whom no one, with the possible exception of the Duke of Hamilton, received more in royalties from coal – well over £100,000 a year. His vast country estates, five in all, included extensive land in the county of Glamorgan fairly bursting with coal. He had two substantial town houses as well. He was a kind and well-meaning man, but his astonishing remoteness from ordinary life is difficult to conjure up fifty years later. Such remoteness was accentuated by his wife's constant efforts toward regal grandeur. She could barely bring herself to speak, except in the most condescending tones, even to middle-class people, let alone to anyone less 'worthy'. The world of the 'lower classes' was naturally unknown to her and, in keeping with tradition, she never spoke to servants except to issue orders. Servants, in fact, had no identity of their own, all of them, male and female, being known, as was then the custom, by their surnames only, with no prefix of any kind. As for the miners who ultimately provided such a sizeable share of the Butes' annual income, they might have been undiscovered aboriginals. John and Augusta Bute, in other words, if extreme in some respects, were not untypical of the coalowning aristocrats of the twenties.

The latters' connection with coal, on the other hand, was, in practice, only indirect, even if they could be counted upon to use their considerable prestige and influence, should the need arise, against any radical change in the basic system. They rarely took any active part in the actual mining of coal which lay under their land, this being entirely managed by the colliery companies who leased from them the relevant portions of the land, and 'wayleaves' for the right of access thereto. Britain was the only European country to uphold this principle of the private ownership of mineral rights, a principle long since abandoned on the continent and anathema to such men as Henry George – and of course the Duke of Northumberland's new-found friend, Andrew McLaren.

In the early nineteen-twenties, roughly 6d. was paid in royalties to the corresponding landowner for every ton of coal brought to the surface. The system behind this had grown up piecemeal with the advance of the industrial revolution and the discovery of more and more coal in all parts of Britain. Unfortunately, however, 'growth had been haphazard . . . being largely dependent upon the boundaries of the properties of the surface owners'.[6] No factor was more important than this in dictating the development of the whole coal industry on a *regional* rather than on a national basis. Herein lay the nub of the great showdown struggle of the twenties; and the result was sectional against general interest. Thus 'the outside observer must keep the regional character of the coal industry constantly in mind if he is to understand its recent history. Not only does this regionalism mean that the economic interests of the different fields and pits are often divergent and sometimes opposed, but these divergencies and clashes have found striking expression throughout the industrial relations and the politics of a highly contentious and most political industry.'[7] This point cannot possibly be exaggerated when assessing the arguments so forcefully presented in the twenties for nationalising an industry whose unique regional structure had produced so divisive and chaotic a pattern. The only unifying element was the labour question, with the miners desperately seeking settlement of their wage needs on a national basis and not district by district. Such a notion was bitterly opposed by the colliery owners, who, though they fought each other tooth and nail for the high stakes made possible by regional competitiveness, closed ranks when threatened with concerted action by the colliers.

For their part, the owners felt that, having individually negotiated their leases with the landlords in the past, they were entitled, in return for the irksome burden of paying heavy royalties, to the maximum profit from such management skill and investment as had gone into their own particular coalfields. Rationalisation or amalgamation, let alone full nationalisation, would knock the bottom out of the whole system, even though many of them realised, on objective analysis, that only some such reorganisation could prevent headlong dispute with the mining communities on a wide and possibly tragic scale. Nevertheless they would fight to the end for regional existence, since those with the best pickings would thus be saved from any unwarranted competition, while those in the less prosperous areas could make up for their difficulties by keeping wages as low as possible.

This had not meant that all the companies had remained independent, but rather the opposite. The tendency to combine gradually put more and more coal into ultimately fewer and fewer hands. By 1924 there were in Britain 2,481 mines producing coal as a principal product, belonging to about 1,400 colliery undertakings. But of these, 323 undertakings produced, in the year 1923, over eighty-four per cent of the output.[8] The increasing combinations, moreover, as was observed at the time,[9] 'do not necessarily abolish competition; indeed, they tend rather to intensify it. For competition is no longer between small independent firms – a competition which is more or less haphazard, unconscious and accidental. The competitive struggle now resolves itself into a mighty struggle of gigantic combines. Competition becomes deliberate, systematic, organised.'

Who then were the men – so greatly maligned by some left-wing propagandists – who owned and operated these companies and combines? They have been maligned if only because of the misleading generalisations made about them. For they varied greatly amongst themselves not only as individuals but also as businessmen confronted with the widely divergent conditions of the different areas. Generally speaking, they were a notch or so down from the aristocratic owners of the actual land from which they dug their coal. Taken as a whole they were anything but industrial villains grinding the faces of the poor. Why then, it must immediately be asked, did the miners suffer such undoubted privations and harbour such legitimate grievances? And why did men of generally goodwill find it seemingly impossible to mitigate such grievances? The answer is at once simple and extremely complicated: 'The whole economic structure raised in a century of titanic capitalist enterprises was too intricate and interdependent for anyone to be able to produce, let alone execute, a plan capable of mending any one of its defective parts without injuring, perhaps irreparably, some other. However delicately one stepped, the floor of the commercial edifice was alive with vested interests, every one of which was apparently sacred and defended by a whole chorus of jealous hierophants.'[10] Nowhere was this truer than within the web-like world of the mining industry where there were 'decent and progressive coalowners ready to move forward'[11] but no Earl of Shaftesbury ready to risk the opprobrium of his own class in the cause of such progress. Yet, relatively speaking, the colliers at this time were no less deserving of some such champion from outside their own ranks.

As it was the voices of moderation were drowned by the 'hard-faced men' who were more forceful than their fellow owners when there was any tough bargaining to be done. The milder men were, almost by definition, unable or unwilling to stand up to the self-appointed guardians of the delicate web of vested interests. Here the field was led by such personalities as the formidable seventh Marquess of Londonderry whose forebear, the third Marquess, had fought every inch of the way against Shaftesbury's Bill to ban female and child labour in the mines. Lord Londonderry (the seventh Marquess) found strong allies before the Great War in such fellow owners as the dynamic Lord Rhondda (formerly David Thomas) and, later on, in the egregious Evan Williams, a vulgar and aggressive busybody who managed to push himself in 1919 into the presidency of the Mining Association, which had been founded in 1854. He thus claimed to 'represent' all the owners, except, as it turned out, when it seemed more convenient to pretend that the Association could not act in any such representative capacity. In vain did such enlightened owners as Yorkshire's Sir Philip Cunliffe-Lister (later Lord Swinton) protest that refusal of the miners' perfectly reasonable demand for a national minimum wage agreement would inevitably mean 'starvation wages' in some districts. In vain did an equally enlightened owner from South Wales, David (later Lord) Davies, point out the saddest and most paradoxical element of all this, namely that the owners' case was not necessarily a bad one and certainly not an evil one; but in the hands of Evan Williams, whose arrogance and offensiveness were driving the miners' leaders to extremism, it was being presented in its worst possible light.

It is often argued that the rank-and-file among workers are duped by their militant leaders. In the crisis period of 1921, when miners and owners were set on collision course, it was the owners who found themselves in this uncomfortable position. So closely knit, however, was the fabric of interests interwoven with and spinning off from the mining industry that it would have been asking too much of human nature to expect a major beneficiary of the system to lead the much needed campaign for thoroughgoing reform. Apart from anything else, where would such a person have started? A brief look at the ramifications of the industry, its links with some of the supposedly indispensable props of the establishment, and the big guns it could bring to its aid from social and political armouries, shows up some of the difficulties such a person might have faced. Throughout the twenties and thirties, such ramifications somehow enabled the 'floor of the commercial edifice' to go on supporting a vast super-structure of interwoven interests and immense, if often concealed, profits. Those at the very bottom of the pile, such as miners, were meanwhile blandly told that unless their wages were cut, and cut again, the country would experience economic collapse. Why and how this happened can be seen by looking at some of the typical companies in the chief coalfields of Great Britain.

Many of these were linked with other influential concerns through a pattern of interlocking directorships with important and far-reaching consequences. It would have taken a brave man to move outside the plush pastures of Establishment to suggest any attempted unscrambling of such golden eggs.

The examples given below illustrate a general pattern, familiar enough in the inter-war period. They exemplify the ordinary capitalist framework against which mining's industrial disputes were conducted throughout this whole period without necessarily accounting for any particular occurrence at any particular juncture. Of particular interest is the fact that even when the 1926 Lock-Out was finally over, and even in the areas where the miners came off worst, big profits continued to be made. In the key area of South Wales, for example, where the depression hit the miners hardest, the important Amalgamated Anthracite Collieries Limited managed to prosper, controlling, as it did, about ninety per cent of the total output of East Welsh anthracite coal and thirteen anthracite companies. This company 'may be taken as typical of a purely coal-producing firm with no structural con-nections with other branches of industry'.[12] Though annual net – as opposed to trading – profits only once fell below £200,000 between 1929 and 1934, such figures, as well as returns on the ordinary and preference shares, were considered too low to enter-tain any claims for wage increases. But such reasoning ignored the huge sums paid meanwhile to the debenture holders. It also ignored the past prosperity of the company. A capitalised bonus, in fact, of ten per cent had been paid in 1926, the very year of the Lock-Out.

The company's chairman at that time was Sir Alfred Mond, later Lord Melchett. He was a man of brilliance and vision who, during the General Strike, demonstrated that enlightened and radical ideas were compatible with the self-interest even of the mineowners. But his arguments for a compromise settlement of the dispute met with scant sympathy either from the Government or his fellow owners. Mond was succeeded, in 1930, and followed onto the Board of Amalgamated Anthracite, by his son, the second Lord Melchett, who was also a director of Barclays Bank, Imperial Chemical Industries, International Nickel and the International Finance and Investment Corporation. Other important links existed for Amalgamated Anthracite through Sir David Llewellyn and Lord Camrose, with Guest, Keen and Nettlefold, which owned a very large group of steel and engineering concerns and, in Welsh Associated Collieries Limited, a useful steam coal subsidiary; through T. P. Cook, with the Cook Shipping Company of Swansea, E. W. Cook and Company, and foreign coalhandlers for vital French coal and anthracite markets; through W. M. Llewellyn, with the factoring concern of Bradbury Son and Company (1920) Limited. Sir David Llewellyn also provided a link with one of the world's greatest distributors in Gueret, Llewellyn and Merrett. The object of such directorial connections was to obtain markets for Amalgamated Anthracite while securing coal for their other interests at the lowest possible prices. Thus, with wages based in the last resort on coal prices, it is easy to see how the miners were almost always at a disadvantage in pressing their claims.

The alliance between mineowning interests and the press was always an intriguing one. Following the first Lord Melchett as chairman of Amalgamated Anthracite was F. A. Szarvasy, a director of the *Daily Mail* and General Trust Limited. This was – and is – the central holding concern of the Rothermere group of newspapers which, at that time, included nationally the *Daily Mail* – most right-wing of the popular dailies – the *Daily Mirror* – originally launched as a women's newspaper – and the *Sunday Dispatch*. The Lord Camrose already mentioned – originally

William Berry – was chairman of the Allied Newspapers group. Within this orbit, generally known as the 'Berry group', were such nationals as the *Daily Sketch*, the *Financial Times*, the *Daily Telegraph* and the *Sunday Times*. Specially interesting to Wales was the Berry ownership of the *Western Mail and Echo*, an intrepid mouthpiece for the hard-line mining viewpoint, notably in the campaign against nationalisation.

Powell Duffryn was another famous South Wales concern, which made great strides in the twenties by gobbling up several useful but struggling companies with the help of the banks to whom they owed money. The principal bank to force these companies, such as the Great Western Colliery Company and Lewis Merthyr Consolidated Collieries Limited, into receivership was Lloyds; and a director of both Powell Duffryn and Lloyds Bank was none other than Evan Williams.

Lord Davies, on the other hand (the critic of Evan Williams' extremism) ultimately became chairman of yet another leading South Wales combine, Ocean Coal and Wilsons Limited. This company was one of many whose operations and ancillary activities were intended to go hand in hand with employer-employee co-operation. Such co-operation in one of its forms came to be called 'Mondism', after the first Lord Melchett, who inspired it. But it was bitterly opposed by Communists and other militants as it split the Labour movement, and involved what was sometimes called 'company' or non-political, as opposed to traditional, more left-wing, trade unionism. Such non-political unionism played a part in the history of Ocean Coal which controlled United National Collieries. This company, in turn, controlled Burnyeat Brown and Company, which owned the Nine Mile Point pit where a famous 'staydown' strike occurred in 1934.[13] A prominent 'company unionist' who was an employee of Ocean Coal was one William Gregory. His plan was to gather up 'individualists' and he opposed the official 'hard' line of the South Wales Miners' Federation. He got as short shrift from union militants as did Lord Davies himself from some of his own fellow directors. The path of moderation was a hard one in the terrible and largely unnecessary bitterness that grew up in the nineteen-twenties between Britain's miners and their employers. The supreme irony was that even the militants of both camps had some right on their respective sides, but their intolerance of any form of opposition so often made them impossible to work with. In any collision, embryonic or actual, between miners and owners, governmental and political links with the mineowning confraternity would obviously be significant. Such links were very strong.

The huge Powell Duffryn concern had on its board Lord Hyndley, who was also a director of the Bank of England, a member of the Committee on Industry and Trade during the vital period from 1924 to 1929 and Commercial adviser to the Mines Department from 1918 on into the thirties. Lord Hyndley was also Vice-Chairman of the Powell Duffryn subsidiary, Stephenson, Clarke, which worked in close co-operation with the big coal and oil contractors and exporters, Wm. Cory and Sons, through their joint subsidiary Coal Distributors (South Wales) Ltd. Wm. Cory and Sons was, in its turn, strategically linked with its own buyers by having on its board Sir James Caird, a prominent shipowner, Sir Arthur Cory-Wright, a member of the Port of London Authority and Lord Inchcape of P. & O. The mineowners could never complain that they did not have friends in the right places.

In certain respects Lord Hyndley had an opposite number in Lord Londonderry, whose extensive mining interests lay in the North-east coalfield. The jump is being made to this area from South Wales for two reasons. It would first of all be tedious to describe colliery companies and their directors in different parts of Britain merely to demonstrate signs of an overall pattern broadly similar in all areas. The other reason concerns the distinctive nature of the North-east which, with South Wales, has been the object of special investigation in this book, particularly as regards the actual 1926 Lock-Out.* One distinctive feature was that the association in the North-east, that is Northumberland and Durham, between coal-producing and iron and steel firms was closer than anywhere else, as exemplified by activities connected with Lord Londonderry. He was chairman of Londonderry

*See Chapters 11 and 12.

Collieries Limited, and his son, Lord Castlereagh, was one of the other two directors. But this was a private company issuing no details as to profits. Both men were also directors of the Seaham Harbour Dock Company, a public company whose record of share distributions 1919 and 1928 is intriguing. Holders of preference shares, worth about a quarter of a million pounds in the mid-thirties, were entitled to a four and a half per cent annual dividend. This, however, was paid in only one year between 1918 and 1927, and at the latter date the preference dividend was in arrears as of 31 December 1919. But from 1928 onwards the company suddenly found itself able to pay nine per cent a year, and by 1935 all dividend arrears had been paid off. 1928 was also the year in which Londonderry entered Baldwin's cabinet – as First Commissioner of Works. (Previously he had been Under-Secretary for Air [1920–21] and Minister of Education, Northern Ireland [1921–26]; and with the formation of the first National Government in 1931, he became Secretary of State for Air.) A fellow member of the board of the Seaham Harbour Dock Company was Sir John Barwick, High Sheriff of his county (Durham) in 1922. He was also a director of Broomhill Collieries Limited, Easington Coal Company and Weardale Steel, Coal and Coke Company Limited, as well as being on the local board of Martins Bank. The whole group, which included the South Durham Steel and Iron Company Limited, was dominated by the shipping firm of Furness Withy to constitute a vertical trust ranging from raw materials to finished articles with many by-products in between.

Dorman Long is a good example of a North-eastern iron and steel firm which was also a large coalowner. It dug coal to produce steel with wages (to the miners) based on the profit thereon. The profit could be, and often was, very small on this particular part of the operation, the major portion of the profit being easily transferable to the steel section. This involved the application of a widespread practice based on the importance of what the Samuel Commission called the 'transfer price' of coal, that is, the amount received by one part of a large concern from another when the coal was 'sold'. In 1925 the *Economist* analysed the

financial results of the operations of South Wales colliery companies with interesting results: 'The profits shown by these concerns, however, do not agree with those revealed in the monthly
audits of the joint accountants for wage purposes under the
national agreement. In the aggregate they are substantially more.
There is, however, a simple explanation of the difference. The
audits relate exclusively to the earnings of collieries of the sale of
coal. The profits derived from the manufacture of coke and by-
products and other commercial activities are excluded from the
scope of the audit; while another important factor of which the
audit takes no account is the income derived from investments,
which in the aggregate amount to fairly considerable sums.'[14] This
analysis appeared at a critical moment; a few weeks later the
owners gave notice that they intended to terminate the 'national
agreement' referred to, which had been in force since June of the
previous year. Failing the miners' agreeing to lower wages, they
would be once more under the threat of a lock-out. Thanks,
among other factors, to transfer prices, the miners were thus
'largely at the mercy of the coalowners'.[15]

A similar principle applied to Pease and Partners, whose chairman was the Lord Gainford previously mentioned. To this day
Pease and Partners are not recalled with any enthusiasm by the
many Durham ex-miners whose conversations have been used
as material for this book. They are remembered as soulless and
hard employers. The recollection of their operations in the twenties
brings a flinty look into the face of the seventy-year-olds of today.
Yet Lord Gainford was as 'enlightened' and beneficent as prevailing standards for an employer would generally permit. He certainly believed himself that he had the true interests of his workers
at heart. During the inter-war discussions about greater amalgama-
tions as a substitute for nationalisation, Gainford expressed views
which were taken, at the time, as representative of widely held
feelings among the owners: 'It is impossible to decentralise or
delegate work beyond a certain point, and when large amalgama-
tions occur (often over-capitalised) the output per person becomes
less, the *esprit de corps* and close touch between owners, officials
and workmen disappear, close attention to every detail in business

becomes impossible, waste occurs, product and quality suffer, and therefore the loss is greater than any small gain obtained through slight reduction in some overhead charges.'[16] In the crucial period of the first 'great lock-out' – that of 1921, as occasioned by the abrupt handing back of the mines by the Government to private ownership – 'there was little hope of the owners making any major concessions' and Lord Gainford 'aptly summarised their viewpoint'[17]: 'The coalowners are firmly convinced that the national interests will be best promoted by district settlements. ... Any national system, any pooling, any kind of levy would inevitably prevent the best equipped, the most efficiently managed, and the best class of colliery from producing coal at the lowest and most attractive price to the consumer, and it is therefore only through district settlements that the best national results will be secured and the highest wages fund provided in the interest of the workers.'[18]

Though Lord Gainford meant to speak in the miners' own interests as well as in conformity with business sense, conversations today with both owners and miners reveal the considerable extent to which their respective worlds were segregated in the early nineteen-twenties. Mineowning, as a business, comprised after all of thousands of people who would have no occasion actually to visit a pit or a mining village. Such people were not heartless but merely unfamiliar with local conditions. One author, in what he called 'A Challenge to the Comfortable', exemplifies this by remarking[19] that 'the knowledge of Durham County possessed by many is restricted to that section of the Great North Road which lies between Darlington and Newcastle-on-Tyne'. He recorded, however, how one particular motorist gained a further insight into Durham life, when, as he was driving at night through Chester Moor, a child ran from behind a bus straight into the path of his car and was thrown twenty feet onto the path at the side of the road. There were witnesses to assure him that it was not his fault. He carried the injured girl down a side street to her home. Apart from a scullery, there were only two rooms, with a double bed in one and a single bed in the other. Ten people lived there, husband, wife and eight children, of whom three were mentally deficient. The father earned £2 a week and two of the children brought in 15s. between them. The motorist put the child on the bed and waited for a doctor, whom he helped with the dressing of the girl's leg. The child could only make hoarse animal noises and was unable to say where she was hurt, being dumb and deficient herself. The room was full of neighbours, some crying, some trying to help. 'The smell of cooking fat fought valiantly with the damp serge of the policeman's uniform, the other children clustered round asking questions and getting in the way. I felt sick, sick not only because of the shock of the accident, but sick that human beings should live like this; I never knew before what overcrowding really meant.' He was one of the millions who 'never knew' – and were lucky enough never to find out.

The working classes on the other hand were not nearly so un-aware of what life was like for others. Many miners' sisters and daughters took – as one of the few forms of employment readily available for them – to domestic service. 'What the butler saw' was nothing to what the scullery, kitchen or under-parlour maid came to discover and report back to her families on the rare occasions when she was able to see them. But whereas the miners were well aware of the extreme contrast that separated their way of life from that of their employers, the latter hardly noticed or were concerned with it.

While the workers generally stuck together in their misfortune, there was one notable exception to this solidarity. Employers' unfamiliarity with working-class life arose largely because direct contact was usually avoidable through the operations of such intermediaries as local managers, agents, overmen, etc. The miners took their orders from the 'gaffers'. A natural desire to rise in the world meant a constant trickle over the line separating the employed from the employers. If working conditions further brutalise normal aspirations for betterment, human nature often has its own perverse reflex action in response to change of status. And miners were not fools. They knew what was going on in the upper echelons in the early twenties, even if they could never have proved some of their most strongly held convictions. As one veteran miner from Glamorganshire put it[20]: 'Owners made huge profits and lived well while claiming they could not increase

wages. Their true profits were hidden by the system of keeping
two sets of books. Demoralisation went deep, and bitterness had
ironical side-effects. . . . If workers became bosses they were often
ruthless and inhuman.'

Examples of such ruthlessness were mercifully few during the
actual long Lock-Out when the solidarity during mutual adversity was a minor miracle. The majority of the local owners were,
themselves, sympathetic to the miners during that period; but
they felt bewildered and unable to help the situation in any concrete way. Like the miners themselves they somehow felt that the
decisive fight was going on in remote negotiating centres and
that they were being represented by men whose personal acquain-
tance with the coalfield was in some cases slight.

It was only thus that certain powerful men in London could
possibly have taken, during the General Strike, so coldly detached
a view – perhaps more innocent than ruthless – of the real conflict
that was occurring. Lack of insight and sensitivity was occasionally quite startling. After the Strike had just started, for example,
the newspaper voice of the Government, the *British Gazette*,
printed two sorts of item in curious juxtaposition. One was a
spirited attack on the workers who were out in support of the
miners; the other was the notice, among 'Latest Wills', that
'Alderman William Edwin Pease, ex-M.P. for Darlington, left
£295,213 with net personally £271,796.' Such an amount, which
came from Durham coal, was princely in 1926. At wage rates then
prevailing, it would have taken the average miner two thousand
years to earn such a sum.

In this same year of 1926 it could nevertheless be written with
justification that 'the attitude of the coal owner is not a thing of
mystery; it is the "practical common-sense" which has determined and shaped British industrial development. Differ with him
as you may, quarrel as you may choose with his plans and pro-
cedures, you yet must recognise in him a working faith. He is not
the "stupid", "incredible" opportunist he is sometimes painted. To
see him as simply clinging to established possessions and privileges
is to fail altogether to see him as he sees himself – working within
a great tradition.'[21]

3

Economic dynamite

During the nineteenth century, it was not only the coalowners but also the miners among whom there was a special class of 'aristocrats'. These were the North-Eastern miners who, in the 1850s, no longer pressed for a general minimum wage, but found it more advantageous to bargain within their own area on the principle that 'prices should rule wages'.[1] This marked a decline in mining unionism's early development and the resulting 'sliding-scales' – the varying of wages with prices – were to become a major bone of contention in future years. But for the time being, having been accepted in the north-east, they were imposed on the lower-wage miners of other districts by employers. From this point on into the 1880s the mineowners went from strength to strength while the union side was divided and demoralised. The Amalgamated Miners' Association, the only rival to the north-eastern aristocrats, was too weak to support the 1875 South Wales miners' dispute and collapsed. Mining trade unionism, except in the north-east, withered to little more than nominal proportions for over twenty years.

Into this vacuum had thundered a new age – the 'iron age' – which, with railway lines now beginning to appear like veins over the whole country, was beginning, literally, to get up its first mighty head of steam. The ensuing 'coal rush' brought a new pioneering spirit as enterprising businessmen began to scent the magnitude of the fortune to be dug out from the earth. Between 1850 and 1880, annual coal output trebled from 50 to 150 million tons.[2] The new 'villages' – soulless plantations of dead-straight terraces, row on row – mushroomed in the wake of the 'prospectors', to house the migratory labour that had already become a by-product of the boom years. By the end of the century the coal-owners had become a class apart, an immensely powerful and, when needed, tightly-knit group. It had all happened with such relative swiftness that few realised the immense social implications of it all. The revolutionary socialist poet, William Morris, was almost a lone voice when forecasting, in his letter on 'The Deeper Meaning of the Struggle', the future fortunes of the British mine-workers.

The scattered labour forces of the mines, though faced with growing dangers, both economic and physical, were slow to weld themselves into new and solid communities, let alone to produce any effective reply to the forming (in 1854) of the owners' Mining Association. The miners spoke, if at all, with the voice of total disunity; and it was not until 1888 that there came a revival of general miners' unionism with the forming of the Miners' Federation of Great Britain. This year became the great landmark, the definitive point of departure. It introduced a much needed but long delayed campaign for less dangerous conditions of work and shorter hours, to say nothing of improved wages; but the owners were already well ahead in the contest, ever racing on to new and more spectacular conquests. With an industry so rapidly developing and diversifying, the employers were able to impose their own working conditions almost at will.

The history of British mining between 1890 and 1925 thus turned out to be largely one of the stockpiling of economic dynamite liable to explode if pressure became excessive or an intentional fuse were lit. The tangled history of those thirty-five years has been told and re-told in numerous volumes, sometimes with tantalising sketchiness, more often with an overpowering deluge of detail. The mind is bombarded with a bewildering succession of reports, commissions, strikes, lock-outs, enquiries, plans, promises, legal actions, legislation and, then, as if in a nightmare, the whole process starts up all over again in yet another apparently self-defeating cycle.

One needs to pinpoint certain 'flags' to chart the course of what, in retrospect, can be seen as a sort of relay race, with a new set of events, rather than participants, taking up the running in three gigantic 'laps'. 1888 marked the 'off' and the first lap ended with the miners winning an eight-hour day in 1908. Then came the period straddling the Great War with the years of 'labour unrest' and ending with portents of a better, more co-operative future with the auspicious findings of the Sankey Commission in 1919. The last lap, however, brought the protagonists closer together in tight, ever more deadly, formation. Total disillusionment on the miners' side was followed by a Government-backed 'employers' offensive'. The Prime Minister, acting as referee, called a halt in 1925, in the hope that a normal competitive process would not end in a bloody and brawling free-for-all, wreaking havoc among the public at large. And at that point, economic, social and political factors blended together into a potentially volcanic mass. Only one side, however, prepared in earnest for the eruption that seemed pre-destined to follow.

The MFGB's earliest efforts were hampered by the confining of their unions chiefly to the Lancashire, Yorkshire and Midlands areas. Their initial demands for better conditions drew a complete blank with the owners, who realised that areas such as the north-east were still agreeable to certain shifts lasting as much as ten hours, whereas the eight-hour day was at this time one of the federation's primary objectives. But unfortunately a new element soon entered into the whole relationship between the colliers and their bosses.

The latter were men who compelled admiration for their boldness and rugged enterprise. They now began to conceive the idea, which was to turn into an unshakable conviction, that the miners were indeed different from all others of their class if only because they were thoroughly selfish and never thought of the problems of other workers. It was perhaps a natural reaction on the part of a newly powerful class bemused by the great bubble of ever-expanding prosperity based on coal – a bubble which they could never imagine bursting. The miners, for their part, hitting out from a position of isolation and making many tactical errors in the absence of any properly co-ordinated union strategy, were easily out-manoeuvred and out-gunned. Demands, often made in desperation, were taken by the other side to have been made with complete indifference to the fate of other workers. Hence a conviction on the owners' part that 'the creed of the miners of the 'nineties was as the creed of the miners thirty-five years later. Without coining the slogan "The mines for the miners", they worked sedulously in that direction. . . . There was no altruism then: there was none in 1912 or 1921 or 1926. The wage rates of other men, even the opportunity of earning wages at all, did not enter into consideration.'[3] Apart from other factors, however, 'other men' did not have to face the hazards and special hardships of the miners; such factors were not, at this time, thought to be worthy of any kind of special consideration. And so a vicious circle of misunderstanding and bitterness crept into industrial relations in the mining world in a manner that never happened in other industries. Each move and counter-move in this first twenty-year 'lap' seemed only to polarise the situation further, until, by the nineteen-twenties, with each side threatened by increasingly adverse economic factors, no quarter was given or expected. In the eighteen-nineties, however, Britain was riding high and its coalowning trail-blazers were the darlings of a still mighty empire. 'In 1890 Britain was producing more coal than France, United States, Japan and Russia combined.' But by 1913 her production, though still increasing, was a little more than half that of the United States and only slightly more than the production of Germany. Worse was to follow when Britain 'staggered out of the war overwhelmed by debt, her economic life disorganised, her world position forfeited. . . . An imperial cycle had ended. The British Empire was defeated in the race for supremacy.'[4]

Psychologically, however, the upper and middle classes continued the imperial dream. They resented any intrusion into it and would do anything rather than have reality rubbed in their faces. Hardship and danger to life in the mines in the twenties? Why, civilians were still largely ignorant of what had been endured by the men in the trenches! Only a spate of war books, plays and poems served to draw this particular curtain aside. The miners, meanwhile, were always having to re-fight yesterday's lost battles. If they did so less violently than might be expected today, it was the vestiges of Empire that reminded them that there were many other British subjects even worse off than they were. Nowadays, since the emancipation and emigration–immigration of the Commonwealth era, British workers tend to feel that, with all the progress of half a century, they are in fact on the bottom layer in a sense that even their grandparents were not. The fact that such feeling is, of course, largely psychological renders it no less potent in practice.

In 1908 the miners got their eight-hour day and, of greater importance on the unions' tactical front, the north-east followed South Wales in giving delayed but henceforth unswerving support for a now greatly strengthened MFGB. Meanwhile, in the wake of the great Liberal landslide of 1906, an important Trade Disputes Act had become law, protecting union funds during a strike. This was the Act that Lord Birkenhead was to come to resent so bitterly as shown in his later writings, thus explaining his conspiratorial and hawk-like attitude towards the TUC in 1926.

'The unity achieved by the Miners' Federation of Great Britain after the Eight Hours Act enabled it to take up one of the most oppressive conditions under which the miners suffered.'[5] The torch passed on at this stage of the 'relay race' now proclaimed a new objective: the Minimum Wage. For the miner, at this time, was paid for the coal he sent to the surface regardless of the particular spot or area where he had to work. Such areas, however, differed widely; and a miner might well find himself working in an 'abnormal place', such as one where there was an unusually large amount of stone and very little coal. At the end of his shift, he would emerge from the pit with the grime moving about his body, following the rivulets of sweat, not just exhausted, like his mates, but totally frustrated as well. With very little coal to show for his labours, his payment for the shift would be negligible.

This state of affairs often went on day after day, so that at the end of each period the amount of pay he brought home to his family was pitifully small: an insult as well as an injury. I have spoken to old-timers, men and women, from that colliers' world who recall such scenes vividly. One miner's day had been much as usual, though hacking at stone rather than coal for most of the morning. The twenty-minute 'snap' – break (for a meal) – had been preceded, as was also usual in many pits, by grace said openly and without shame by the men. God was thanked for the famous 'coal-dust sandwiches' and then work would re-commence on the barren face. It was pay day, and when the collier got home he placed the few shillings on the table, all he and his family had to live on for the next fortnight, he looked up at his wife but did not speak. Her eyes were, if anything, more redolent of suppressed strain than his, her attempts to keep their tiny house neat and tidy an ironical commentary on the fact of having nothing to wear, practically nothing to eat and little to hope for. The silent miner sat for some time in the chair sobbing quietly but uncontrollably while his wife looked down at him. Her eyes were soft toward him but her heart was hard toward others, as stony in fact as the 'coal-faces' that yielded no coal.

The hardship involved was widespread and genuine, and yet another example of factors distinguishing mining from other industries. Little progress, however, could be made toward its mitigation – except by locally agreed special 'considerations' while the mining unions were still disunited. But 'the great struggle that developed on the question of abnormal places became possible when the unions were strong enough to regard an injury to one as an injury to all.'[6] The 1912 Minimum Wage Act went a long way toward meeting the principal grievances, but only after some of the bitterest struggles yet seen in the coalfields. They initially occurred in South Wales, at pits belonging to the Cambrian combine of which D. A. Thomas (Lord Rhondda) was chairman. It was the rugged individualism displayed by men such as this dynamic coalowner of daring skill and high ambition that helped to generate a general indifference to risks and hardships of one kind or another. But to men, such as miners, with no chance of alternative employment, the burden was particularly heavy. After protracted negotiations, strike notices were handed in and, at the end of March 1912, for the first time in history, work had stopped at every pit in Britain.[7] The Act of Parliament, when it came, compelled the owners to pay a minimum, but they obtained a vital concession, only accepted with reluctance by the

Federation, that the actual amount of such minimum was to be
settled county by county. (Thus the 'minimum wage' which was
now conceded in principle – known to pitmen thereafter as the
'mini' – must be distinguished from the concept of a *national*
minimum which was the object of an unrelenting, but unsuccessful, campaign between the wars.)

The events of the 1910–12 period are discussed and argued
over with vehemence to this day in the numerous Working
Men's Clubs of the Rhondda Valley. I have listened to many such
conversations, contributed to in some cases by octogenarians who
had already started work at the time. Many of their theories,
however, tend to be hotly disputed by others. Some, for example,
like to claim that it was not really Churchill who made the final
decision (as Home Secretary) to send troops to Tonypandy. But
the troops were there, the riots were bloody and ferocious as
pickets were confronted by imported 'blacklegs'. Scarcely a
window in Tonypandy was left intact. Non-participants, including children, were beaten up by panicking police. Their conduct
was resented but somehow less despised than the Home Secretary's
evasive answers in Parliament as to what had really happened and
why in what came to be called 'Tonypandymonium'.

Thus was added a sizeable slice to what veteran miners of the
1970s look back on as their legacy from the past. The late Sir
William Lawther explained to the author what he conceived this
legacy to be.[8] He believed that people should not be encouraged
to forget their heritage but are entitled to cherish whatever
lessons it might impart. For royalty, it may be service and
pageantry; for soldiers, martial glory. For the miners it is a
'legacy of misery'.

1911–12 was one of the many key turning-points, and from
that date until 1945, mining – accounting for forty-two per cent
of the total of days lost in strikes – was the cockpit of British
industry. The miners now constituted a vast army of men, the
largest group among the nation's workers. As for their leadership,
the 1912 strike proved to be the final thrust of the acute 'labour
pains' accompanying a new birth of the Miners' Federation. It
was just at this time that the owners, for their part, became aware

that, though their industry dominated the home trade, foreign competitors were making alarming inroads into their share of world markets. They thus entrenched themselves from this point onwards to defend the prosperity to which they understandably felt that the hard, slogging pioneer days had at long last entitled them. They rightly sensed that they may well have reached a peak and would now have to fight every inch of the way to keep their profits up, and, if possible, increase them. Indeed, 'in the year 1913, which was the year that marked the highest point of production ever attained in the history of the industry, coal was plentiful and comparatively cheap; profits were high, no less than 1s. 11·38d per ton of mineral raised; wages were low, averaging only 6s. 4·9d per day, or £82 per annum per person employed.'[9]

By 1920, however, production had fallen drastically, though profits had risen by fifty per cent. Wages had also risen; in fact they had doubled, but the cost of living had increased even more quickly.[10] Thus the post-war pattern found miners relatively less well off than in the very badly paid pre-war days, and with mine-owners facing an extremely uncertain and inauspicious future. The resulting spectacle of an industry with declining productivity yet still managing to increase its profit margin was symptomatic of concealed illness, with life being maintained by a form of artificial respiration. Why had the miners not taken more advantage of this period which straddled the war, when the new-born MFGB had already begun to show its power and the owners were starting to go on the defensive? The answer is that the miners were still far from united. Generally speaking they were not, as yet, even very politically conscious, and were easily be-wildered by politico-economic solutions being thrown up for their alleged salvation. In 1912, the 'Miners' Next Step',[11] a sensational pamphlet written by Noah Ablett and others, was published in South Wales. Its effect, largely because of extended comment in conservative papers, notably – for many years afterwards – the *Morning Post*, served only to confuse the whole issue confronting the miners. For it introduced very strongly the note of worker-ownership of industry, known on the continent as Syndicalism. This notion was strongly repudiated in an important part of the presidential address to that same year's (October) Conference of the MFGB. Ironically, however, 'it was not until the artillery of Lenin was brought to bear on it in 1920 that the Syndicalist doctrine was overcome. But for a period of ten years* there was a ferment in the trade unions, appearing in a variety of forms; industrial unionism versus craft unionism; the amalgamation drive ("too many unions, too few trade unionists"); the One Big Union; the longing for the General Strike; the demand for workers' control in industry, etc. etc.'[12] Though all these elements were to burst with the exploding bubble of the 1926 Strike, they were, which is even more important, to continue festering throughout the long Lock-Out which followed. Many former feuds, thought by some to be dead, such as the rivalry of 'craft', and 'new' unionism, were to rear their heads, and to show that working-class solidarity during that traumatic period, even in the mining communities, was nothing like as complete as has so often been claimed. There persisted, however, the unifying effect of the central drive for shorter hours and better conditions. Nationalisation remained the principal objective as a final and overall remedy peculiarly suited – for reasons unconnected with political dogma – to the mining industry. 'The formation of the Triple Alliance just before the Great War between the MFGB, the National Union of Railmen and the National Transport Workers' Federation for the purpose of joint industrial action in support of each others' demands had the same centralising effect.'[13]

Discussion of aims went on unabated all through the war, and was intensified by the return of the miners from the trenches. Some of them brought home tales of their military leaders' incapacity at such places as Passchendaele; this heightened reluctance to tolerate a continuance of the old oppressive conditions at the hands of 'civilian generals'. With highly successful Government control of the mines (as of 1916) bearing out the maxim that 'necessity knows no law', the MFGB came in quickly after the war with their demands for a 2s. increase in wages per shift, a six-hour day and nationalisation. The tide was running strongly in the miners' favour at this particular juncture. The Federation was

*This refers to the decade prior to 1920.

not only the most powerful trade union in the country but, which was of much greater psychological importance, 'the miner's work, by its unpleasant and dangerous nature, gained him the respectful sympathy of people unconcerned with the industry, who felt no such sympathy with the wage claims of shop assistants, or even railwaymen'.[14] The demands being made, moreover, could be, and were, backed up by more than merely empty threats of strike action. They were threats which the Prime Minister, Mr Lloyd George, did not care to take lightly in the jittery, post-war climate of opinion which feared revolution. He consequently set up a Royal Commission on the coal industry, half of whose members would be chosen by the MFGB. So startling was this unprecedented piece of supposed conciliation, it was surprising that it was not immediately suspected as being a trap. The Commission, which became famous as the Sankey Commission after its chairman, Mr Justice Sankey, a distinguished High Court Judge, afterwards Lord Chancellor, was to make a detailed examination of the Federation's demands.

The promise was made on the Government's behalf, in Parliament, by its 'second man',[15] Mr Bonar Law, that whatever the Royal Commission proposed would be carried into law. Never had the mining community had more cause for optimism than at this moment. After all their struggles, it seemed as if a possibly spectacular breakthrough was imminent. For 'without parallel in the history of Commissions appointed by Act of Parliament, this Commission had opportunities of surveying an entire industry, both in its general aspects in relation to the nation in the past, in the present and in the future, and in its general structure down to the smallest conceivable detail.'[16] The Government's unambiguous pledge to implement the Commission's findings had won over those in the Miners' Federation who were originally doubtful about co-operating with the copious enquiry that now got under way.

Final unanimity could hardly have been expected from a Commission made up, as it was, of six miners' nominees, three coalowners and three industrialists. The latter were Mr (later Sir) Arthur Balfour, a steel manufacturer who described himself in

Who's Who as 'a Freemason, a Churchman and a Conservative'; Sir Arthur Duckham, a noted engineer, and Sir Thomas Royden, Chairman of Cunard, whose hobbies were 'hunting, shooting and polo'. They combined with the Commission's Chairman to produce, in March, one of the three interim reports, and declared, in Clause 9, that 'Even upon the evidence already given, the present system of ownership and working in the coal industry stands condemned, and some other system must be substituted for it, either Nationalisation or a method of unification by national purchase and/or by joint control.' This sentence, coming from the source it did, was the most significant, if, to some, the most disturbing of all the comments to be included in the written findings of this historic Commission. There were four final reports, the net effect of the Commission being a recommendation for the increase of wages already asked for (2s. per day); immediate reduction of hours from eight to seven with a further reduction to six if certain conditions were fulfilled; and, in the last resort most importantly but most contentiously of all, *nationalisation of the mines*.

The miners had won – or so it seemed. Admittedly the majority on the Commission in favour of public ownership of the mines was only seven out of the thirteen members (though there was unanimous approval for nationalising the coal royalties). Nothing had been said about the need for unanimity when the Government had pledged itself to be bound by the Commission. There was some embarrassment, it is true, for the 'hard-faced men', as Baldwin called them, who dominated Lloyd George's Coalition, since their economic kith-and-kin were involved in the vested interests of coalmining. But a solemn pledge is a solemn pledge, and this particular one had been given in unqualified form, to be binding in 'letter and in spirit'. It was on the basis of this pledge that key MFGB leaders had staged a special conference on their attitude to the Commission and, 'displaying a touching faith in the usefulness of Royal Commissions, pleaded for the miners' full participation in the enquiry'.[17]

Then the almost incredible happened. The Prime Minister not only repudiated the Government's pledge now that the Commission had reached conclusions it had not expected; he even, at a later stage, asserted blandly that no firmly binding pledge had ever been given. The cleverest part, however, of Lloyd George's strategy at this delicate stage, when revolution could not be ruled out if a major blunder were made, was the manner in which, very gradually, he extricated himself from the dilemma posed by Sankey. Arguing that the Report was not unanimous, the Premier ruled that it would remain for the moment under 'consideration'. As he played for time, every passing week showed that the tactical tide was on the turn and that the miners had lost, perhaps for ever, the best opportunity that had yet come their way. The owners, however, were still in a state of shock at the thought of how nearly the policy of nationalisation had had to be adopted. From that moment can be dated the Mining Association's determination to fight to the bitterest of finishes any resurgent threat of a similar kind.

At the same time, among the public at large, 'the distress of the miners excited a unique passion and bitterness. There was a feeling, which extended far beyond the Labour movement, that the unpleasantness and danger of digging into the bowels of the earth deserved better reward than an average of 60 shillings. This feeling was reinforced by the inefficiency and arrogance with which the coalowners managed their affairs and Lloyd George's blatant duplicity in 1919.'[18] Actually the Prime Minister had not quite come to the end of his tight-rope walk. In the early summer of 1920 he was forced to pause perilously in mid-air by the threat of a general strike if British troops were sent to support the cause of 'reaction' in Poland in its war against Russia. This first ever threat of industrial action to secure political ends was symbolically successful in that a boat bound for Poland, the *Jolly George*, could not sail as the London dockers refused to load her with the required munitions of war. In fact the changing military situation in Poland made British assistance unnecessary in any event. 'But the Government had stumbled on the "Constitutional issue", which was used with such potent effect in 1926.'[19]

Then, in the autumn, a short but inconclusive miners' strike enabled Lloyd George to introduce far-reaching Emergency Powers arming the Government with potential 'police state' powers in case of domestic crisis. He now felt in a strong enough position to make a direct challenge to the newly revived 'Triple Alliance', by bringing government control of the mines to a premature end. This had originally been due to happen in August 1919. The Government decided instead to bow to political pressure and break another set of pledges.[20] 'De-control was sudden, violent and brutal. Three months were allowed for the whole process; the industry was handed back to the owners with no provision made for improved production or distribution.'[21] The owners announced severe wage cuts in face of declining overseas markets and the poorer demand at home resulting from trade depression. The cuts were to become operative from the date of de-control (31 March), but the Miners' Federation was quite unable to agree to such a sudden reversal of fortune and drastic decrease in the miners' standard of living. For this is what the fight was now about from their point of view. In consequence of the ensuing deadlock the miners were locked out of work as of 1 April 1921. This was the first of the two Great Lock-Outs in the coalmining industry, a dress rehearsal, as it turned out, for 1926. Theoretically, the 'Triple Alliance' should now have come to the immediate assistance of the miners. In this event the General Strike would have occurred then and not in 1926; and had it done so it would have been successful. It would have enforced an equitable economic solution to the mounting problem of depression, demoralisation and sub-standard living in the mining communities.

As far as the other 'side' was concerned, however, the struggle was now primarily a political one. Though the economic dynamite continued to accumulate, a slow-burning political fuse was about to be attached to the pile. The only real danger to the cause of the Establishment was the premature explosion of a 'general strike' in 1921, when labour would have won. Public opinion was heavily on the miners' side at this moment, and the Government's plans to meet an 'emergency' with organised force had barely begun. Time had to be bought, principally by exploiting differences between the MFGB and the other unions of the Triple Alliance. Standing ready to down tools in sympathy with the miners, the dockers, railwaymen and transport workers waited with mixed feelings for the approaching deadline of 10 p.m. on Friday, 15 May. 'Nobody doubted that a widespread strike was to develop and the only question was how long it would last. It was one of the most dramatic days in trade unionism. During the afternoon Mr Thomas came running down the stairs at Unity House and remarked: "Gentlemen, the strike is off!"'[22]

What had happened was that J. H. (Jimmy) Thomas, the wily, ambitious and powerful general secretary of the National Union of Railwaymen, had seized on an unguarded remark made by the MFGB's secretary, Frank Hodges. The latter, at an evening meeting at the House of Commons, had made a favourable impression on a worried group of (mostly Conservative) M.P.s. (Evan Williams, putting the mineowners' case, had cut a less favourable figure with the same audience earlier in the day.) But at an advanced hour during the evening meeting, Hodges had intimated, in an answer to a well-timed and probably well-prepared question,[23] that his Federation's Executive *might* favourably consider a temporary abandonment of the demand for a national 'pool' (to level out wages in all the coalfields) in return for a 'satisfactory wage settlement'. Such an opportunity was all that Jimmy Thomas needed as a pretext for shattering the already fragile Triple Alliance. The day of the decision to retreat has gone down in trade union annals as 'Black Friday'.

All thereafter was anti-climax. The miners struggled on alone in their lock-out for three months. Lloyd George enjoyed the advantages of his own form of 'triple alliance', consisting of the press, the key members of his coalition government and the socially ambitious newly rich. His friend, Lord Northcliffe, controlling the *Daily Mail* and *The Times*, was not stinting in his support; the coalitionists envisaged an almost indefinite extension of political power in the absence of industrial chaos; and the Duke of Northumberland was as scandalised as many others by Lloyd George's open auctioning of titles and honours.

The Welsh wizard contemplated the year 1922 with regained equanimity, his spectacular tight-rope walk successfully concluded. Little did he think that by the end of that year he would be out of office. Still less could he or anyone else have imagined that in the course of the following year, the 'Baldwin era' would have begun, and that by early 1925 this comparative newcomer to Britain's political scene would be facing another touch-and-go mining crisis, but facing it from a position of great strength. The whole mining situation was thus transferred squarely into the political arena with the appearance of the inscrutable and paradoxical figure who was to dominate and mastermind the events of 1926.

4

The political fuse

Stanley Baldwin, soon after his expected General Election defeat in 1923, was extremely optimistic about the Conservative Party whose leader he had so recently become. He even predicted a 'great victory' at about the time when his Labour opponents might otherwise, 'through want of action on our part', have been swept into power by 'the discontent in the country'. And the year in which this 'great victory' would occur, according to Baldwin's prediction, was to be 1926.

It was this year of 1926 which saw Britain's million miners locked out of work for seven months. Fleetingly, at the very beginning of this period, they enjoyed the support of certain other industries and the backing of the General Council of the TUC. This, though it represented a solid downing of tools by three and a half million men, did not amount to a strike that was truly 'general', and the stoppage of work was never described, in trade union circles, as anything but a 'national' one. It has nevertheless passed into history and, in some senses, into mythology, as 'The General Strike'. It was terminated after nine days by the same General Council who had so reluctantly called it in the first place. But the termination, involving unconditional surrender to the Government, was made with no agreement from those on whose behalf the strike had been staged. These latter, the miners, whose enforced stoppage of work had preceded the mass stoppage ordered by the TUC, thereafter embarked on a further period of struggle which was to last more than another six months.

This Great Lock-Out, as it came to be called, overlapped the short period of the actual General Strike, and can be seen, after

fifty years, to have eclipsed it in ultimate importance. Evolving
into a virtual hunger strike over a prolonged period and on a
nationwide scale, the Lock-Out came to develop its own distinctive character and to have its own special long-term effects. It
produced a story that was extraordinary and in some respects
incredible, without any exact parallel in the rest of British history.
It possessed aspects and elements to which full justice has yet to be
accorded by chroniclers. But it was doomed from the start to
almost certain failure and ended in just that: a humiliating and
complete capitulation. A turning of the tables in the other direction came about only years later, when the legacy of the Lock-
Out finally bore fruit.

Quite obviously no exact falling out of future events could have
been foreseen by Baldwin when he picked 1926 as the probable
point at which his party would come in for a 'great victory'. But
most accounts of his fateful 1923 decision to call a surprise General
Election still underestimate the full depths of his very considerable political astuteness. There is general agreement only on the
inscrutability of his true motives. 'Baldwin's decision to hold a
General Election in the autumn of 1923 was widely condemned
at the time as an act of gratuitous folly; and it has since puzzled
historians, who have been reluctant to believe that the reasons he
gave at the time were sufficient to justify so risky a step.'[1] The
most favoured explanation sees Baldwin reasoning that only a
protective tariff on imports would fully re-unite the Conservatives
as an entity independent of former allegiances under the Lloyd
George Coalition and at the same time be the best hedge against
the threat of mounting unemployment. There have, however,
been other theories. 'It has even been suggested that Baldwin
courted electoral defeat in 1923, foreseeing the troubles ahead and
calculating that, if another party held office and failed to overcome them, the Conservatives would be swept back into power,
all the stronger for their brief surrender of it.' So writes Professor
C. L. Mowat;[2] but he adds forthwith: 'The truth was otherwise.'
A. J. P. Taylor, while concluding that Baldwin's 'motives for this
sudden decision must remain obscure',[3] refers to the 'more sophisticated' explanation that the Prime Minister deliberately provoked

F. E. Smith arrives at the Carlton Club, 1922

electoral defeat in order to bounce back more strongly when others had made a mess of things. But he dismissed this as a 'doubtful story', although it is a story that has been left not so much in doubt as, with notable exceptions,[4] unexamined in detail.

Britain and Europe had remained in a chronic state of crisis ever since the ending of the Great War. Reparations against Germany were beginning to have a boomerang effect inasmuch as they threatened to reduce that country to such economic chaos as would court violent revolution. And yet the victorious nations themselves owed vast sums to the United States, and the attempt to repay these was draining Europe of its precious gold reserves. Baldwin was in a peculiarly delicate situation having personally* handled the negotiations for the repayment of the American debt. He shrewdly realised that, in the entirely new situation created by the Russian Revolution, Anglo-American co-operation for re-establishing Europe was essential if the capitalist system was to survive. But how, as has been asked,[5] could this be achieved 'other than by reversing the flow of gold across the Atlantic, cleansing the German plague-spot by liberal and repeated applications of assisting in this sanitary operation?' The trick was ultimately worked by a Plan associated with the American General Dawes. His name, however, was sufficiently anathema among British labour- and working-class circles as to make the sponsoring of any scheme associated with him virtually impossible for any but a heavily entrenched Tory Government. It was little wonder that the Prime Minister had many worries over which to ponder during his solitary walks in Aix-les-Bains where he went as usual for his summer holiday.

To the risk of failing to stabilise capitalism in Europe there was added the certain worsening of the domestic situation. The post-war boom had been quickly replaced by deepening depression and disillusionment. Wages had been falling ever since 1921, and no-

---

*During the Premiership of Bonar Law – November 1922–May 1923 – Baldwin was Chancellor of the Exchequer. Early in 1923 he agreed to the repayment of Britain's debt to the United States on terms highly favourable to the latter but ultimately productive of greater involvement of the United States in European affairs despite prior American withdrawal from Versailles.

where, with a brief respite in 1923, more rapidly than in the mining industry. Unemployment, which had dropped from the 1921 figure of two million already mentioned, was showing unmistakable signs that it could only go up again ominously in the near future. It was in such a climate that the workers were observably beginning to take their own kind of offensive. The rate, in fact, at which the Labour vote was increasing pointed to a Labour majority at the next General Election, on the assumption that Parliament lived out its normal term until 1926 or 1927. And the Prime Minister would then be a man, Ramsay MacDonald, who had been gaining ground on all fronts. Baldwin could recognise in him a possible adversary possessing many of his own instincts for political survival: a man in fact who, once he had become leader of a majority Labour Government, could well dominate British politics for the next decade or more. Such a prospect could only be viewed with unmitigated alarm by the 'men of property'. For, though MacDonald was respected in Establishment circles, he could not, at a time of seething unrest among the working-class rank-and-file, have failed – in office with a sizeable majority – to have followed an uncompromisingly Socialist path. For if he did fail to do so, the Communist Party, at that time gaining some strength despite being disbarred from any form of affiliation with the Labour Party, might well find its once-for-all opportunity of gaining the substantial foothold it desired – but, in the end, never achieved – in British politics.

In 1923, however, there was no chance whatever of Labour gaining anything like an overall majority at a General Election. The most likely result of any poll taken at this time was that the Labour Party would do well enough to form a minority Government, but to 'govern' only by the grace and favour of the Liberals. The chances were that such a Government would not long retain office and enjoy, meanwhile, no real power. To state categorically that the effecting of such a situation was Baldwin's definite plan, would be impossible. It is equally impossible to deny categorically that this, in general terms, was the main motivation of Baldwin's otherwise inexplicable decision to fly in the face of all advice and plunge his party into an unnecessary General

Election at the end of 1923. To make such a denial would be vastly to underrate the man whose 'simple exterior concealed a skilful operator'[6] and whom Lloyd George – of all people – called 'the most formidable antagonist I have ever encountered'. To do so, moreover, would be to take quite unquestioningly at its face value Baldwin's official explanation for the election decision, namely his decision to commit his Party to the principle of protection. For within twelve months Baldwin had miraculously been converted to free trade. Having detached such key men as Birkenhead and Austen Chamberlain from their former allegiance to Lloyd George and the Coalition by the first decision, he completed the re-unification of the Conservative Party by getting Churchill back into the fold when free trade suddenly became the order of the day. MacDonald had meanwhile duly won a larger number of seats than either of the other parties at the General Election of December 1923, and ultimately formed a minority Government dependent for its continuation on Liberal goodwill. Far from being dismayed by this turn of events, Baldwin publicly interpreted them in the words partly quoted at the beginning of this chapter. It was to the post-Election meeting of the Conservative Party that he said: 'It was on unemployment that the Labour Party relied on coming to power within two or three years. Their calculations were that the discontent in the country coupled with want of action on our part would have swept them into power and us out by 1926. And I believe myself that that would have happened, and believe that in spite of the losses in this election we shall emerge all the stronger and able to bring to pass a great victory about the time when in my view nothing but disaster could have overtaken us.'

If indeed something like what has been described was in the back of Baldwin's mind, his instincts did not deceive him. 'It was a daring solution, requiring all the skill in political manoeuvring in which the British governing class has so long excelled. Even if it was not conceived in these clear terms the point remains that no other hypothesis explains the turn of events. . . . At the time, however, this skilful manoeuvre was scarcely perceived, except by those on the extreme Left.'[7] The final vindication for Baldwin

came at the General Election of October 1924, when the Conservatives won an overwhelming victory.

Stanley Baldwin could thereafter relax in his favourite role as
a man of peace, a role he quite honestly and genuinely wished to
play as long as it was humanly possible to do so. And he could
now afford to be generous toward the Labour and trade union
movement, the first plank in his strategy toward whom was that
of containment rather than confrontation. Such a strategy well
accords with his character and corresponds to the general course
of his early career. A brief look at the latter helps to disentangle
the political threads of the early twenties as constituting a prelude
to the decisive confrontation of 1926. It also helps to explain how
Baldwin became so ideally suited for his eventual role as the 'man
for the post-war Establishment'.[8] As such, he was the key to the
causes, course and effects of the Great Lock-Out drama.

Baldwin was a Harrovian who, like Churchill, was not an outstanding scholar either then or later at Cambridge. His undergraduate leanings toward the church were replaced by a more
unspecified sense of vocation. This first took the form of paternal-
istic goodwill toward the workers in the family firm when, in the
guise of ironmaster for the next twenty years, he made himself
cultivate the more benevolent characteristics of a typical Victorian
businessman. In course of time he was to become Chairman of the
Great Western Railway, the Metropolitan Bank and the Aldridge
Colliery Company. His family enjoyed a solid and respected
status in the county of Worcestershire, but his first attempt to
enter Parliament (as Unionist candidate for Kidderminster in
1906) was a discomforting failure in that year of the great Liberal
landslide. He eventually became a member of the House of
Commons by means which raised no eyebrows at the time but
would be unthinkable today. For in 1908 his father died and
Stanley, at the age of forty, inherited not only the family business
but also his father's constituency of Bewdley. Out of respect for
Baldwin's father, the Liberals put up no candidate of their own,
and Stanley was declared elected unopposed. His uneventful and
undistinguished first decade in Parliament became a blessing in
disguise later on. For it helped to build up the bucolic image that

led many more spectacular politicians into fatally misjudging him. It was less that they underrated his political skills than that they failed to perceive that they were there at all. Churchill, so often contemptuous of Baldwin in the twenties, lived to praise him in terms no less significant than the highly revealing tribute of Lloyd George already quoted. When a memorial was dedicated to Baldwin in Worcestershire in 1948, Churchill said of him: 'He was the most formidable politician I have ever known in public life.'

Having entered Parliament by means seemingly unconnected with political ability as such, Baldwin achieved office in somewhat analagous circumstances. He was still a relatively obscure backbencher when Lloyd George took over the Premiership from Asquith in 1916, and chose Andrew Bonar Law (the Unionist leader) as Chancellor of the Exchequer. The latter, a man who happened to loathe entertaining, had been a friend of Baldwin's father. He needed a junior colleague and showed a preference for his old friend's son, a man rich enough to do the entertaining he himself so much disliked. Baldwin was thus appointed Financial Secretary to the Treasury by Lloyd George, while holding which post he made, soon after the Armistice, an extraordinary gesture which appeared to be entirely quixotic in motive. He anonymously donated to the nation a sum of £120,000 – no less than a fifth of his personal fortune. Some light is shed on the nature of his political instincts when, with great care, he subsequently arranged that his 'secret' action should become publicly known. By the time he had become President of the Board of Trade in 1921 he had also become completely disenchanted with the political morality of Lloyd George, who was still Prime Minister. It was thus that, with catlike tread, Baldwin was soon to steal his way onto the very centre of the stage and, within a couple of years, to astonish both friend and foe alike.

Lloyd George had become Premier in 1916 as the man most likely to win the war, but without the advantage of being the leader of any party. His strength derived from his dominance of a Coalition containing a large number of Conservatives – or Unionists as they were still more generally called – and he adroitly

cashed in on his wartime success by triumphantly going to the
country at the end of 1918 on the basis of continuing to lead a
Coalition to cope with the transition to the new problems of
peace. This meant that his own party was now split into 'Coalition
Liberals' and those others now in Opposition – who joined the
Liberal rump led by the deposed Asquith. The new element in the
Opposition was a small but growing Labour Party which soon
found that seething social unrest and popular disillusionment
throughout the country might quickly be transformable into
tangible political power.

It was obvious, however, that Lloyd George would have to rely
more and more on the continuation of official Conservative
support in the flurry of foreign and domestic worries that taxed
his mercurial brilliance to the utmost. Such official support came
to be viewed with increasing alarm by the Conservative rank-and-
file who, with an apprehensive eye on the rising hopes of the
Labour Party, lacked a prophetic advocate of their own strong
independence. For, thanks to Lloyd George's wizardry, 'attitudes
within the Unionist party by 1922 were the reverse of 1916: in
1916 mass support for Lloyd George had come from the backbenchers longing for dynamic leadership and the leaders had been
hesitant – in 1922 the backbenchers had had enough of dynamism
but the leaders were under the magician's spell.'[9] How and by
whom was this spell to be broken? Almost the last person who
could have been predicted to emerge as giant-killer was Stanley
Baldwin who was nevertheless (in the autumn of 1922) 'alarmed
to hear of the plans for an immediate general election to perpetuate the coalition, feeling that Lloyd George, who had already
smashed the Liberal Party, was well on the way to smashing the
Conservative party also'.[10] On the advice of friends, in an atmosphere of high political intrigue, Baldwin made a dramatic speech
at the meeting so critical for Conservatives which was held at the
Carlton Club on 19 October 1922. He gave a blunt warning that
if the 'present association' were continued, the old Conservative
Party would be 'smashed to atoms and lost in ruins'. No one
could have imagined Baldwin himself emerging at this moment
as the possible leader of a newly independent Conservative Party.

The mantle was to fall on Bonar Law, even though he had only reluctantly come to the Carlton Club meeting which, in the event, voted overwhelmingly for an end to the Conservative association with Lloyd George and his Coalition. In the ensuing General Election, the Conservatives' boldness was rewarded by their obtaining a majority of eighty-eight over all the other parties. 'The old order had returned,' in the phrase of Professor Mowat,[11] who adds, 'and thus ended the reign of the great ones, the giants of the Edwardian era and of the war; and the rule of the pygmies, of the "second-class brains" began, to continue until 1940.'

This return of the 'old order' was accompanied by an entirely new factor in British politics, and one that was being watched with great care and much apprehension in certain circles, by no one more than by Stanley Baldwin. For the true significance of the 1922 election was the great stride forward made by the Labour party, 149 of whose candidates were elected to Parliament as against 59 in 1918; and Labour, in the intervening period, had won no less than 14 by-elections, losing only one. Everything now pointed to the Labour party's becoming the Conservatives' principal opponents in place of the Liberals, who were disastrously weakened and split by the break-up of the Coalition. The latter received, in 1922, less votes than Labour and returned far fewer members. Even the rising star, Winston Churchill, still a Liberal, lost his seat at Dundee. The 1922–23 period thus turned out to be a vital one, with the occurrence of three general elections and 'the terrible portent of a Labour Government'.[12] Baldwin had every justification for his fears and, as Prime Minister after May 1923, every chance to do something about allaying them. His fateful decision, already described, precipitated a general election in December of that same year, giving Labour their expected Pyrrhic victory. They now had 191 M.P.s, becoming the second largest party, but able to outvote the 258 Conservatives only with support from enough of the 159 Liberals who managed to scrape back into this Parliament.

Discernible from this point onwards is the gradual lining up of forces, almost all on one side, which were to play such a prominent part in the 1926 showdown. The 'side' which was active was that which feared some revolutionary move from the Left. But there was a curious time lag in such thinking and the re-established 'old order' had not yet had time correctly to sum up the true political character of the 'new men' now, for the time being, in power. Even today there is confusion about the philosophy of the official Labour party in the mid-twenties, for it is certainly not true that 'the new men repudiated both capitalism and traditional foreign policy'.[13]

What was happening was that the men of Baldwin's world had not yet got over the fright of the immediate post-war period when, indeed, a bitterly rebellious spirit was stirring throughout the country. There was plenty to keep such a spirit on the boil. 'The workers were within an ace of being ready for revolution. ... The people of England had borne the agony of the war on the promise that they would be given homes fit for heroes to live in, but almost as soon as the war was over the promises were scrapped with other war material, and repeated attacks were made upon their standard of living.'[14] Once more, as after the Reform Act of 1832, the public at large had been fooled; but on this occasion they were determined to fight for what was theirs, and the Russian Revolution had brought its clear lesson of what could be achieved – though formerly thought impossible – when vast sections of a nation are driven to desperation point. In circumstances dominated by economic factors, this revolutionary period lasted from 1918 to 1921, but not beyond the latter year. Lloyd George had adroitly distributed enough palliatives to sugar the pill of military preparations backing the declared state of national emergency; the danger of key unions irrevocably combining together had been pre-empted for the time being; and there was sufficient, if reluctant, acceptance of the new wage structure to put off the possibility of violent confrontation. Traditionalist circles, however, were far from put at their ease as they noted the forming, in 1921, of the British Communist Party. Their uneasiness was in no way alleviated even when it became apparent, from 1922 onwards, that official Labour intended in no way to have any Communist affiliation. Rather was it the Labour Party, at its 1923 level, that represented to them everything that was most undesirable and dangerous in British post-war political life. In reality, this particular set of 'new men' were surprisingly cosmopolitan and no longer drawn only from one class and almost exclusively from trade union backgrounds. It was quickly evident that Labour's first Prime Minister, the eloquent and respectable Ramsay MacDonald, was anything but a revolutionary. But it was naturally still feared that his party would soon drag him down the road of socialism; and socialism, it was axiomatic, meant communism in the long run.

It was thus that Lloyd George's skeleton plan to meet a national emergency resulting from industrial action was set up and never dismantled. In the dangerous months of 1919 he brought into being a Supply and Transport Committee to keep essential services moving during a crisis; and in 1920 he had rushed an Emergency Powers Act on to the Statute Book. This Act 'made permanent the dictatorial powers the Government already possessed under wartime Defence of the Realm Acts'.[15] At any future threat of strike action on a scale thought likely to endanger security, the Government could proceed by orders-in-council to establish summary courts and take any other measures felt necessary to meet the country's day-to-day requirements. It soon became clear that the most competent judges as to the utility of such contingency planning were not necessarily felt to be the Government ministers of the day. For it is a vital adjunct of 'Establishment' that it can function, if necessary, quite independently of any particular government. There thus were certain people who felt, in 1923, that a Labour Government could not be trusted with the secrets of emergency plans against possible future strikes, in particular against a general strike. They were therefore willing to take matters into their own hands if and when the need arose. All of course was well while Baldwin was at Downing Street from May to December 1923, and during this time the Prime Minister decided to revive the dormant Supply and Transport Committee. To whom could the custodianship of this key organisation be safely entrusted?

Every Prime Minister, it is said or thought, has a person on whom he leans as his most intimate confidant in political matters.

In the case of Baldwin, this person was John Davidson* whom Baldwin, soon after becoming Prime Minister, made Chancellor of the Duchy of Lancaster. Davidson himself gives a very full and candid account of how his duties were to be extended in another very important direction.[16] The Prime Minister asked him to take on the position of Chief Civil Commissioner, his first assignment being to revive and revise the dormant emergency plans. Davidson forthwith took up this task in strict secrecy, drawing his salary as Chief Commissioner not from the public purse but from Conservative Party funds.

As Baldwin's unofficial but powerful right-hand man, he set to work with his usual thoroughness, and has recorded that:[17]

> The Government had the duty to protect the people against any attempt at direct action by revolutionary methods to put in an anti-democratic body to control the country. . . . An attempt to substitute an oligarchy with no claim to represent the majority of the people had to be resisted at all costs. . . .
>
> Within days [of Baldwin's becoming Prime Minister] I was appointed Chief Civil Commissioner, and I spent practically the whole of my energies in supporting John Anderson,† my assistant . . . who was responsible for the detail in preparing a largely voluntary organisation to meet the General Strike. The country was divided into twelve areas, each under a Commissioner who was responsible for maintaining all the public services, if these were interrupted, by controlling and organising transport, food supplies and essential services like light and power. London had a method by which they co-operated with surrounding areas for the supply of food and essential services to the capital. There was no publicity given to the scheme. Arrangements were made to take over the BBC and possibly to produce a Government news sheet if the newspapers ceased to appear. Work continued unremittingly until the fall of the Government in 1923.

*J. C. C. (later first Viscount) Davidson.
†Sir John Anderson, the brilliant Permanent Under-Secretary to the Home Office.

The urgency prompting the laying of this groundwork – ultimately leading to a giant overkill operation – was supplied by the
fear that a Communist plot was in existence. This fear was based
on Scotland Yard and MI5 reports, notably that of December
1922, that 'the Communist Party of Great Britain is organising a
"Secret Service" which will be composed of members who are,
in the opinion of the Executive, 100 per cent Communists'. It was
also reported that Communists were participating in the National
Unemployed Workers' Movement. Ironically, however, the
revolutionary thrust in British politics had, as mentioned earlier,
already played itself out by the end of 1921 and the British
Communist Party, in 1922, commissioned an internal report of
its own. This had been necessitated by Communist demoralisation
and disarray at a time when 'the membership was rapidly fading
away, the finances of the party were chaotic and the organisation
had almost completely broken down'.[18] The report in fact concluded that during the first two years of the party's existence
(1920–1922) 'with all these opportunities and with the tireless
activities and energy of individual workers, the party has made
no real progress either numerically or in terms of influence'. To
the extent, moreover, that the police reports reaching Davidson
were true, they were a sign of the weakness rather than the strength
of the Communist Party. For such Communist activity as was
supposedly 'secret', or aimed at influence through infiltration,
'engendered increasingly strong opposition from the Labour
Party and the trade unions, when they became aware that the
Communist Party was organising groups within their organisations'.[19]

By a further irony, however, it was the Labour Party which
Davidson and his colleagues feared most with respect to the
immediate fate of their emergency regulations. A strange situation
thus arose with the Conservative electoral defeat at the end of
1922, when Davidson received a secret memorandum of some
significance. The sender of the memorandum was one Colonel
Launcelot Storr, a man who can be said to have stood at the heart
and core of the contemporary Establishment. But who was he?
His early career had been in the Indian army and in the Great War

he served with the War Cabinet, the Committee of Imperial Defence, and at the Peace Conference. He resigned from the army in 1921 and as of 1924 he became a key figure in the inner counsels of his party as head of the first Conservative Policy Secretariat. Official records are discreetly silent as to his activities during the extremely important interim period; but he appears to have acted as personal assistant to Davidson, for, in 1920, 'he approached Davidson with the object of securing a political appointment in England, which Davidson was able to arrange. He became a close friend, a loyal ally and a reliable informant.'[20] The Communists in fact were not the only body to enjoy the advantages of a 'secret service'. The memorandum which Storr sent to Davidson in December 1923, warned of the possible dangers for the emergency organisation posed by an incoming Labour Government. It pointed out that if the new Government decided to retain the organisation, it might appoint some prominent trade unionist such as Robert Smillie or Frank Hodges to the post of Chief Civil Commissioner. 'In this event, whoever was appointed would at once become acquainted with all the machinery for quelling that very crisis which he himself, when in opposition, may have done his best to foment.' Such logic was not questioned at the time, for, in the circles wherein Storr moved, it was readily assumed, however mistakenly, that the Labour Party and the trade unions were hand in glove and that the latter were, in the very nature of things, virtually committed to revolutionary action if necessary. Storr consequently commended to Davidson the wisdom of ensuring that the strike-breaking organisation 'be wrapped in temporary obscurity and silence', and that pressure be exerted through the Home Office for the appointment of a suitable successor to Davidson.

Davidson, however, decided to make a private approach to the man eventually chosen to be Labour's Chancellor of the Duchy of Lancaster. No choice could have been luckier for Davidson as it fell on Josiah Wedgwood, an old friend, scion of the famous pottery family and maverick figure in the Labour movement of the day. Davidson begged Wedgwood 'not to destroy all I had done and not to inform his Cabinet of it. This,' added Davidson (referring, in fact, to an assignment he had been given as a direct employee of the Conservative Party) 'did not concern party but was a national matter'.[21] Davidson's instincts did not betray him. Wedgwood could not pledge himself to continue the work in question but did promise not to interfere with what had already been done. When Davidson was back at his old desk on Labour's defeat, in November 1924, he found that 'Josh' had honoured his pledge, telling him that 'I haven't destroyed any of your plans. In fact, I haven't done a bloody thing about them.'

In most other respects the action, or inaction, of the first Labour Government, lasting for ten months, gave little reason for its political opponents to fear for the safety of the Constitution. Apart from anything else, the Prime Minister, Ramsay Mac-Donald, gave anything but comfort to would-be revolutionaries by his threat, soon after taking office, to use the Emergency Powers to deal with threatened strike action in the docks. Nevertheless Labour, having accorded recognition to the new government of Soviet Russia, proposed further links by treaty with that country. This policy, coupled with inept handling of what became celebrated in legal annals as 'the Campbell case',* revived fears that MacDonald's government had secret Communist sympathies after all. The Conservatives and Liberals combined to out-vote the government by no less than 369 to 191, and an early general election became inevitable.

This was the election which became famous for its association with the name of the president of the Communist International, Grigory Evseevich Apfelbaum, better known by his pseudonym of Zinoviev. A few days before polling day, a letter from Zinoviev was reportedly sent the Russian *chargé d'affaires* in London advocating revolutionary propaganda and other seditious activities. In vain did Labour party supporters, smarting under the reflected discredit engendered by the letter, protest that it was a forgery, which it was; all they could do was to use the 'Red letter' as an

---

*The acting editor of the *Workers' Weekly*, J. R. Campbell, was charged with incitement to mutiny, but when the prosecution was dropped, the Tories censured the government and the latter lost the resulting vote by an overwhelming majority.

excuse – for years to come – for their Party's failure, and quote its
use at that election as an example of unscrupulous Tory tactics.
But it was a lame excuse, and there was certainly no Tory plot
involved, even if there was an unexpectedly large quota of Tory
luck. Baldwin's gamble thus came off in spectacular fashion,
Conservatives returning 413 members to the new House of
Commons.

The new Prime Minister found himself in a position of enormous strength. He had brought back into the Conservative fold
not only the former opponents of the Coalition, but its key
supporters as well. Soon he was to win over Churchill into the
bargain. He could face the year 1925 with confidence despite the
warning signals that greeted him on several sides, particularly on
the industrial front; and though it is dangerous to be selective
in quoting statements attributed to Stanley Baldwin, it is worthwhile adverting to his declaration after the passing of the 1927
Trade Disputes Act that 'I provoked a general election in November 1923 as a means of demoralising the Labour Movement and
securing the commitment of the Labour Party to our imperialist
policy in deed and word. I provoked a General Strike in 1926 as
a means of demoralising the trade union leaders and breaking up
the unity of the unions which had become so manifest in 1925.
There is now no important organised political opposition either
inside or outside Parliament. Whatever strength may be gained
by the revolutionary forces, which as yet are very small, it will
take considerable time before they can seriously hamper any
policy we wish to pursue.'[22]

In 1925, however, it was still a question of maintaining the con-
tinuity of a carefully laid political fuse should an explosive
economic situation ever seem to invite victory to whichever side
acted boldly and acted first. Baldwin was prepared to be ruthless
if necessary but, as already stated, he preferred the ways of containment as long as they were possible. He vigorously rejected an
opportunity presented early in March 1925 to deal the Labour
movement an immediate and crippling blow. A Conservative
backbencher, Frederick Macquisten, introduced a private member's bill aimed at drastically curtailing the trade union political

levy, the main source of Labour party funds. The Bill was defeated by an eloquent speech from the Prime Minister which appealed for justice and an all-party re-echoing of his prayer 'Give us peace in our time, O Lord'. When Baldwin incorporated into the 1927 Trade Disputes Act the very bill he was now so decisively reject-ing, it was after a dramatic interval during which the defensive attack against supposed subversive forces had won its greatest victory of modern times. The immense suffering caused by the great 1926 overkill was a hostage to future fortune; but Baldwin was determined, in 1925, to show that all the options were still open. If political considerations could dictate the switch from Protection to Free Trade in a matter of months, patriotic consider-ations could be shown to demand the transition from industrial peace to all-out war in a matter of days if ever the need should arise.

5

Explosion

In 1923 and 1924, the mining industry enjoyed a burst of heady but shallow-rooted prosperity. The 1923 French occupation of the German mines of the Ruhr, as part of the reparations package, and the American strike in 1924, suddenly opened up new markets for British coal. 'The industry went drunk on the profits . . . 1925 saw the morning after and the hangover. The British coal industry had spent the last two years frittering away its substance in riotous living, in excessive profits, bonuses and over-capitalisation; it should have spent them in a vigorous and urgent programme of modernisation, mechanisation and new development. The profits that had been taken out of the industry in high dividends should have been ploughed back.'[1] Put in another way 'the worthy sentiments of a euphoric spring evening in Westminster were soon negated by the economic and political realities of 1925. The harshest and most immediate economic reality was the progressive decline of the mining industry in the face of resumed German competition after French withdrawal from the Ruhr and the determination of the owners to maintain profits at the expense of the miners. The most disturbing political reality was the greatest resurgence of trade union militancy since Black Friday.'[2]

The 'worthy sentiments' referred to were those of the Prime Minister, Stanley Baldwin, in his speech opposing the anti-trade union Bill introduced by his own backbencher, Frederick Macquisten. It was in this speech that he (Baldwin) uttered his famous cry: 'There are many in all ranks, and all parties who will re-echo my prayer: "Give us peace in our time, O Lord." ' All chance of peace on the industrial front, however, was soon killed by the decision to return sterling to the Gold Standard at the pre-war rate of exchange. This decision was made by Baldwin's surprising choice as his new Chancellor of the Exchequer, Winston Churchill; it involved an over-valuation of the currency to the extent of about ten per cent, and the setting of an excessive price abroad for exports. 'The economic consequences of Mr Churchill,' in the phrase made famous by the title of J. M. Keynes's pamphlet, were 'to force down money-wages and money values. . . . Engaging in a struggle with each separate group in turn, with no prospect that the final result will be fair, and no guarantee that the stronger groups will not gain at the expense of the weaker . . . and it must be war until those who are economically weakest are beaten to the ground.' The particular vulnerability of the miners became immediately apparent. Their plank in the 1921 (post-Sankey) shipwreck had been the agreement with the owners that wages were not to fall below a national minimum percentage additional to the 'standard' level, that is the 1914 'piece' and day-wage rates. This percentage had originally been fixed at 20; but the greater prosperity of 1924 brought pressure from the miners for an increase, and the new figure agreed on was 33⅓ per cent. Within two months of the new Chancellor's panic-provoking announcement of a return to the Gold Standard, the owners announced that the prevailing agreement would end on the last day of July. Thereafter wages would be cut by up to twenty-five per cent, hours increased from seven to eight, and there would be a return to purely district, as opposed to national, settlement of wages. This would mean crippling falls in wages in the economically weaker areas, the very contingency avoidable by the proposed pooling of profits to help level out wages.

All of this meant that *profits* in coalmining would not drop despite the revaluation of the pound. But there would be a dramatic fall in the living standards of the miners, who were once more faced with a threatened lock-out. The unions of the Triple Alliance pledged their support to the MFGB. After a re-run of the 1921 cliff-hanging negotiations, a general stoppage of work on August 1 was averted only by a last-minute Government decision to buy time. A subsidy was to run until 30 April 1926 to cover the difference between the 1924 wage level and the new level now proposed by the owners. All-out war had been averted, or rather, postponed. Why did the Government not stand and fight then and there in a cause which, though unduly favourable to the coalowners, they averred to be in the national interest? Baldwin's own answer was 'we were not ready'.[3] The day came to be known in Trade Union annals, as 'Red Friday'.

The miners' case is well known. What of the case for the coalowners? Its most succinct expression has come from the best-qualified advocate, W. A. Lee, who had a foot in both government and coalmining camps. He was secretary of the Coal Mines Department at the end of the First World War, and between the wars was the Mining Association's chief executive officer. He maintained that the fundamental cause of the troubles in the coal industry at the delicate 1925 stage was 'to be found in general economic conditions outside the coal industry itself and beyond its control' and that 'the situation was further bedevilled by the avowed policy at the time of leaders of the Miners' Federation to force nationalisation of the industry on the Government by making it economically impossible to conduct it under private enterprise.'[4] From the miners' side, nationalisation was the only ultimate guarantee that the appalling accident rate in the mines could be brought down to acceptable proportions. Yet this factor and other elements in the intense human drama behind the 1925–26 negotiations has been strangely neglected. One particular accident, in fact, which occurred in March 1925 got scant attention even at the time and is never mentioned at all in subsequent accounts, which are mainly concerned with economic data, negotiating figures and corresponding statistics. There is perhaps a special reason for the omission, whose significance can be better appreciated by a glance at the miners' world in general and the accident figures in particular for the general period in question. Despite repeated condemnations of miners' housing standards, notably by the Sankey Commission, nothing had been done since the war to improve these or other conditions. As for the accident rate, there had been the shocking number of 3,603 miners killed in the three years 1922, 1923 and 1924 and 597,198 injured, with no records being kept of injuries keeping a man away from the pit for less than seven days.[5] Apart from accidents, silicosis and pneumoconiosis, contracted respectively from stone and coal dust, were killer diseases well known to every miner and his family.

If such accidents had been unavoidable, it might have been a different matter. The miners, however, were able to produce figures to prove that, among other things, individual accidents occurred more frequently in the last hour of the shift. And now the owners were asking for an extra hour to be added on. That there were other, strictly avoidable, causes of accidents was shown by the Montagu Pit Disaster at Scotswood in West Durham in the March of 1925. Part of its significance in overall historical terms was the little attention that it attracted at the time, for 'In terms of mining tragedy, it was a nonentity. In the league of northern mining disasters, the death roll of 38 was small beer. To a region almost inured to mass death in the mines – 205 at Hartley Colliery, 168 at West Stanley in 1909, 164 at Seaham in the 1880s – the events at Scotswood in 1925 held local headlines for a couple of days only.'[6] The background of this very disaster, however, was to come to life for the thousands of readers of A. J. Cronin's *The Stars Look Down*. As a story with a moral, moreover, it holds an important place in mining history; for it tells of a disaster that could not have happened had the mines been publicly owned and properly supervised. As it was, the free-for-all competition of the previous century had permitted the reckless sinking of more and more shafts into likely coal-yielding areas. The process of separately leasing the minerals to several colliery companies had simultaneously meant that insufficient information was exchanged as to the whereabouts of 'barriers' between abandoned workings and new ones being explored by other companies. The old workings became filled with water and thus a powerful source of potential danger. Even under the inadequate mining legislation of the 1880s it was required that a forty-yard barrier of coal must be left between abandoned flooded workings and approaching miners. Unknown to them, some of the colliers in the Montagu Pit on 30 March 1926 were exploring an area where the life-saving barrier had been 'whittled' down to a wafer-thin six inches, and they were chiselling away at the walls of a dam behind which lay three-and-a-half million tons of evil-smelling, swirling flood-water. When this dam inevitably burst, the water poured through sweeping all before it and claiming 38 dead. The subsequent enquiry uncovered long-lost documents whose existence would have provided a warning of the danger.

The supreme irony of all was that nationalisation would not only have put safety higher, but would have cut out one of the major sources of waste in terms of potentially useful coal unnecessarily left in the earth. The total amount of coal estimated in 1920 to have been left in such barriers was between 3,500 million and 4,000 million tons. 'It is perfectly true that some of these "barriers" could not have been worked without considerable risk either to the surface or to the underground workings, but it is the lack of co-ordination as between one mineral owner and another and, consequently, between different colliery owners, that makes it impossible to undertake those scientific surveys which alone can correctly determine which "barriers" should be worked and which should be left in the earth.'[7]

Had nationalisation or some radical form of reorganisation in fact come about in the wake of Sankey, the same men who were already involved in 'management' would, because of a need for their expertise, have been reabsorbed into the newly constituted industry. Profits to certain key individuals, however, would not, after the dismantling of the vested interest structure, have been so vast. It was thus the interplay of political and mineowning interests that now dominated every approach to an attempted settlement of the festering problem of the coal industry. The main point at issue between miners and owners was concerned with this one matter of reorganisation. Its equitable and statesmanlike solution during the respite afforded by the subsidy as of 1 August 1925, could still prevent an explosive confrontation. But the political fuse attached to the economic dynamite was already alight and had only nine months to run.

How were these months employed by those pledged to the concept of 'peace in our time'?

The Government prepared secretly and in great detail for a showdown with organised labour. It felt that if efforts, spear-headed by the appointment, now made, of yet another Royal Commission, failed to prevent such an eventuality, a decisive conflict was justified. Baldwin, in other words, was fully pre-pared for all-out war provided he safeguarded his reputation as a peacemaker by first appearing to exhaust all possibilities of an honourable settlement all round. The bones of his policy during the nine months, which were distinctly Machiavellian, were comfortably covered by an abundance of Micawberish flesh. 'The object of Baldwin's statesmanship, after all, was to postpone dealing with issues until they were no longer relevant. By this definition, far from being the "sell-out to syndicalism" its right-wing critics claimed, Red Friday was the apotheosis of Baldwinian statecraft.'[8]

The Prime Minister's move cleared the way for a nine-month period taken up with a fascinating example of Establishment co-operation in action. The beauty of such co-operation was that it needed no official organising. Indeed most of its strength consisted in the extent to which it was unofficial. Association with the same or similar schools, regiments and clubs combined with total identity of interest to produce a solidarity that needed no words to explain or direct it. Like a vast flock of birds wheeling with simultaneous and perfect unison in a new direction, the interested persons, regardless of individual status or occupation, reacted as a single entity. Side by side with the Government's refurbishing of existing emergency machinery, there sprang up, with no need for secrecy, a body that became famous as the Organisation for the Maintenance of Supplies. Its inception and growth dovetailed with perfect symmetry into the pattern of Government preparation. Its titular head was the distinguished former diplomat, Lord Hardinge of Penshurst. On its Council were such men as Admiral of the Fleet Lord Jellicoe, hero of Jutland and a subsequent, not very successful, First Sea Lord; General Sir Francis Lloyd, who commanded the London District during the war and was, immediately afterwards, Food Com-

missioner for London and the Home Counties; Sir Lynden Mac-
assey, an Ulsterman, Leader of the Parliamentary Bar, wartime
member of the Ministry of Munitions and sometime Chairman
of the Government Commission for Dilution of Labour on the
Clyde; Colonel Sir Courtauld Thomson, Chief Commissioner
from 1915 to 1919 for Malta, Egypt, Italy, Macedonia and the
Near East; Dr Walter Seton, the Balkan expert who secured
Mary Stuart's Penicuik Jewels for Scotland; Sir Rennell Rodd,
the well-known diplomatist who asserted that the OMS had no
connection with the Fascists; and Mr Geoffrey Drage, a former
Secretary of the Royal Commission on Labour. Such men were
neither die-hards nor cranks, but were, 'all of them, trusted
servants of the bourgeoisie, carrying the highest reputation for
faithful service in their respective professions. They were all of
them on half-pay; their participation did not involve the Government directly, and any one of them might conceivably have
acted for once in his life in an irresponsible manner; but by all
the canons of commonsense, their participation *en bloc* did
involve the Government indirectly.'[9]

The press supplied the necessary propaganda cover for the
successful launching of the strike-breaking organisation; and the
OMS sent a circular to the papers, published on 25 September
1925, announcing its response to the 'numerous suggestions' that
had been 'made from various quarters for organising those
citizens who would be prepared to volunteer to maintain supplies
and vital services in the event of a general strike. It seems, therefore, that the movement has already been constituted and is at
work in many metropolitan boroughs, while steps are being
taken to create corresponding organisations in all the principal
centres of the Kingdom.' The counter-propagandists of the
Daily Herald exhibited the *naïveté* of so many left-wingers of this
time by trying to explain away the OMS as an 'insulting inti-
mation' that the Prime Minister was unfit for his job. Little did
they understand the arcane ways of Establishment. All, however,
was made clear a few days after the OMS announcement, when the
formidable Home Secretary, Sir William Joynson-Hicks, decided
to issue a public reply to a worried anonymous correspondent:[10]

Thank you for your letter of yesterday in reference to the organisation known as the O.M.S. I will be perfectly frank with you. I have known of the inauguration of this body for many weeks past; in fact, the promoters consulted me as to their desire to form some such organisation. I told them quite frankly that it was the duty of the Government to preserve order and to maintain the necessary supplies for keeping the life of the country going in an emergency. This duty the Government is prepared to carry out. My plans have been long since made, and have been approved by the Government as a whole.

On the other hand, we have not thought it necessary or desirable to make a public parade of our willingness and ability to do that which is our duty, nor have we desired to assume what might be considered a provocative attitude by enrolling several hundred thousand men who would be willing to assist in maintaining the services vital to the country's life. This being so, I told the promoters of the O.M.S. that there was no objection on the part of the Government to their desire to inaugurate the body to which you refer; that, if and when an emergency arose, the Government would discharge the responsibility which is theirs and theirs alone, but that it would be a very great assistance to us to receive from the O.M.S., or from any other body of well-disposed citizens, classified lists of men in different parts of the country who would be willing to place their services at the disposal of the Government.

From this statement you will see that not only is there no reason why you should object to the O.M.S. but that you, or any other citizen who would desire the maintenance of peace, order, and good government in times of difficulty, would be performing a patriotic act by allying yourselves with this or any other similar body, formed for the sole purpose of helping the public authorities in the way I have suggested.

The OMS went about its task with military thoroughness bolstered up by its claim, in which some of the organisers genuinely believed, to represent the entire community and to be motivated by patriotism not politics. 'But, to the disadvantage of the Government, it was the patriotism of the prosperous and the majority of volunteers lacked precisely those skills which were most needed. The great bulk lived in the south and east of England, the largest single number – over 7,000 – being provided by the City of Westminster.'[11]

The Communists, hitherto regarded with distaste and suspicion by official Labour, were meanwhile turned into martyrs and heroes by the Home Secretary's decision to arrest some of their leaders on the general ground of what they represented rather than what they had actually done. (The technical charges were seditious libel and incitement to mutiny.) It was at the Tory Conference in October 1925 that Baldwin promised that their prosecution would be considered, and it in fact followed shortly afterwards. The accused were awarded heavy sentences at the Old Bailey, seven of the twelve defendants refusing the judge's significant offer to bind them over instead of imprisoning them if they promised to renounce all further association with 'an illegal party'. 'A desire to placate his own extremists for the humiliation of Red Friday undoubtedly played a part in Baldwin's decision to launch the first overtly political trial in England since the days of the Chartists.'[12]

A new and heady atmosphere was now developing dramatically and rapidly. It was becoming apparent that the non-occurrence of a General Strike (a Strike for which the Trade Union movement was doing nothing whatever to prepare) would come as a most disappointing anti-climax to many. In one view 'the more hot-headed of the Tories were going about in a great state of jubilation in the autumn of 1925, boasting that a fight was coming which would smash trade union power for ever. They welcomed it, knowing that the casualties in that fight would be drawn from the ranks of starving miners, not from themselves.'[13] This was no mere hyberbolic apostrophe such as might have been thrown away by the fiery MFGB Secretary, Arthur Cook. Its author was J. R. Clynes, the fiercely anti-Communist deputy leader of the Labour Party whose integrity was widely recognised by fellow Parliamentarians. It was written of him that 'there are many sturdy democrats, some honest men, and an occasional successful statesman. Mr Clynes is all three.'[14] He was right in singling out the miners as the group who would have to bear the brunt of any major industrial battle. They were made of sterner stuff than members of unions whose sympathetic support could not be taken as a foregone conclusion.

The Government meanwhile intensified such preparations as it was entitled to make under the 1920 Emergency Powers Act whereby Lloyd George had 'made permanent the dictatorial powers which the Government had possession in wartime under the Defence of the Realm Acts – as big a blow against the traditional constitution as any ever levelled.'[15] (The Act of course could not be invoked to the full without a Royal Proclamation that 'a state of emergency existed'.) The country was divided up into districts each with its own headquarters and staff headed by a specially appointed Civil Commissioner. Food and other stocks, contingency plans for manning such key points as power stations, and the planning of emergency routes, food supplies, and essential transport were the matters officially discussed at regular meetings. Complementary to all this were the far-reaching potentialities of the OMS which, as was clearly understood, would officially link up with the Government if and when the time came. The Home Secretary could tell the Cabinet in February 1926 that 'little remained to be done' to deal effectively with a General Strike. The situation can be summed up by saying that 'in 1925 the Government were fearful that a General Strike would succeed, in 1926 they were confident it would fail. They could safely let it happen, and indeed made sure that it did.'[16]

One might well think that this elaborate and detailed 'arming' of the country for a decisive if bloodless 'civil war' betokened some sort of massive 'build-up' on the other 'side'. In fact the TUC were making no preparations whatever for a General Strike. They had no desire for such a strike and lived in hopes that some factor would preclude their ever having to call one as a result of the Triple Alliance unions' pledge to support the MFGB. Such hopes were pinned chiefly – in yet another demonstration of left-wing *naïveté* – on the findings of the latest Royal Commission on Coal appointed by the Government. This

Commission, which started its deliberations on 15 October 1925, differed in one vital respect from other tribunals set up by the Government since the war to look into the problems of the coal industry. It contained no representatives of either miners or owners in view of the Government's claim that it was to be an 'impartial' body. Its chairman was the distinguished Liberal, Sir Herbert (later Lord) Samuel, who had extensive family connections in the financial world and wide experience in government, both British and colonial. Its other three members were Sir William Beveridge, the noted economist and former *Morning Post* leader-writer; General Sir Herbert Lawrence, the much decorated soldier son of Lord Lawrence of Kingsgate, who, on retirement from the army, became a managing partner of the Glyn Mills Banking house and a director of ten other important concerns; and Mr Kenneth Lee, chairman of Tootal, Broadhurst, Lee (the large cotton firm) and of the District Bank. Certain of the concerns on whose boards Lawrence and Lee sat were grouped within the Federation of British Industries; and Lawrence had some direct knowledge of coal by virtue of his financial interest therein through Vickers Limited.

It looked as if the Government, at last, had found the right formula for the composition of a Commission on coal. The Government, in fact, was rather in the position of a frustrated patient who had gone to many doctors but had finally found one likely to give the diagnosis he wanted to hear. The general scope of the diagnosis was that the coal industry was in need of reorganisation but that this could be put off until a later date; the immediate need was for a drastic reduction of wages. The report demonstrated that the dispute with the miners had now become almost completely dominated by political considerations. Baldwin was already reaping the first fruits of his calculated risk in 1923. Having narrowly averted a possibly fatal showdown with the miners in August 1925, he was by the winter in an unassailable position. If the other unions ever again came to the assistance of the miners and seemed genuinely determined on national industrial action, his Government, backed by powerful allies, was in a position of total paramilitary preparedness. In fact, had Baldwin shown equal determination to ensure preparedness against another sort of war in the late thirties, recent history would have been very different.

The Samuel Commission not only made reduced wages its principal recommendation, but skilfully framed its findings so as to present wages as the central feature of the whole report. It was a far cry from Sankey, whose realism and objectivity had given such hope to the miners and given those politicians concerned with the 'wider issues' the problem of how not to implement its findings. Samuel was subtler. It ranged over the whole field under review, having asserted that the problem had a permanent and a temporary aspect. It gave commendable attention to the permanent aspect under the headings of mineral ownership, amalgamation, combination, research, distribution, labour and general organisation. But then it stated that it would take years to make fully operational any of the proposed reforms under this general heading. It thus, thereafter, found itself free to bring all the various avenues of exploration back to the one and only route then thought desirable, namely by way of drastic reduction of miners' wages. This was something that the miners themselves felt, not so much that they would not, but that they *could* not accept under prevailing and often totally miserable living conditions, exacerbated by the danger-ridden and disease-prone nature of their particular type of employment. The Royal Commission, however, was looking to broader horizons. It concerned itself, though naturally indirectly and by what it left out, not only with the Government's domestic political needs, but with its foreign ones as well.

One of the coalowners' arguments in favour of reduced wages was the inhibiting effect, for example, of the loss of certain foreign markets. The Samuel Commission did not, for political reasons, recommend an expansion of coal exports in two particular directions where, in fact, such expansion would have been possible. One was Fascist Italy and the other was Communist Russia. Britain had an arrangement providing for the repayment of the Italian Debt in return for concessions made to Britain by Italy over Abyssinia; and the plans for the Anglo-Italian partitioning of Abyssinia were finally made public in 1926. (Sir Herbert Samuel, as High Commissioner of Palestine, was not ignorant of these developments.) Italy, meanwhile, was only able to repay her debt to Britain by receiving reparations from Germany, under the Dawes Plan, in the form of free coal. This left a huge gap in Britain's potential coal export market. But the Samuel Commission did not recommend an adjustment of the Dawes and Reparations arrangements, let alone a revision of the Versailles Treaty, for the sake of saving the living standards of four million Britons. The arguments in favour of such a recommendation, however, would not have been unreasonable.

As for Russia, the situation was, in one sense, simpler. The Soviet Union was willing, on deferred credit terms ultimately very favourable to Britain, to take quantities of iron and steel manufactured goods up to about £100 million. As four tons of coal went into the making of every ton of steel, a strong recommendation by the Commission for a trade agreement with Russia would have made possible a massive boom in both the home and export markets of the British coal industry. The whole situation, however, was not quite so simple when it came to the political considerations of which the Royal Commissioners were fully aware. In recommending a suitable trade agreement with the Soviet Union 'they would in as many words have been setting the seal of their approval on the economic policy (as regards Russian trade) of the Labour Government of 1924, and disapproving of the economic policy of the Government by which they had been set up as a Commission. The Commissioners, therefore, were discreetly silent.'[17] None of this necessarily implies general criticism of overall British policy at the time; but it does help to show that the reasons for industrial attitudes for which Britain's miners eventually paid a high price in terms of hardship were influenced by more far-reaching factors than those most often stressed in accounts of the period.

Ironically, nevertheless, the 1925 Royal Commission came to be looked upon as the last word on the coal industry: an authoritative and unprejudiced assessment. It also served the purpose of dividing the Labour movement on the vital question of whether a repetition should be attempted of the coercive action of the previous July. Trade Union morale was duly weakened to a significant extent, and the bulk of the movement would have accepted the Commission's findings, leaving the miners to fend for themselves, had it not been for the hard official line taken by the coalowners at the end of March 1926.

Baldwin's Cabinet had, in the middle of the month, signified their approval of the Report provided the miners and owners agreed to it. Briefed by the Minister of Labour, Sir Arthur Steel-Maitland – himself a coalowner – the Prime Minister then, unhurriedly, approached both sides. The owners announced that their policy was based on wage cuts, longer hours and a return to district settlements. The miners' most forthright leader, MFGB Secretary, Arthur Cook, bravely proclaimed that 'we are going to be slaves no longer and our men will starve before they accept any reduction of wages.' The latter was exactly what actually happened when the Lock-Out whimpered to a finish many months later. But in March, the miners were willing, as far as practical negotiations were concerned, to talk about substantial concessions provided there was a definite Government guarantee that reorganisation would take place.

Baldwin would not consider any such guarantee until the two sides had agreed on the immediate question of wage cuts. The pistol was already at the miners' heads and events from this point moved swiftly onwards to an explosion that, after all the Government and OMS preparations, came almost as an anti-climax. The TUC became, as each day passed, more and more lukewarm in its once fervently proclaimed determination to stand by the miners. The latter, in turn, felt the whole ground rapidly slipping away from under them. Increasingly urgent negotiations went on through April but made no headway. Finally, the General Council of the TUC summoned the executives of the affiliated Unions to a summit conference in London on the 29th. Two days previously, it had at last drafted plans to meet a possible struggle. It was not even the 'eleventh hour'. That had already passed; it was now nearly 'midnight' with the mineowners' Lock-Out notices already posted as of mid-April and due to

expire the next day. If they did so in the absence of an agreement
the dreaded Lock-Out would be a reality.

It was dreaded because the shadow of a possible second Black
Friday was now looming over the whole operation. 30 April, the
second day of the TUC Conference and also a Friday, would be
the day of decision, the previous day's proceedings having ended
with a resolution:

> That this Conference of Executives of Unions affiliated to the
> Trades Union Congress endorses the efforts of the General
> Council to secure an honourable settlement of the differences
> in the coalmining industry. It further instructs the Industrial
> Committee of the General Council to continue its efforts, and
> declares its readiness for the negotiations to continue providing
> that the impending lock-out of the mine-workers is not enforced.
>
> That this Conference hereby adjourns until tomorrow, and
> agrees to remain in London to enable the General Council to
> consult, report and take instructions. (Thursday, 29 April
> 1926.)

Meanwhile, however, the solid and eloquent Ernest Bevin,
general secretary of his own brainchild, the key Transport and
General Workers' Union, had reminded the assembled executives
of the 'extraordinary position' in which they found themselves.
He pointed out that within twenty-four hours they might no
longer be representing separate unions; that united action on
behalf of the miners meant that they would all have become one
giant union; that the miners would have to throw in their lot
with the general movement; and that this general movement
would have to take on the responsibility for seeing the whole
thing through. 30 April came and went with the deadlock
unresolved. The Prime Minister relayed to the TUC General
Council the last-minute 'offer' – actually an ultimatum – issued
by the owners. The miners' reply was an inevitable protestation
that the terms were unacceptable; but these last hours contained a
vital plea by the TUC that the Lock-Out notices should be
suspended so that negotiations could continue. The Cabinet,

however, before it came formally to reject this plea, had already taken the first overt steps in the direction of general conflict. It had presented a proclamation for signature by King George V enabling the Government to make full use of the Emergency Powers Act; to assume, in other words, arbitrary authority to act without recourse to Parliament or through normal constitutional channels. The Royal Proclamation stated that 'the present immediate threat of cessation of work in Coal Mines does, in Our opinion, constitute a state of emergency within the meaning of the said Act'. This was significant in that 'The declaration by royal proclamation of a "state of emergency" has the same effect in civil strife as a "mobilisation" order on the brink of war.'[18]

On the same day, 30 April, the Government issued detailed instructions through its various departments. The Ministry of Health sent local authorities a reminder of its famous (many have said 'notorious') Circular 636. (This had originally gone out on 20 November 1925, outlining the plans already made to meet a national strike and now up-dated by Sir John Anderson's subcommittee.) The names of the Civil Commissioners were published together with lists of their staffs and headquarters in the twelve divisions of the country; an official announcement was made as to troop movements; *and a placard of the strike-breaking OMS was posted throughout the country*. The response of the General Council of the TUC, close on midnight of this same Friday, 30 April, was to hand the Executive what amounted to an instruction for a national strike. The expression 'general strike' was never used by the TUC, and the instruction drawn up was for a stoppage that was specifically intended not to be 'general'. Areas in which it was envisaged that work should cease completely were transport, printing, iron and steel, metal and the heavy chemical industries; electric power, light and gas were to be rationed; the health, food and sanitary services were to be continued. The ironical fact, almost superfluous to add, was that the miners themselves were never on strike at all at any stage throughout 1926; for being 'locked-out' from work is, of course, very different from being on strike. The 'cessation of work' in the mines – the threat of which, not the threat of a general strike,

was the official reason for the state of emergency – came about
at the moment when the owners' lock-out notices expired. At
that moment the nation's colliers were, in effect, sacked. They
could be re-employed only on the basis of longer hours at
drastically reduced pay.

The long and wearisome session of the union executives'
special conference meanwhile limped to its end in the small
hours of the morning of 1 May without any actual vote of the
constituencies as to whether or not a general strike was to be
approved. Instead the day's proceedings were concluded by an
astonishingly unstirring speech from Jimmy Thomas, whose
final words were:

> Tomorrow you will be called upon to review the situation.
> You, as Executive Committees, will be called upon to take the
> most momentous decision that any body of trade unionists was
> ever called to make up their minds upon. Do not do it in
> passion or in heat. Do not think that this issue is one to trifle
> with – not one for glib phrases, not one for hotheads, because,
> whatever the result, there are still the cold, hard, economic
> facts to face afterwards. Don't lose your heads. We have
> striven, we have pleaded, we have begged for peace because
> we want peace. We still want peace. The Nation wants peace.
> Those who want war must take the responsibility.

'It was almost a pathetic finale to the long-drawn-out negotiations. Here was the great negotiator – the leader of a great union –
the leader of a combination of tremendous power – and he was
almost squirming before the prospect of mass workers' action. It
was not the breakdown of the talks that worried Thomas – it
was the thought of what a General Strike would involve so far
as leadership was concerned. And he shrank from it.'[19] The
circumstances in which the four-million-strong mining community of Britain faced the prospect of a possibly prolonged period
of idleness in the pits – far worse even than ordinary unemployment, since there would not even be any dole money – could
hardly have been more inauspicious.

Duke of Northumberland addresses Coal Manufacturers

Duke and Duchess of Northumberland

6

Lock-Out

The Great Lock-Out of 1926 thus began at midnight on 30 April. Its first two days were embittered by misunderstandings and confusion within the greater trade union movement. Its first big test came in the form of doubt as to whether or not the much vaunted 'general strike' would actually happen. For no sooner was the strike officially 'on' than it seemed as if it might suddenly be off again, and this without the miners' being able to do anything about it.

It was not that there was any doubt about the feelings of the rank and file. When the Conference of Executives reassembled on Saturday, 1 May – May Day – it had placed before it the unprecedented proposal for a national strike. Depending on the voting, the partial strike, involving only those workers specifically mentioned in the previous night's memorandum, would take effect as of midnight on the following Monday. The block votes of the unions represented produced 3,653,527 in favour of the proposal, with 49,911 against. (The latter were the votes cast on behalf of the Seamen's Union by their curious president, Havelock Wilson.) Strike orders accordingly went out to such unions as were to take part in the stoppage. The result of the vote – 'the greatest dramatic event since the days of the Chartist Movement'[1] – was accompanied by passionate words. Ernest Bevin proclaimed:

I desire to point out, that with a view to doing nothing at all which would aggravate the position, these proposals were not ready to hand to the General Secretaries, or rather the documents in the form in which you received it, until after we had received in our room the news that the Emergency Powers Act had been signed, and after the OMS had already placed upon the printing press their preparatory literature. We looked upon that, and I think rightly, while our people were down there and we did not know what was really happening, as indicating that the Government, behind the scenes, was mobilising the forces of war. I think it was a right deduction in view of subsequent happenings. Sometimes it is said, that he who draws the sword perishes by the sword, and we all looked upon the action of the Government last night as equal in stupidity to the actions of the well-remembered Lord North and George III combined, and the result may be fraught with as serious consequences as the action of George III in the history of this country. . . .

We look upon your 'yes' as meaning that you have placed your all upon the altar of this great movement and, having placed it there, even if every penny goes, if every asset goes, history will ultimately write up that it was a magnificent generation that was prepared to do it rather than see the miners driven down like slaves.

It nevertheless remained to be seen how such rousing rhetoric would stand up to the acid test of action. In view of possible further discussions with the Government, Herbert Smith, the miners' President, agreed that 'all negotiations would now be carried on through the General Council, but that the Miners' Federation would be consulted'. In practice all power devolved for the time being on the TUC's specially appointed Negotiating Committee. This, in turn, appointed, for the purpose of detailed discussion with the Government, a sub-committee consisting of Arthur Pugh, the mild and moderate friend of the Prime Minister and Chairman of the TUC General Council; the social-climbing and mercurial former Government minister and railwaymen's leader, Jimmy Thomas; and the militantly left-wing President of the Engineers' Union, Alonzo Swales. They made an odd trio. Though acting with plenipotentiary powers, liaison with the miners broke down. Arthur Cook, who did not share the General Council's euphoric view that the May Day meeting was supposed to be a bridge between workers and the Government– Employer axis, did not get certain vital messages. Thus, all unknown to him, the TUC negotiators became, on the same Saturday evening, deeply involved in talks with the Government at Downing Street to see how the strike could be averted. 'The issue dividing the Government and the TUC remained precisely what it had been the previous night; The Negotiating Committee continued to insist that the Lock-Out notices should be withdrawn so that unfettered negotiations could proceed on the Samuel Report; the Government would not consider lifting the lock-out notices without a prior acceptance of wage cuts.'[2]

The impasse was still seemingly absolute; but the physical and psychological background to the whole debate was now very different from the gloomy Memorial Hall in Farringdon Road where the Union Executives had sat out the previous frustrating three days. At Downing Street, the atmosphere was a heady one for Thomas, Pugh and Swales, whose immediate opposite numbers were the Prime Minister himself, Lord Birkenhead, the brilliant former Lord Chancellor, now Secretary for India, and the Minister of Labour, Sir Arthur Steel-Maitland. A certain bogus *bonhomie* was cultivated as between Birkenhead and Thomas – 'Fred' and 'Jimmy' – which the latter purringly lapped up. (Birkenhead had successfully used the same technique with Michael Collins during the negotiations over Home Rule for Ireland.) The Secretary for India subtly administered further anodyne by declaring his sympathy for the miners as his great grandfather had been a collier and a respected 'bare fist' prize fighter in Yorkshire. Thus, unguardedly relaxed, the TUC negotiators sat down to a strange poker game in which the Cabinet members held all the best cards: if a general strike were to be averted, it could only be on terms which, however dis- guised or fudged, were favourable to the Government; but if a general strike had to come, the Government was ready, even anxious, to meet it head on.

The TUC delegates left Downing Street in the early hours of

the Sunday morning with the apparently victorious acquisition
of an emollient formula: the Prime Minister had 'satisfied
himself as a result of the conversations he has had with the
representatives of the Trade Union Congress, that if negotiations
are continued (it being understood that the notices cease to be
operative) the representatives of the Trade Union Congress are
confident that a settlement can be reached on the lines of the
Report within a fortnight.' The first wedge was thus deftly
inserted into the papered-over façade of supposedly solid Trade
Unionist sentiment. The wedge was driven deeper by a further
formula, drafted by Birkenhead on the basis of a comment from
Thomas, which emerged in the course of the resumed talks at
Downing Street late in the evening of Sunday, 2 May.

The Miners' executive had, in the meantime, returned hastily
to London, having left the day before under the impression that
there were to be no further negotiations with the Government.
The General Council thereupon gave qualified approval to the
first formula, despite Arthur Cook's strong misgivings, and the
evening session at Downing Street was intended to elicit a clearer
interpretation of its meaning. But Cabinet attitudes had hardened
in the interval, and the excluded miners' representatives were
deeply apprehensive. They were not the only ones. Walter
Citrine, acting Secretary of the TUC, was present at all the
Downing Street discussions, taking a note on behalf of the
General Council, a function performed on the Government's
behalf by Sir Horace Wilson. Lord Citrine has provided an
invaluable and detailed account of the Downing Street negotiating based on very full shorthand notes taken at the time.[3] 'We
had visions,' he has written, 'of Black Friday, 1921, in our minds.
On the present occasion the miners had expressly handed their
powers over to the General Council, but it would not do to
attempt to force a decision upon them.'

The second 'formula' – the so-called 'Birkenhead Formula' –
was read out, but not actually handed in writing, to the TUC
sub-committee by Birkenhead as discussions dragged on late
into the Sunday night. It asked the miners to authorise a decision
on the understanding that the Samuel Report would be the

basis of settlement and that the decision be approached 'with the knowledge that it may involve some reduction in wages'. The two sub-committees then separated, with the Cabinet members going off to confer with their colleagues in another part of the building. The TUC delegates went through an intercommunicating door into No. 11 Downing Street to report back to the General Council, who were waiting for them upstairs. They were shortly joined by the miners' executive. These latter were remarkable men of the old type, having little in common with their modern bureaucratic-minded and often rather self-important counterparts. They were towering heroes to their own 'butties' in the pits; they had come up the same hard way and were not among those labour leaders whose flowery oratory went hand in hand with a yearning for something of the sweet life that only 'belonging, higher up' can produce. To any suggestion felt to be inimical to the miners' fundamental interests, the Federation's president, Herbert Smith, would reply with his favourite expression 'Nowt doin'.' Without feeling able to put heavy pressure on them, the sub-committee members were desperately hoping that the miners would say, or even hint at, something which would enable them, with a clear conscience, to call off or at least postpone the strike, now due to commence in less than twenty-four hours. While they were still talking, in an atmosphere of considerable tenseness, a message arrived saying that the Prime Minister wanted to see them. Pugh, Thomas, Swales and Citrine duly went down and across, back to No. 10, to meet Baldwin, who grimly handed them a letter. It turned out to be an ultimatum which came as a bombshell to the Trade Union leaders. Arthur Pugh describes the sequence of events as follows:[4] 'Many exchanges of opinion took place between the two sub-committees as to the suitable formula. As the miners' representatives were now present in the building we left the Government representatives so that we could consult the miners, *and were actually making an arrangement*** when, without warning, we received the ultimatum of the Government.' This demanded the immediate calling off of the strike as constituting 'a challenge to the con-

*Author's italics.

stitutional rights and freedom of the nation'; it added that 'overt acts' which had already taken place, including gross interference with the freedom of the Press, 'meant that no further talks could take place prior to an unconditional surrender'.

One of the 'overt acts' referred to was the sending out of strike notices on the Saturday afternoon; but this was readily explainable as an inevitable measure of counter-mobilisation in response to the Government's prior actions, and a routine part of contingency planning for the contemplated strike. Much more serious was the news, just received by the Cabinet, of an incident in the offices of the *Daily Mail*, which had occurred without the knowledge of the TUC and had no connection with the preparations for the strike. It was evident to Citrine that Baldwin's mind was already made up, and the sub-committee was dismissed. As its members filed out in bewilderment and consternation to report back to their colleagues, the Prime Minister said to Citrine: 'I have been happy to meet you, and I believe if we live we shall meet again and settle it.' Then he added solemnly, 'If we live.' These melodramatic words were Baldwin's last contribution to the evening's proceedings. When Citrine returned to demand, on the TUC's behalf, a further explanation and a chance to continue proper discussions, the Prime Minister had gone to bed. The Trade Union and miners' leaders had no alternative but to show themselves out of Downing Street where, by now, only the caretaker and resident detective were to be found. Before they left, somebody shouted, 'Here it is, on the tape.'

'Sure enough the whole incident was recorded,' writes Lord Citrine. 'That meant that Baldwin's letter must have been handed to the Press even before we had received it. It told us something further – that the Cabinet probably had been drafting that letter long before we had retired from our first meeting with Baldwin earlier in the evening. I felt we had been cruelly let down and that the other side had been manoeuvring for position. It was only later that I found that Churchill had been to the *Daily Mail* office. The compositors had refused to set an article which vindictively and viciously accused the General Council of organising a movement against the King and the Constitution.'[5] Despite discoordinated efforts for reprieve during the rest of that day (Monday, 3 May), it was clear that, at long last, the 'General Strike' was 'on'. And yet 'the leaders were terrified. Mr Thomas frankly avowed his dread of what should happen if the government should lose, and Mr MacDonald wailed, "I don't like General Strikes. . . . I don't like it; honestly I don't; but, honestly, what can be done?" The right, however, revelled in it; the time they had been waiting for and preparing for had come. . . .'[6]

'Revelled' is perhaps not quite the right word. The 'right' displayed more of a quiet, self-righteous determination to teach the agitators a lesson, while disavowing any animosity against the misled rank-and-file. 'I couldn't regard a large section of my fellow countrymen as enemies,' as Duff Cooper put it.[7] Such attitudes were comfortingly backed by complete confidence that nothing could go wrong with the authorities' preparations. Churchill brushed aside the probings of the Labour party chairman, Arthur Henderson, as midnight approached on 3 May. 'You will be better prepared,' he said, 'to talk to us in two or three weeks.'[8] But had the key members of powerful and complacent Establishment made a gigantic miscalculation?

They were correct in observing on the other side of the fence a total lack of trade union preparedness and a body of leaders mouthing brave words with something less than total conviction. And they were accustomed to supposing that trade union leaders were more militant than those whom they claimed to lead. By conventional logic, the 'general strike' had to be the flop of flops. What happened on 4 May stunned not only the Establishment, but also many of the most experienced of trade unionists. What might, in the organisational confusion, have been only an uneven cessation of work, turned out to be a 'flood tide' involving three and a half million workers. 'They flowed to the centre of the towns and cities and the great murmur began. It was not a murmur against the strike but against the limited character of the strike and the contradictory positions into which large numbers of the workers were thrust. Especially was this the case in the engineering and shipbuilding industry.'[9] The enormity of what they themselves had largely precipitated quickly dawned on the powers that be. 'Astonishingly complete and orderly' was J. H. Laski's description of the beginning of the strike. 'In general, over 90 per cent of those asked to stop work did so. Not the least difficult task of the council was to keep at work the literally hundreds of thousands who were insistent in their desire actively to stand with their fellows.'[10] The depth of fellow feeling in so large and heterogeneous a group demonstrated a 'solidarity unequalled in our industrial history. It was from first to last a soldiers' battle. No leader emerged to personify the common will. Of organisation there was little, and what there was, was improvised. . . . These millions of men were risking their livelihood for the single end of winning for the miners a living wage.'[11]

The fact that this central objective was never lost sight of by the troops in the field in what was, indeed, a 'soldiers' battle', was an embarrassment for others. These 'others' proved not to be limited to the upper and middle classes, as became even more apparent when the actual 'soldiers' battle' was over and the long siege of the locked-out section of the 'troops' got under way. For there were many of all classes whose financial, political and social status was adversely affected by the enforced idleness of a million key workers. Overlapping in both directions was that other amorphous group 'the British public' whose overall sympathy was claimed with equal confidence by strikers and strike-breakers alike.

As for the locked-out miners, their struggle was comparable to a modern but bloodless Peasants' Revolt. Many of the elements of the great rising of 1381 were present in 1926. The solidarity with which miners were supported by millions of their fellow countrymen, including many from the professional classes, gave the nine-day battle an authentically national character. The unifying factor was a widespread sense of injustice; without this there could have been no such solidarity on the part of a huge but scattered group of men and women, ill-prepared and lukewarmly led. The effective contribution of Communists and fellow travellers was negligible. The support of the Parliamentary Labour Party was derisory, since many of its leading members were themselves either adherents or aspirants to the Establish-

ment. Even the radical Clydesiders were not directly involved,
for when 'the General Council blundered into the General
Strike like a moth into a lamp, the ILP was not invited to help.
. . . The Strike with its real danger and farce, and its extraordinary legends, passed them by.'[12] But the rank-and-file
attitude was that 'the miners had been locked out and we were
going to their assistance; an injury to one was an injury to all.'[13]
As Steel-Maitland had put it after the lock-out had become
operative, 'A taper has been lit this day in England.'[14]

The taper, lit by the lock-out, did not start a raging fire as had
the extortionate Poll Tax of 1381. Rather did it generate – pious
legends to the contrary notwithstanding – a sullen white-hot
anger, smouldering in all areas, which might well prove harder
to extinguish than a conflagration. Even extensive mobilisation,
which had included military and naval deployment, was no
match for a sub-community bent on passive resistance to the
bitter end. The grievances of seven years had at last come home
to roost. The lid was off. Post-war industrial unrest had reached
a climax whose spontaneity even supine leadership could not
dampen. Well might the demagogic Arthur Cook, a great
coiner of phrases, have employed the couplet:

> Be ware or you be woe;
> Know your friend from your foe.

This was part of one of the messages whereby John Ball, 'the
mad priest of Kent', had inflamed the Peasants into Revolt in
the fourteenth century. 'But the Poll Tax was not the cause of
the rising; it was only the match which set alight a great deal of
material ripe for a bonfire. Not the serfs, only, but the Free
peasants and artisans, the tenant farmers, petty landowners,
traders, small manufacturers, apprentices, and poor clergy, were
effervescent with discontent.'[15] In 1926, also, discontent was much
deeper and more widespread than is generally allowed. The
Government's newspaper, the *British Gazette*, on its first day and
on the front page, headlined a 'Hold-up of the Nation', declaring
the strike to be 'an effort to force upon some 42,000,000 British

citizens the will of less than 4,000,000 others.' In fact, however, the combined numbers of men on strike or locked out, together with those not yet on strike but in sympathy, and the families of all concerned, amounted to something approaching half the nation.

The John Ball of 1926 was Arthur Cook, who had replaced Frank Hodges in 1924 as Secretary of the Miners' Federation. His oratory was wild but spell-binding when he spoke *to* the miners by speaking *for* them. According to Sir William Lawther[16] he seldom knew what he was going to say next and often sat down without knowing what he had said while on his feet. But 1926 lacked its leader of genius who, in 1381, had appeared in the form of Wat Tyler. The most forceful member of the TUC General Council was Ernest Bevin, but he was considered something of a 'rogue elephant' by both right and left. Nevertheless it was he, along with the hypocritical Jimmy Thomas and the General Council's Chairman, Arthur Pugh, who dominated the scene as far as overall strategy was concerned. And the General Council desired to keep this as centralised as possible (in London) while waiting for its best moment to sue for terms with the Government. The local 'Councils of Action' – sometimes calling themselves Strike or Emergency Committees – were the effective, though hurriedly improvised, instruments of day to day strike tactics. They had great success outside London, particularly in the North-East. Everywhere in fact where the mining communities were prominent the lock-out gave a keen fighting edge to the strike.

It was London where the forces of 'law and order' mounted their principal offensive; where lack of public transport took its main psychological toll; where armoured cars conveyed food but failed to elicit more than contemptuous jeers from the solid citizens of the East End; where undergraduates had their famous fling trying to drive buses and trains; where the shopgirls had the time of their lives meeting new boy friends as they got lifts to work; where the romance lingered on long after the enforced holiday-cum-spree, and the legends and myths sprang to life. It was also in London that the middle-class do-gooders gave of their best and the well-meaning but unimaginative General Council lost heart so quickly. The latter rejoiced in the return to England of Sir Herbert Samuel. They eagerly sought his help and clutched at the straw of his new Memorandum as a peace-making formula. The miners were not impressed. Without them, however, the General Council went ahead and made its unconditional surrender, even though the Samuel scheme was but a re-hash of the Commission's recommendations, and anyway not binding on the Government.

The TUC attempted to show that their surrender was a portent of better things to come for the miners. In fact it was a more deadly blow than Black Friday, 1921. The rank and file were stunned and took a long time to assimilate the fact that the struggle was over when in many areas it was just beginning to succeed. For the miners it meant that the General Strike was little more than a side-show – courageous but ultimately almost farcical – to the main drama which still had to be acted out. As far as the leaders were concerned, it was far from being 'unconstitutional', let alone revolutionary. And there was no thought at all of such things by those in the thick of the soldiers' battle, however much they may have hated the blacklegs and other 'traitors' within their own ranks. Such, however, is the force of legend and the inevitable picture of the 'patriots' in plus-fours, that the depths of bitterness understandably rankling amongst the lock-out victims, the central figures in the whole affair, is all too easy to forget or ignore.

Among the thousands of stories illustrating the supposed spirit of the General Strike – humorous, sad, hearty – few are more ultimately significant than that of an incident occurring one evening on a lonely stretch of railway line some miles north of Newcastle. Preoccupation with trains during the General Strike centred chiefly on which commuter services might be operating in and out of London and other big cities. Highly optimistic announcements appeared, as to services supposedly running, in the best vehicle of contemporary fiction to emerge from the Strike, the Churchill-edited *British Gazette*. Corrections from other sources did something to redress the balance and most

councils of action issued news bulletins of their own. They
tended to show that the enthusiastic railway volunteers were
nothing if not conscientious. 'We understand,' said one report,
'that luncheon cars are to be put on trains running between
Westminster and Blackfriars.'[17] The strike-breakers fared badly
in trying to run the London buses but had better luck with the
Underground, one train actually being used by Churchill himself. It proved to be an educative if bewildering experience, as
his wife recounted later on: 'He knows nothing of the life of
ordinary people. He's never been on a bus, and only once in an
Underground. This was during the General Strike, when I
deposited him at South Kensington. He went round and round
(it happened to be the Circle Line) not knowing where to get
out and had to be rescued eventually.'[18]

No train, however, could compete in fame and romance
with the majestic Flying Scotsman. In the North-East, that is,
in Northumberland and Durham – where, along with South
Wales, hardship for the miners had been particularly intense in
the past – the Strike was well organised. Feelings ran high and
no one was more despised than the 'scabs' or blacklegs, and
strike-breakers of various kinds. On the morning of 10 May 1926,
there was a meeting of miners at West Colliery near the pit
village of Cramlington, about twelve miles north of Newcastle.
There was a discussion about such trains as were being manned
by blacklegs. About fifteen miners left the meeting determined
to do something about it on their own initiative. Later in the
day the Flying Scotsman, travelling south on what was then the
LNER main line from Edinburgh to King's Cross, was derailed
near Cramlington. Four weeks later nine miners were arrested
and charged with maliciously displacing a rail on the said line.
Eight of them were quickly brought to trial in Newcastle when
several local miners gave evidence for the prosecution that the
defendants had been in the group who had removed the rail.
All were found guilty, and one of the three sentenced to
eight years' imprisonment, Mr Arthur Wilson, now lives in
Dudley, just south of Cramlington. His house overlooks a section
of the very line from which he helped to remove that famous

rail fifty years ago. Would he do it again if he had the chance? His answer is 'yes'[21] in the sense that he has no regrets over his action. So miserable and desperate had life become for him and his kind that nothing was to be lost even by a possibly murderous act of this nature. What if someone had been killed? 'We'd have been hanged of course,' is his immediate and stoical reply. As it happened, the train, which had already been halted further up the track and warned of possible danger, was travelling slowly. Wilson and his comrades, having lifted out the rail, watched its approach from a disused colliery 'drift' nearby. The noble engine, as it reached the displaced rail, toppled sedately off the line and two of the carriages jack-knifed. The passengers had all been removed to the rear of the train and no one was killed or even injured.

The story, however, did not end even with the release of Wilson and the others from prison (after serving five of the full eight years). In fact the story is still unfinished in that there are those locally who will not talk to each other to this day as the recriminatory bitterness of 1926 lives on. 'Some day, the truth of what happened in these mining communities after the train wreck – the whirlpools of local intrigue, the attitudes struck for and against, the adulation or condemnation, accorded to the participants – will emerge. The time is not yet ripe. Suffice it to say that Arthur and his fellow wreckers held no love for those who gave evidence against them. Cruel stories are told of funerals held during which men turned their backs on the cortège; of men who proffered friendship and wanted bygones to be bygones – but were scorned.'[22]

In the North-East in general there was widespread and successful picketing of blackleg transport. 'Had the strike gone on into another week, the grip of the pickets on the roads through the mining areas would have tightened and led to even more determined attempts by the authorities to break it.'[23] This tendency, spreading in other areas, could have had the same effect as the 'authorised reprisals' had had during the guerilla war in Ireland in 1920 and 1921. (Many of the special constables and other temporary Government auxiliaries during the General Strike were ex-Black and Tans or men of a similar type.) Though the government of the day – Lloyd George's – had been complacent and, when pressed,[24] deceitful about the terrorising of the Irish population in the name of law and order, the British public was horrified when it discovered the truth. Lloyd George had to eat humble pie and agree to negotiations with a provisional Irish Government. Only subtlety, combined with intimidation on the part of some of his Cabinet colleagues, notably Birkenhead and Churchill, prevented the less experienced Irish negotiators from taking full advantage of their position. (Shades of the 1–2 May negotiations in 1926.) But the Establishment had been badly shaken, and could hardly have faced a similar risk in future without some apprehension. Such a risk would unquestionably have appeared had the General Strike been prolonged.

As it was, its premature termination would have paved the way for an immediate collapse of working-class morale and a decisive check on trade union strength for many years to come – but for one thing: the miners refused to surrender so tamely, and the Lock-Out went on. The soldiers' battle, lost by default, gave way to a protracted siege of those determined somehow to live without work and its proceeds for as long as might be needed.

The Great Lock-Out was only just beginning.

PART II

THE SIEGE

7

Digging in

1926 obviously marked a distinctive turning point in British history. Surprisingly many modern memories of it are philosophical rather than bitter.

That 'The first month after the General Strike was a fabulous spell of freedom' is a typical ex-miner's recollection of the period. The fact that this 'holiday' was in the May and June of an exceptionally balmy summer is of particular significance. For one of the many factors distinguishing the miner's job from all others is the feeling of almost continual night. During nearly half the year the average collier went to and returned from work in the dark; he only saw the light of day on Saturday afternoons – usually spent at a football match – and on Sundays. But now fresh air and light, all day and every day, were unaccustomed luxuries; and there were no bad money worries as yet to tarnish with a form of Midas' curse the gold to which everything was suddenly turned by constant sunshine. The Rhondda collier could daily see for himself how green was his valley 'for like most miners he loves the daylight. On Sunday, and other holidays, when the weather is good, the miner loves to walk upon the mountains on each side of the valley. Clad in his Sunday best, he presents a strange spectacle against the rough and rugged fissured slopes. He goes there to catch the sun which he is hungry for.'[1] He had not, for years, had such a good opportunity as in 1926.

Soon, however, this same collier was walking up from the valley in anything but his 'Sunday best'. For there was work that could be profitably but unofficially done at the 'levels', or 'drifts', where the coal outcropped on the surface of the hillsides.

Such activity was tacitly permitted by most of the owners, at least in the early days. Vital coal was thus obtained for storage against the winter, and for sale wherever possible at about a shilling, sometimes 1s. 6d. per hundredweight sack. But it was a patchy and chancy business, increasingly difficult as time went on. If the men tried to cut too deeply into the hillside, they could soon be in danger, apart from the difficulty of seeing. The only available form of illumination – in the obvious absence of the usual lamps – was supplied by candles, which came to acquire a premium value. Soon men who had been getting coal from the drifts or tips were pleased to accept two candles – or even one candle – rather than the shilling for a bag of coal. Some of the men were lucky enough to be able to bring some coal down every day. Conditions, however, varied greatly from one area to another, and the supplies of burnable coal quickly began to give out. It was gruelling, man's work, with ever-diminishing returns, and only the toughest men stuck at it day after day. But one particular person became famous in Rhondda for the amount of coal obtained in this way – a woman, not a man. With flaming hair, she was known as 'Red Mary', and could dig and carry coal 'as good as any man', even as far as two miles. Men laugh about it all now over their beer in the Working Men's Clubs in the towns and villages of the Rhondda Valley.

Was any beer available during the Lock-Out, when, theoretically, the breweries could obtain no coal to continue operating? The answer is yes, for somehow – no one asked too closely just how – coal got delivered to the breweries, and beer continued to be available! But as for coal deliveries elsewhere, there was often bitterness and recrimination, going to the very heart of what the whole struggle was about.

Coal was needed for certain essential, as well as general commercial, purposes, and the owners were only too anxious for its continued provision provided the workers would agree to their new terms of employment. And a tiny, if detested, minority was willing to agree to these terms. Such blacklegs, or 'scabs', became lepers in their own communities. There were attempts to dump the coal that started, though in very small quantities, to come out of such pits as managed to reopen. Some of the locked-out men even wanted to 'dump' coal destined for the canteens that became for so many the only lifeline between subsistence and starvation. But such militancy, as we would call it now, was considered as plain 'daft' by most people, and the canteens were never disrupted for this reason. Confusion meanwhile inevitably arose between those secretly digging or scraping some coal here and there and the genuine blacklegs. Much depended on individual interpretations of the use to be made of coal unofficially collected.

The young Aneurin Bevan, in Tredegar, took, as may be expected, an uncompromising view. As chairman of the Combine Executive Lodge, he transformed his Council of Action into a Relief Committee, whose main function was to open and maintain feeding kitchens. 'He was not afraid to show his authority to others besides the police. Some miners were in the habit of getting coal for themselves from "the patches" on the mountain sides. A few started doing it on a bigger scale and selling it to others. Bevan decided to take the matter in hand personally. He went up the mountain and shouted down to a miner at work in one of the holes. "You wait, you bugger, I'll come up and deal with you," came the voice from below. "Don't trouble," said Bevan, "I'm coming down," and with that he jumped into the hole onto the back of the would-be blackleg. It was one of the very few brawls during those tense months in Tredegar.'[2]

While most of the country basked in the euphoric aftermath of a 'settlement' to the General Strike, the former tenseness only increased in the mining communities. Once more we were 'two nations', but this time with a vengeance. Naturally the plight of the miners soon ceased to be of news value in the daily press. Even in retrospect, priority of interest fails to be given to starving colliers, as in the description, for the middle months of 1926, of 'the summer of frustration which ended in triumph'.[3] The 'frustration' refers to the initial failure of the England Test Match team in its battle against the visiting Australians. The 'triumph' came in August when the Ashes were won back by the home team amidst scenes of unrestrained jubilation at the Oval. Sport, nevertheless, cast its spell on others besides the employed and well-to-do. In Rhondda 'the Oval' meant not the famous cricket ground at Kennington but a patch of land in Tonypandy where locals competed at climbing 'the greasy pole'. Such games were a source of profit as well as relaxation, for that matter, and profit in forms almost more valuable than money. Shopkeepers gave, as prizes, the shirts, boots, caps and other articles which there was no money to buy.

Though 1926 saw the worst stoppage of its kind, and the one that brought the most suffering, the legacy from five years before had yet to be wiped out in most areas. 'We were in poorer shape for a stoppage in 1926 than we had been in 1921. None of us had any reserve funds, and few had paid much back off the debts. We had carried all the old timber that was to be found on the mountains, and the coal-tips had been picked as clean as possible. The old pits we had used to get coal from had been blown in to stop anyone going down. This was a wise precaution, for the men would have kept risking their lives for that coal as long as they were able to go down.'[4]

As the seemingly interminable summer dragged on without work and without a settlement, the men continued to walk up the mountains; but the novelty of daylight had worn off and soon there was no more coal to be had. They now walked up for a different reason: 'because the grass was soft and because we could not endure the sight of those prosperous looking cars flashing along'.[5] What one might think were small privations began to assume major proportions. Men experimented in numerous ingenious ways to satisfy their craving for nicotine. They tried cutting up herbs and smoking these; and a cigarette end in the gutter would cause a rush to reach it first. It was no unusual sight to see four men hungrily but happily sharing a single cigarette. The occasional gift of half-a-crown from a well-off benefactor would provoke a stampede for the nearest Woodbines.

Though this strange period following the end of the General Strike hit various parts of the country in different ways, the over-all pattern was similar in all the mining areas. It was something like what happened to the whole country in the autumn of 1939.

There was an obvious awareness that an emergency existed, but no way of telling at first how it would develop. Indeed a sense of excitement and challenge exhilarated many people to begin with. The enforced holiday acted as a tonic; for miners the day-long lungfuls of fresh air brought the breath of new hopes for the future. It was only as the Lock-Out dragged on that all vestiges of a 'honeymoon' period* came to an end.

'How did the miners survive? By the end of July their union strike benefit was exhausted. But in mining areas the whole community was behind the colliers. They sank or swam together, and there was no problem about keeping up appearances.'[6] Men of about seventy in, for example, Tonypandy now, remember the period as if it were yesterday. The Rhondda Valley of today still teems with the memories of 1926.

The most vivid sensation experienced by the miners was that of even greater isolation than ever from the rest of the community. Despite the action of the TUC leaders, however, they managed to remain morally united with their fellow workers and erstwhile fellow strikers. Such unity, however precarious, delayed the drastic action contemplated by the Government to render any repetition of the General Strike impossible. Baldwin's cabinet did not want any more years like 1926, when 160 million working days were lost in strikes. The weapon in preparation was a Trade Disputes Act to illegalise any future attempted General Strike (a tacit admission that there was no settled law already on this point, although John Simon had contended that there was). The Government had even intended to introduce such legislation during the General Strike itself. The decision was made by the Cabinet on 11 May to define as illegal any strike 'intended to intimidate or coerce the Government or the community' and to make the use of trade union funds in such a strike an indictable offence. King George V had, unknown to the public,[7] intervened personally with a warning to the Home Secretary and the Attorney-General that 'anything done to touch the pockets of those who are now only existing on strike pay might cause exasperation and serious reprisals on the part of the sufferers'.

*See Chapter 10.

He strongly advised the Prime Minister not to provoke the strikers 'who until now had been remarkably quiet'.[8] The proposed Bill would thus have to be kept back until the right moment had arrived. For 'while the miners were still fighting no Government dared to introduce such vindictive legislation, for it would have precipitated the very thing it aimed at killing – working-class unity. The Miners' struggle through those six long months of incredible hardship would deserve a volume to itself. In November 1926 when they were finally driven back to work by sheer starvation and exhaustion they ended one of the most magnificent epics in working-class struggle.'[9]

This at least is one view of what happened. Stress on starvation as the *main* reason for a return to work exemplifies traces of Left-wing myth. The fact remains that the 'hunger-strike' aspect of the long Lock-Out was easily its most dramatic feature. It was like 1921 all over again, on 1 April of which year over a million miners had been forced into idleness and left 'gazing at the gaunt and silent machinery on their pithead'.[10] But conditions had deteriorated sharply since then and the mining communities in 1926 were much less well equipped to conduct what looked like being a conflict of unprecedented roughness. The facts were stark. A million miners and their three million dependants were without any normal means of support; but they were apparently bent on a suicidal course. Their determination confounded calculations in Whitehall. The end of the national strike should have signalled the falling into line of the miners. Nothing could have been neater or tidier than the 'package' envisaged by the Prime Minister, in his broadcast of 12 May, as immediately following the surrender by the TUC. But it was not to be. And the Great Lock-Out, rather than the General Strike, was to become the 1926 event of principal significance for the future.

Its repercussions were not only domestic but affected foreign policy as far away even as the Pacific Ocean. China had been in a state of revolution since 1911. At the end of 1925 Sun Yat-Sen's Nationalist movement came to be aimed sharply against Great Britain, and in the summer of 1926, as it so happened, British

interests were directly imperilled. Chiang Kai-shek led an
apparently invincible Nationalist army northward, putting the
numerous British merchants in immediate peril. They looked in
vain for help from home where the Government's preoccupation
was elsewhere. It is not an exaggeration that the locked-out
miners provided a 'shield to the Chinese Revolution'.[11] For the
breaking of the 'strike' was the Government's all-eclipsing
objective for the time being.

The immediate problem for the miners was how they were
going to subsist at all during what had to be envisaged as a
possibly prolonged dispute. Ordinary Strike funds had been
depleted by the 1921 stoppage. It now took only just over two
months – May to June 1926 – for them to become exhausted.
During this time the TUC itself contributed nearly £50,000,
the General and Municipal Workers £20,000, and the Weavers'
Association £10,000. The Miners' Federation of Great Britain
managed, with the help of local subscriptions, to feed £30,000
to some of the district federations. The MFGB also received, in
this period, a quarter of a million pounds from Soviet trade unions
for distribution where needed. But Russian support for the British
miners, which was, of course, politically motivated, was deeply
resented by the Baldwin cabinet.

What meanwhile was the attitude of this cabinet to the new turn
of events? Though the miners' continued defiance was a setback
to the Government's calculations, such calculations still envisaged
a speedy capitulation by the beleaguered colliers. They were
upset only when Baldwin fell disastrously between the two
stools of resistance as represented by the miners and the owners.
As far as the former were concerned, 'the publication of the
Prime Minister's proposals for the settlement of the dispute
quickly reassured them of the justice of their fight'.[12] These
proposals involved a subsidy of £3,000,000 for three weeks to
facilitate a return to work, but at a reduction of ten per cent in
the minimum wages, with further reductions to follow. A
National Wages Board would meanwhile draw up a national
wages and hours agreement; but the wages of the lowest-paid

men were no longer to be guaranteed if they exceeded 45s. a week. The Government promised legislation to implement the Samuel Commission's recommendations for reorganising the industry, but only *after* such legislation had been vetted by the Coal Advisory Committee of the Secretary for Mines.

The Government proposals were not only considerably less liberal than the original Samuel Commission's recommendations; they fell short even of the subsequent Samuel Memorandum produced during the General Strike as a possible basis for honourable settlement. The temporary subsidy was no longer a guarantee that the men resumed work at their previous rate of wages, nor were the wages of the lowest-paid men to be safeguarded. The proposals, furthermore, involved immediate wage cuts, the introduction of district settlements instead of a national agreement, and substitution of compulsory arbitration for traditional collective bargaining as a means for settling disputes. Most important of all, however, was the central and ominous fact that wage reductions were now definitely to *precede* any reorganisation of the industry rather than to follow it. This struck directly at the principle upheld all along on the miners' side: that without reorganisation as a necessary pre-condition for all other remedial action, there could be no hope that the tortured mining industry could ever be operated successfully, and in accordance with basic justice.

These proposals were rejected by the Miners' Federation whose Executive Committee nevertheless stated significantly that:

We are largely in agreement with the legislative and administrative proposals set forth and are prepared to render every assistance possible to ensure their success, but see no reason why such measures should be first reviewed by the Coal Advisory Committee.

We are unable to recommend the mine-workers to accept his proposal that a Board with an independent chairman shall be empowered to abolish the National Minimum and enforce varying minima throughout the districts.

We consider that, in making these proposals, the Prime Minister is not honouring the pledge he gave to the country in the message broadcast on the 8th May as follows:

'I wish to make it as clear as I can that the Government is not fighting to lower the standard of living of the miners, or of any other section of the workers.' (20 May 1926)

This rejection by the miners was scarcely surprising. The Government was less prepared for the haughty attitude taken by the coalowners. They not only rejected the proposals through their Association, they also put in a gratuitous demand for 'freedom from political interference'. After making a counter-proposal for an eight-hour day and wage reductions which would 'not exceed 10 per cent when wages are at the minimum in the worst placed districts', they added the somewhat patronising conclusion that:

The proposals of 14 May, calculated as they are to limit freedom of administration, will not be helpful in securing the increased efficiency of the industry. It will be impossible to continue the conduct of the industry under private enterprise unless it is accorded the same freedom from political interference as is enjoyed by other industries.

Those who gave this answer – claiming, rightly or wrongly, to be speaking on behalf of all coalowners – knew perfectly well that their industry was different from all others; that it directly concerned national issues as well as sensitive social questions; and that without political 'interference' private ownership would no longer even exist. But these were the last things their Association would officially admit at this delicate juncture, when, at least for the moment, they found themselves on the defensive. They considered it just possible that Baldwin might really have meant it when he asserted his determination to protect the miners' living standards; and they knew that the arguments in favour of thorough reorganisation were formidable.

But they gambled on the ultimate identity of interests which they realised existed between themselves as a group and the Government, even though such an identity was seldom expressly mentioned.

The gamble came off. The Prime Minister swallowed his pride and put all the blame on the miners. He said that he was 'aware that the immediate cause of the present deadlock is the refusal of the Miners' Federation to consider any concession', whereas 'the colliery owners have made some advances from their original position in order to try to reach a settlement'.[13] The owners thus slipped neatly out of a tight corner, just as it seemed as if the Government might have used this favourable moment to grasp the long-standing nettle and impose an equitable settlement on the coal industry. They would, had they judged things correctly, have had the backing of public opinion for such an attitude. Indeed an extraordinary by-election occurred on 28 May at Hammersmith North. The Conservative candidate, defending a 2,000 majority in this 'suburban' rather than working-class constituency, made the Strike and the Coal Crisis the main issues of the campaign. In the event the Labour candidate, J. P. Gardner, gained the seat for Labour with a majority of nearly 4,000. (At each of the six by-elections held during the remainder of 1926 the Labour party increased its share of the votes, while the Conservatives, in each case, lost ground.)[14]

The Government, however, decided to move in a very different direction. On the basis that a long war of attrition might lie ahead, it made the necessary preparations. It arranged for the importation of foreign coal[15] and for restricting the allowance of coal for domestic purposes to one hundredweight a fortnight. The latter move was a useful softening up of public opinion in case of a prolonged dispute as regulations were issued emphasising the critical nature of the situation. Then on the last day of May the Government's special powers were kept in being by a renewal of the Emergency Powers Act.

The owners were meanwhile left in an extremely strong position. Whatever they may have said about political 'interference' they could be confident that in practice the Government would have to fight most of their battle for them. They could afford to sit back and await the developments while the miners faced up to an economic siege. There was added significance in the fact that the miners were not on strike but were locked out. This left the owners holding all the high cards; for while a strike is initiated by the workers to bring pressure on the employers, a lock-out is a weapon designed to bring such hardship on the workers that they will be forced to return to work on the employers' terms. Legally, however, 'the workers are on strike even if they are only refusing to accept a change in conditions which their employers are seeking to enforce'.[16]

Thus the miners got the worst of both worlds, since no unemployment insurance or other benefits were payable when they were considered to be on strike, even if they did not see themselves in this position. Throughout the whole seven-month period, the distinction between lock-out and strike was blurred; and to this day the stoppage is often referred to, incorrectly, as a 'strike' on the part of the miners. The real strength of the owners' position, however, lay in the tacit understanding which automatically allied them to the most influential circles in the country, notably the Government itself. This understanding was to receive dramatic expression when, in the following September, Winston Churchill, deputising for the Prime Minister in negotiations to try and end the deadlock, was to blurt out the truth. He assumed that discussions with the owners were to be taken as discussions as between natural allies, and referred specifically to 'the basis of understanding which has subsisted between H.M. Government and the Mining Association during this long-drawn and protracted dispute'.*

By the autumn, in other words, the Government and the Mining Association were back together in undisguised double harness. In the early days of the Lock-Out, however, there was an interesting realignment of forces as against what had been the position during the General Strike. The contest then had been, as it were, a 'mixed doubles' between Government and coalowners on one side, and miners and General Council of the TUC

*See Chapter 14.

on the other. Now the owners and the General Council had retired to the side lines, leaving the Government and the colliers to fulfil the respective roles of besiegers and besieged. These two combatants now dug themselves in for a decisive confrontation.

8

Honeymoon period

There is a sense in which, while there was no preparation by the TUC for the General Strike, there was a whole century of fortuitous preparation for the Lock-Out of 1926. That event – which became, because of its ultimate legacy, the turning point in the whole history of the British coal industry – came to the mining valleys somewhat as did war to the country as a whole in 1939. There was no sudden or violent blitzkrieg, but rather an eerie stillness and air of defiant uncertainty. Conversations with dozens of veteran miners in different parts of England and Wales help to evoke a picture of surprising uniformity. Though scattered far and wide, the miners and their families formed one indivisible community, and this despite the fact that 'no two collieries are alike'.[1] When the Lock-Out came, it was all for one and one for all.

There was inevitably much fear, particularly among the womenfolk, although they were equally the most determined to resist to the end. The phenomenon of people freely talking to each other and discussing their common danger and common battle was then no novelty, as it was for men-in-the-street in 1939. The camaraderie of the colliers was nothing new; but it had never, until 1926, been put to so severe a test, since few envisaged a short sharp dispute, still less an easy victory. It was for such reasons that the analogy of a group under siege is no exaggeration.

The average member of such a group at that period has been pictured as deriving almost superhuman strength from awareness of past endeavours. 'The miner looks back a century and sees his predecessor of that period working twelve to fourteen, even eighteen hours a day, sometimes under bond, in mines where there were few safety devices and no inspection.'[2] Sidney Webb recalls that 'It was then customary not to trouble about a coroner's inquest if the corpse "was only that of a collier". The newspapers as we learn from one of them were asked not to mention such things.'[3] The collier of the twenties realised that his predecessors of the earlier years were 'a rude, bold, savage set of beings, apparently cut off from their fellow men in their interests and feelings'.[4] He knew the landmarks of that subsequent history whereby they and he were affected: how the families of the men who were killed or permanently injured, as well as the aged among the miners, were left in destitution; of the abuses in the weighing of coal, the heavy fines for short measures, and the arbitrary confiscation of tubs; of the long and bitter fight to achieve an independent 'checkweighman' to ensure full payment for coal brought up; of the 'truck shops' where the miners were forced to buy goods at prices fixed by the mineowners; of the miseries of eviction from owners' houses at a time when eviction meant homelessness; of the blocking of attempts by miners to secure a proper education because of its 'prejudicial effect on profits'. Summing up his feelings toward these earlier days a pitman remarked, 'I read of women dragging along their length in chains, prostituted and bestialised by conditions now happily eradicated – of children cooped up in the pit, trap-door boys, fire tenders, companions of the darkness and the rats so long that they saw the daylight only in the week-end interval, and I blush with shame for the community upon whose annals such monstrosities are bound to be recorded.'[5] The past, in other words, was a vividly living reality for the miners of the twenties. It conditioned and moulded their outlook; its hardships had toughened them for present conflicts; its burdens had not yet crushed their spirit to resist and fight back. They knew, however, that this particular conflict – the Lock-Out of 1926 – might well be different from any that had gone before; that it could well be a make-or-break affair. Failure in a protracted dispute would almost certainly, at long last, break the spirit of resistance which had withstood a century and more of constant buffeting. The miners' whole past, as well as their status for the foreseeable future, was wrapped up in the conflict that lay ahead. This was the great gamble they were taking.

It was thus that 'after the high level of activity of the General Strike the population settled down to the hard slog of what proved to be a seven month lock-out. The transport pickets were called off and no pickets were needed at the pits in view of the men's solidarity. Big colourful rallies and demonstrations were held. Spirits were high. . . .'[6] An almost carnival atmosphere, in fact, invaded the mining areas, despite the serious undertones of the situation. The weather, which had remained cold throughout the Strike, gave way to a heat-wave at Whitsun. Savings, though sparse, had not yet been dipped into as for an emergency; and miners with their families from Rhondda and other Welsh mining valleys converged on Barry for the Whitsun holidays. On the surface it might have been thought that they had not a care in the world. Even demonstrations assumed a gala aspect. A latent love for music, marching, dancing and sport was given full vent. Jazz bands and glee clubs made full use of their unaccustomed leisure. At the beginning of June the Rhondda Glee Singers, who had been away since the previous September, came back from a victorious tour of the U.S.A. and Canada. Their return to a valley where virtually everyone was out of work produced an astonishing scene. The streets were thronged to give a festive welcome to the local heroes. Fancy-dress parades and competitions, along with singing and dancing contests, provided more than just idle entertainment. The organisers were shrewd and practical. They were looking ahead to a time – perhaps within a few weeks – when no money whatsoever would be circulating in most areas. Shopkeepers and relatively prosperous well-wishers gave household goods and articles of clothing as prizes.

The honeymoon period could have brought a welcome and overdue sense of classless solidarity to the mining areas. Many owners were sympathetic to the men and their families. But there was an unwritten code among the owners analogous to that prevailing among the unions. Honour forbade a selling of the pass or a division in the ranks, even in a supposedly philanthropic cause. The official owners' (Mining Association) line was that a speedy return to work was in the men's best interest, even at the new conditions being laid down. Therein lay the only chance of resumed and increased production and thus, ultimately, an improvement in living standards for all concerned. Every idle week, on the other hand, only piled up greater potential hardship for the future; to have encouraged false hopes would, therefore, it was reasoned, be a cruel form of 'kindness'. As a result the owners were conspicuous by their absence while the workless miners went out and about to find outlets for their pent-up energy. The miners, as a still surviving legend has it,[7] presumed that they were all off on their yachts, or staying at villas in Nice and Cannes. More often, in reality, they stayed out of the way, at home or in London, worried for themselves and for their employees about a situation they felt largely powerless to influence. Most of them were convinced that the stoppage could not last long and were content to sit it out. The more perspicacious, however, could see ominous signs in the miners' carefree optimism which, they knew, accompanied a steely determination.

It was, in fact, the great hour for Arthur Cook, the voice of the mining communities. Extravagant and irresponsible he may have been in his utterances, making him almost a caricature of a demagogue. But the moment was psychologically right for his kind of showmanship, and he told people what they wanted to hear. Audiences whose frustrations and fears found expression and relief in his spell-binding oratory reacted as did so many to Ian Paisley in Ulster fifty years later. His gasconade manner seemed ridiculous to sophisticated observers but was intoxicating to the besieged warriors of the coalfields. He swooped down on South Wales four days after the Strike was over to tell the people of Treorchy that he was their man, rather than their own M.P. This stroke of syndicalist cheek went down well, and he went on to tell the Rhondda miners that there was *hope*.

Hope! The feeling fed on the unnaturally festive atmosphere of the moment. It needed no logic, and would have found none,

Arthur Cook arrives at 10 Downing Street

Canteen at the Infants' School, Trealaw, Rhondda Valley

Soup kitchen, October 1926

Coal selling cheap

to support it. Cook rode the euphoric wave for everything it was worth. All would be well if people ignored 'the gramophone voices' of the politicians. His stridency increased as the peace overtures of early June came to nothing. His scorn for politicians was not reserved to those of Conservative hue, but turned its fire on Ramsay MacDonald when the Labour leader tried to argue that the miners' dispute was a business and not a political matter. MacDonald was as out of touch with colliers' thinking as the Prime Minister himself, for whom Cook hurled out the warning, 'If Mr Baldwin attempts by legislation to force longer hours, it will be the start of a British revolution.'[8] There were signs, however, that Cook was beginning to alienate powerful forces in the TUC whose continuing general support was essential if the hopeful momentum was to be kept up. It was a delicate moment, and the pending post-mortem on the General Council's action in terminating the national strike was already provoking bitter controversy. Mounting apprehension accumulated as to the Conference of Trade Union Executives planned for Friday, 25 June. An open split between the miners and the rest, increasingly thought likely, would have brought all traces of the 'honeymoon period' to a violent end. The announcement of the Government's planned legislation to lengthen the miners' working day had an electrifying effect. A united front was restored, and the day of reckoning and possible recrimination was put off until the mining dispute was settled.

The ensuing truce was not universally popular, but was accepted in most areas. Cook's account of the Strike from the miners' point of view, *The Nine Days*, was withdrawn from circulation. It had been hastily and impetuously compiled and sold – at 6d. – for the Miners' Wives and Children Fund. In it Cook had written: 'Since May 12 we have been left to continue our struggle alone – but not alone, as the rank-and-file are still with us. They did not let us down. . . . We still continue, believing that the whole rank and file will help us all they can. . . . We hope still that those leaders of the TUC who feel that a mistake has been made will rally to our cause and help us to victory.'[9] There was still enough optimism about for this to be a tenable belief.

The ubiquitous buntings and red flags were symptomatic of the great parade the Communists had to put on to make up for their negligible hold on the minds and hearts of most miners. But the colourful presence of the flags, shorn of political inference, was appropriate to the light-headedness lasting into the flaming June that followed the Whitsun heat-wave. The miners were still very definitely on the offensive. Theirs was the psychological advantage at this stage, and the studied appearances of 'normalcy' in other quarters produced some anomalous situations. On 7 June, the Prime Minister, who had spent such a nonchalant country weekend just before the Lock-Out had started, and had visited the London Zoo one afternoon while the Strike was on, was, with much fanfare, made a freeman of the City of Cardiff, then dominated by coal and shipping interests. The next day, however, the mineowners were openly pessimistic about the chances of an early peace, and Cook began another whirlwind round of inflammatory speeches. But some of the edges were losing their sharpness, and he came out with the statement that 'Only half the pits could be worked under the old conditions.'[10]

This was a concession of sorts, as it implied that under prevailing circumstances the owners had no alternative but to lower wages. Proper reorganisation, on the other hand, preferably nationalisation, would have saved the day for the country, the miners, and, indirectly, for the owners as well; the latter had only to make a small sacrifice to their standards of living compared to what they were asking of the colliers. As it was, and without reorganisation, Cook admitted that a return to work on former terms would throw 200,000 miners out of work in South Wales alone. In the midst of such depressing news, William Randolph Hearst, the American newspaper tycoon, entertained a mainly Rhondda male choir at his Welsh retreat, St Donat's Castle in the fertile Vale of Glamorgan.

The honeymoon period lasted about a month. It was such a month as could not happen today. Despite the enormous and dangerous implications of it all, there was little violence and a minimum disruption of business and middle-class life. Colliers in the Midlands took daily to the cricket pitch. The legendarily militant Durham miners tranquilly enjoyed the sun and fresh air. They stayed out all day. Street vs. street football was played daily until mid-June, when the weather got so unusually hot that the railwaylines began to warp. The ponies were brought up to the surface to be properly looked after. The owners even encouraged the locked-out miners to keep them occupied and exercised. The ponies presented a strange and pathetic sight. They were scarcely recognisable to those who had previously seen them only underground. Some were already going blind – the fate of most of them after a lifetime in darkness. They were bewildered by the sunlight as they stood about, thin and listless. But soon, with the fresh air, better feeding and proper exercise, they began to flourish. They were ridden in specially organised races with the miners as jockeys; a popular diversion and even a source of profit through the improvised punting.

It was a rare sight to see the darlings of the pits thus employed. For in the coalmines of the twenties no mere human being was pampered as were the ponies. The best part of the colliery was allotted to the underground stables, which had their own specially trained keepers. Their value was always at a premium; human life seemed cheap by comparison, as many a miner of the period attests today. A man called Joe was the victim of an accident, fortunately one of the less serious kind, in a Leicestershire pit in 1925. As he struggled to get himself free of the debris he heard comrades asking about his safety. Then he heard the 'gaffer' saying: 'Bugger the lad, is the pony all right?' In fact the pony had been killed.

Recounting the incident in the office above ground later, he was told that he should have made more of an effort to save the pony. Recording the incident in his 'black book' the manager said, 'You could have saved the colliery £20 by saving that horse.' The carpeted collier spat out by way of reply: 'My mum couldn't have bought a Joe for £20 could she?' Recalling the incident fifty years later he added: 'And I shut his bloody book for him.'[11]

The pit-pony races became a favourite recreation during the Lock-Out, especially in the early weeks. They gave a novel dimension to the important relationship between pony and driver that was a well-known feature of life in the mines. Each driver got to know and love his own pony. The temptation to ride him part of the way to his work spot in the pit was always great, but strictly forbidden. Had it been allowed there would have been more time for actually working at or near the face, and thus allowable in the official computation of time spent at 'work'. As it was, 'travelling time' – not included as 'work' – could take as much as two hours underground every day since walking or crawling two miles in both directions could take as long as this. An attempted surreptitious lift on a pony could get swift reaction from the sticks of the gaffers, ever vigilant from various vantage points.

During the Lock-Out, however, the pitmen could ride their ponies to their hearts' content. It represented a concession by the owners, but had an ironical sequence. When the ponies returned underground after seven months of fresh air and light many never settled down again in the darkness and fetid air of the pits.

The atmosphere prevalent among the miners during this first month or so of the Lock-Out had its counterpart among people in other areas and of differing classes. They, also, had their 'honeymoon period', but it had different causes and had another kind of result. It sprang from relief that the Strike had been so 'successfully' defeated, and the habit of talking to complete strangers lingered on for some time. The miners were now only of sporadic interest to the press, and thus were largely forgotten by the general public.

Instead of a polarisation of classes, as in the industrial areas, there was, especially in southern England, an exactly opposite tendency. People tacitly congratulated each other on the fruits of their new found camaraderie, and the protagonists of the 'gay twenties' got back to their hell-raising tasks with renewed vigour. The glossy magazines glowed with smug euphoria, and *Punch* archly commented that instead of backing the Strike, the British Public had been striking back. 'Mr Punch' himself, perkier than ever from wing-collar to spats, congratulated a new kind of 'British Worker' on the results of his temporary employment during the nine day crisis. He did so in a cartoon appearing 'with Mr Punch's compliments to the great army of amateur workers who sustained the Nation's life.'[12] There also lingered on for many a sense of welcome and unusual excitement. For the feckless 'bright young things' – who normally had nothing important to do – it had been a week of wonderful work; for those in humdrum jobs immune from strike action, it had been a whirlwind of adventure, with every excuse for turning up late at the office. The scope for yarns and tales of heroics was limitless and was exploited for years to come, though the general absence of violence had robbed many of the chance of genuine blood-and-thunder encounters. It had already been observed by the third day of the Strike that Government tactics 'towards creating the impression of rowdyism seem to be petering out'. Legend, however, could easily fill in the empty gaps: 'The same blackleg bus has been burnt in Poplar, Camberwell and Hammersmith, and the holocaust was witnessed by all the imaginative people who saw the Russians pass through London in 1914.'[13] Most of the banter, however, was surprisingly good humoured, and continued as such long after the incredible nine days. Compared to what would be the case today, hard feelings, again in southern England and other prosperous areas, were negligible. And although there was widespread victimisation of workers seeking back their old jobs after the Strike, there was no great bearing of grudges on the part of men-in-the-street. 'As the strike was not a general one',[14] it had been realised that no useful purpose was to be served by unnecessarily annoying an innocent public.

The only fly in the honeymoon ointment hereabouts was a regret that the first flush had so quickly spent itself. Many lower-middle-class people long looked back with nostalgia on those nine days when every journey from home was an adventure rather than yet another routine piece of drudgery. Such young people as shop girls missed it most of all, and had to be content with the congratulation they were offered by Sir John Simon in the House of Commons a few days after the Strike was over. He also took the opportunity to administer a much-needed rebuke to the wicked strikers. 'They might wear out the girls' shoes, but they could not wear out her spirit,' he proclaimed with extreme unction to loud cheers. A few days before, those who had actually witnessed the scenes in the City and such thorough-fares as the Commercial Road, had seen these same girls in their dizzy dozens, as, 'astride the bars of push bikes, pillioned on motor cycles, tucked away into side-cars, snuggled in motors, ranged in charabancs, the lovely creatures sped upon their way. . . . What a change, what a chance! It was the time of their lives.'[15]

9

Red money and poor law

During most of 1926 the weekly newspaper, the *New Leader*, was edited by the brilliant and cultured H. M. Brailsford. In putting forward the principles of the Independent Labour Party, it reflected the insistence of such of its members as Shinwell and Jimmy Maxton on the tolerant attitude desired by the party's founder, Keir Hardie. Its outlook was summed up by the phrase from an official statement of policy produced at a time of potential discord at the end of 1926: 'We want tolerance within the Labour movement.'[1] Though well to the left by the standards of the day, the *New Leader* was edited at that time with considerable urbanity and a merciful absence of polemical exaggeration. 'Brailsford produced a paper of great literary and artistic merit, loved by school teachers for its Nature Notes, adored by artists for its woodcuts, and revered by intellectuals for its theoretical features.'[2] With a wide range of distinguished contributors, such as Shaw and Bertrand Russell, it was eminently readable; and, allowing for a bias in favour of the miners' case, it can be usefully studied as an unusually searching and valuable chronicle of the General Strike and the subsequent period.

In mid-June it carried an article describing life 'In the Miners' homes.' One incident was recorded as happening on the property of Lord Tredegar, who owned a large estate in Monmouthshire containing abundant coal. Across a corner of it ran a colliery railway yielding £17,000 a year in 'way-leaves', and the mineral royalties amounted to about £80,000. Not far from the railway line, in a small house occupied by a locked-out miner, one of the three children died of pneumonia. The death occurred

at a moment when the lock-out in some parts was just beginning
to bite with some ferocity. Many people were already existing
at lower than subsistence level. Such funds as were now being
made available barely covered weekly outlay on essential food.
Death brought extra expenses unless a pauper's burial were to
be settled for. The bereaved mother of Tredegar decided, instead,
to pawn her wedding ring to buy the tiny coffin.

Death when it came to such houses brought, apart from the
normal sadness, other and curious problems. Such problems
had to be faced with lack of undue sentimentality. In the case of
this particular dead child, one common sort of problem could
be avoided, as the child's body could be put on a sideboard or
out of the way in a corner. When an adult died there was no
convenient place for the body to be put unless the inhabitants
of a two-roomed house were willing for it to remain in the
bed where three or four others had to go on sleeping. The only
other place for the body was the kitchen table, in which case
there was nowhere to eat. And the body could not always be
removed as soon as would have been desirable. Apart from the
great increase of normal strains, such problems as these brought
an extra dimension of eeriness to the lives of many.

It was not that death, as such, produced any particular squeam-
ishness among the mining folk. Quite the opposite was true,
owing to its frequency and constant proximity in normal times.
In the abnormal conditions of the lock-out there was the difference
that between 500 and 600 colliers did not die, as they would
otherwise have done according to the weekly average of fatal
pit accidents at this period.

During the course of July, in almost all areas, 'strike pay'
accumulated from union funds began to dry up, though the
Miners' Relief Fund received income from other sources. Trade
unions in other countries made donations, but none on such a
scale as those in Soviet Russia. This money had been raised to
support the General Strike and was to continue to help the
miners during the Lock-Out. It elicited a strong protest from the
British Government, spearheaded by the Home Secretary
(Joynson-Hicks) who, on 11 June, sent a note to the Soviet

Government regretting that His Majesty's Government 'cannot maintain silence about the actions of the Soviet Government in support of the General Strike. . . . In particular the activity of the Soviet Commissariat of Finance is not conducive to a friendly settlement of the questions outstanding between the two States, which settlement the Soviet Government professes to desire.' The Russian reply stated that 'The Soviet Government, expressing the will of the workmen and peasants of the USSR, could not forbid the Trade Unions which are organised by the millions of workmen of the USSR to send money abroad to render support to the trade unions of another country.' The reply did not of course add that the Soviet Government had every reason to favour financial help to British trade unions. The almost total ineffectiveness of the British Communist Party was an admitted cause of concern in Moscow. It was even referred to by Stalin himself when he expressed 'no doubt that the weakness of the British Communist Party was of no small importance in the defeat of the General Strike'.[3] The story behind the 'Red Money' was nevertheless an intriguing one. The official account from the Russian point of view, involving tales of 'spontaneous' demonstrations and levies by the workers on themselves of double the amount originally agreed, records that by early July, 3,970,000 roubles, or about £400,000, had been sent.[4] (Altogether between May and October, the Russians contributed £832,000 to the miners' fund.) The Russian reply did not satisfy the British Government and a debate on the 'Russian Gold' was held in the House of Commons on 25 June. In the course of it a surprising amount of venom displayed itself not only against the Russian workers but also against the British miners. George Lansbury was stung to exclaim:

I do believe in the class war. I believe the class war is responsible for the starvation of my kith and kin, people who are bone of my bone and flesh of my flesh, down in the coal-fields of Britain. The only thing that is being asked today by the Government and the capitalists is that the workers should sacrifice. I hope to God that the workers will be able to stand out and with

their women defeat the most nefarious campaign that has ever
been waged against them. . . .

The Speaker did not, however, call any of the nearly fifty
members representing mining constituencies. In the ensuing
disorder, the House was adjourned without the Question being
put. The case against the miners thus went unanswered. (The
whole incident was an influential factor in Britain's severance of
diplomatic relations with the Soviet Union in 1927.)

By the end of August, the Russian contributions amounted to
£517,000 out of a total received from all sources by the MFGB
of £879,578.[5] These sources included such bodies as the Women's
Committee, the Trade Union Congress, the International
Miners' Federation, the National Society of Woodworkers, the
Amalgamated Weavers' Association and the American Federation
of Labor. On the basis, however, that the million locked-out
miners had, between them, about three million dependants, these
sums could provide only about 5s. (25p.) per person for the whole
period of the Lock-Out. In practice funds available at any one time
went, directly or indirectly, to the hardest hit districts.

Other sources of financial assistance included, notably, the
Co-Operative Societies with whom the miners often had worthwhile savings in the form of accumulated investments. During
strikes and the 1921 lock-out, the Co-Ops had allowed extended
credit to the miners in the form of food vouchers, whose equiva-
lent was to be repaid by deductions from future dividends.
Similar action was taken in 1926, but not on so large a scale as
before. Individual Co-Ops, however, were able to make special
contributions including even, as in Somerset, a free distribution
of 1,500 loaves of bread a day at one stage. In the atmosphere
of a siege economy, however, it was often the less spectacular
but more personal gestures of support that came as the greatest
boost to morale. Many thousands of miniature miners' lamps
were bought and worn as badges by contributors to the Labour
Women's Fund. There were numerous groups at work at local
level engaged in fund-raising activities. Schools, churches and
private households lent premises and other facilities, and helped

in the organisation of raffles, flag days, sporting events, entertainments. Ultimately, it was the extraordinary solidarity of spirit common to the entire 'archipelago' of the nation's scattered but united mining community that was the greatest weapon of the families under pressure. Nevertheless, the Government, as custodian of the people's health, could not stand by and let four million people literally starve, as they would eventually have done without massive outside help.

The Government, at the same time, was naturally concerned that the coal industry should be made fully operational again as soon as possible. It was therefore anxious not to encourage a prolongation of the stoppage such as would result from the miners and their famillies being properly fed. This posed an unusual dilemma. The situation was in no way similar to that in which men were out of work in the 'normal' course of economic vicissitude. In such a case unemployment insurance would be applicable. This latter was a relatively new concept in the twenties, especially as widened by Lloyd George. For, by extending insurance to virtually the entire working class, he had revolutionised British economic affairs. The unforeseeably high rate at which unemployment was later to run made the 'dole' a regular feature of life between the wars. But the dole was available neither to men on strike nor to men locked out of work by their employers. For the miners, in 1926, therefore, there was, in the final analysis, only one last hope: a desperate one with complicated social implications. This was the only ultimate 'safety-net which prevented them from falling into starvation,'[6] namely the Poor Law.

'The law which we in England call the Poor Law, but which receives more appropriate names in other countries, is that law which regulates the administration or distribution of assistance from public funds to private individuals on the ground of their failure to provide for themselves.'[7] This law had had a chequered history and its very name makes some men shudder to this day. Its name, in fact, is rarely pronounced as such by those who remember the last years of its operation on the old principles. They tend instead to speak of getting 'help from the parish'.

This, in effect, was how the Poor Law worked as of inception in its 'modern' form in 1834. Parishes were grouped into 'unions' to be administered by 'boards of guardians of the poor', such guardians being elected by the ratepayers. The criterion of eligibility was total destitution; and the principal means of supplying assistance was by way of 'indoor' relief, that is being put into the workhouse. 'Outdoor' relief was severely curtailed so as to limit to the minimum those who might choose to live as virtually subsidised paupers; and the 'workhouse test' was imposed on applicants for public alms. 'Such was the remorseless utilitarian logic of the [1834] Poor Law Commissioners, to whom the Act gave power. . . . The need to make life in the workhouse less attractive was the principle on which the Commissioners worked, and as they could not in that era raise the attractiveness of employment by enforcing a minimum wage, they felt obliged to lower the standard of happiness of the workhouse.'[8] The resultant horrors did not become generally known to Victorians until they read Dickens's descriptive attack on workhouse management in *Oliver Twist*. The 'New Poor Law', however, at least created a centralised framework within which reforms could come about. And notable efforts were made in this direction at the end of the nineteenth century and by the signatories to the Poor Law Report of 1909. The overriding aim was to ensure appropriate relief for genuinely deserving cases without encouraging abuses or subsidising indolence.

The 1926 situation, however, was loaded with anomalies and apparent exceptions to the accepted criteria. These provided that out-relief was payable to able-bodied men living in decent and respectable surroundings – in the absence of which the workhouse would be more appropriate – who could not, through no fault of their own, find any means to support themselves and their families. Utter destitution was ultimately the condition that Poor Relief sought to avoid. But what if the men were devoid of support because of strike action?

Theoretically the position was adequately covered in a circular (Circular 703) which the Ministry of Health had issued to all Boards of Guardians in England and Wales on 5 May.[9] The

operative part of this circular attempted to clarify the position
in the particular circumstances of a trade dispute:

> With regard to the limits within which relief may be given
> to persons who are destitute in consequence of a trade dispute,
> the Minister desires to draw attention to the declaration of
> the law contained in the judgement of the Court of
> Appeal in Attorney-General versus Merthyr Tydfil Guardians
> (1900).
>
> The function of the Guardians is the relief of destitution
> within the limits prescribed by law and they are in no way
> concerned in the merits of an industrial dispute, even though
> it results in applications for relief. They cannot, therefore,
> properly give any weight to their views of such merits in
> dealing with the applications made to them.
>
> The questions for the consideration of the Guardians on any
> application for relief made by a person who is destitute in
> consequence of a trade dispute are questions of fact, namely,
> whether the applicant for relief is or is not a person who is
> able-bodied and physically capable of work: whether work
> is or is not available for him and if such work is not available
> for him, whether it is or is not so unavailable through his own
> act or consent.
>
> Where the applicant for relief is able-bodied and physically
> capable of work the grant of relief to him is unlawful if work
> is available for him or he is thrown on the Guardians through
> his own act or consent and penalties are provided by law in
> case of failure to support dependants, though the Guardians
> may lawfully relieve such dependants if they are in fact desti-
> tute.

In practice the position was not by any means clear or straight-
forward. One of the added hardships for miners and their dependants was the confusion and tangle of technicalities in which
civil servants and the Poor Law Guardians found themselves in
their efforts, however, limited to prevent hundreds of thousands
of people from falling into complete destitution as the Lock-Out

dragged on. The Merthyr Tydfil case referred to had arisen out
of an action brought by the Powell Duffryn Steam Coal Company
against the Guardians of the Merthyr Tydfil Union for giving
poor relief to miners during the 1898 strike. The definitive
judgement ultimately emerging in the Court of Appeal laid it
down that the Guardians may not give relief to able-bodied men
on strike for whom work was available. Their wives and children,
however, could be relieved *if destitute*. The men themselves
could also be relieved if, through want, they became physically
unable to work. It was further held that a strike did not create
a case of 'urgent necessity' entitling someone to relief. Strikers,
furthermore, could technically become 'liable to be dealt with
under the Vagrancy Act for neglect of their family'. The Local
Government Board, moreover, 'had no power to extend the
application of the Poor Law statutes to persons not entitled to
relief under them'.

The Guardians soon found themselves beset with troubles and
critics on all sides. They displeased the ratepayers by giving any
relief at all; they upset the audit departments whose sole consideration was accounting for borrowings or the slightest 'irregulari-
ties' incurred in an effort to be just; and they failed to satisfy
hundreds of thousands who were unquestionably bordering on
destitution. The Minister of Health (Neville Chamberlain)
received numerous irate letters from various branches of the
'Property Owners' and Ratepayers' Association' claiming that
the Poor Law was never meant to 'deal with unemployment and
subsidise strikes'. Their sentiments were echoed by complaints
from Coal Owners' Associations in various districts, as well as
such branches of the 'National Unionist Association' as that
presided over by Lord Tredegar. They felt that feeding of the
destitute was unjustified as it might prolong the 'strike'.

The unsatisfactory operation of the Poor Law with regard to
semi-destitute miners was, on the other hand, described to the
Minister in a deputation led by Sidney Webb. He pointed out
Circular 703 had been designed to meet a general strike situation,
whereas the hardship now arising from the Lock-Out was of a
different nature. He complained that although the general strike

had ceased, boards of guardians were still being pressed to continue the policy suggested in the letter in view of the dispute in the coal industry, but many boards of guardians (for instance in rural parts of the South of England) were entirely unaffected by the coal dispute. In those cases there should be no restriction in the amount of relief given in individual cases, though some restriction might be reasonable in industrial unions where heavy calls upon the rates might be anticipated for some time. The circular had been read by boards of guardians to apply to the relief given to persons who were in receipt of it even before the strike began. It was not just that the first cuts in expenditure should be made at the expense of old men and women and invalids. The letter was interpreted by guardians as meaning that relief should not be given to a man on strike, but only to his wife and family, but there were in the mining areas many thousands of boys between the ages of fourteen and sixteen who were not eligible for relief under these conditions, as they were normally employed in or about the mines. It was ridiculous, Webb maintained, to say that these boys, who had no votes in their unions, could if they wished return to work. Further, the unmarried miner living in lodgings had no family who could contribute to his support, and he was faced with sheer destitution. Guardians should not take into account any assistance received by men involved in the dispute from charitable sources or from union funds. If in calculating the number of mouths that had to be filled they ignored the head of the family, it was inequitable that, in reckoning the family income, anything that he received should be taken into account. It was a departure from the principles of the Poor Law that there should be any family maximum of relief. The duty of the boards of guardians was to give relief in accordance with the needs of the applicant. He understood that the Minister had actually insisted in certain cases on boards of guardians making a rule not to give relief beyond a certain amount, no matter what the size of the family. He also complained that some boards of guardians, in giving relief in kind, gave tickets which were exchangeable for food generally, but not for milk.[10]

Mr Chamberlain contented himself with a general but not ungenerous reply. He felt himself the victim of cruel circumstances. The circular, he pointed out, had been issued to meet the emergency of a general strike which, it was true, was no longer in operation. But he believed that a long stoppage in the coal industry would gradually bring about the same condition of affairs as a general strike, and he could not take the responsibility of withdrawing it while matters remained as they were. He was naturally concerned lest the whole social security system as then organised should snap under the strain of such unusual burdens. He denied that there was any 'family maximum' for such relief as could be given. This may have been theoretically true. In fact, however, the circular had specifically stated that:

The Minister considers that at this moment it is necessary to examine the general situation and in this connection he desires first to draw attention to the scale on which unemployment benefit is paid and to suggest that, as is already the practice in a considerable number of Unions, the relief given by the Guardian should be so restricted as to be within this scale. The scale is as follows:– 18/- weekly for a man, 5/- for a wife, 2/- for each child.

In cases where, under the Merthyr Tydfil Judgement, relief may not lawfully be given to the man, it may be found necessary to increase the allowances to the woman and children above the figures of unemployment benefit but it is thought, that such allowances should not exceed the sum of 12/- and 4/- for the woman and each child respectively, these amounts representing what was found reasonable in the emergency of 1921, subject to a reduction corresponding to the fall in the cost of living. Exceptions would naturally be made in this scale, or any other scale that may be adopted by the Guardians, in cases in which sickness or other special need was present in the family.

The Minister further assured the deputation that the question of children between fourteen and sixteen was being considered by his legal advisers; and in the case of such hardship as that experienced by single miners, he considered that 'the proper thing to do was to bring a test case to the Courts'.

Discouraging as were such legalistic reactions, merely verbal battles were swiftly being overtaken by events. The whole population was beginning to feel the indirect effects of the hardships falling directly on the mining communities. At the same time pressure mounted on Neville Chamberlain to stop any more Poor Law payments at all to the miners against whom a new wave of resentment was stirring in the country at large. Typical of representations made to him was that of the 'National Citizens' Union' – which incorporated the 'Middle Classes Union' – whose President was the well known industrialist and arbitrator in many trade disputes, Lord Askwith. The Minister was urged 'to direct Boards of Guardians to cease granting relief to the dependants of Miners and others in places where pits are open'.

Hunger and its attendant hardships, both psychological and physical, were meanwhile being compounded by administrative chaos, especially in some of the hardest-hit areas. The supposedly plain 'fact of destitution' became less and less plain to bewildered Guardians. If a locked-out miner's family was being relieved, he was legally in the position of being 'constructively' relieved himself. The granting of any relief at all was therefore, in such cases, technically illegal. Relief 'in kind' was resorted to to get round practical difficulties, and another indignity was added to an already hated system when housewives turned up at the grocery with a ten shilling voucher known to have come from the Poor Law Guardians. In practice Chamberlain began to solve some of his problems by authorising the reduction to an absolute minimum of relief payments. All in all, inadequate and limited though it was, the figures relating to relief actually given during this period reveal something of the magnitude of the hardship involved.

Whereas outdoor relief had been given to 894,685 persons in the year ended 30 June 1925, the amount of recipients in the succeeding twelve months was 2,203,389.[11] In July 1926, however,

Neville Chamberlain resorted to some drastic surgery. Guardians
in some areas had been using their discretion in favour of the
locked-out miners' dependants, even if it had meant borrowing
funds to do so. The Minister of Health now introduced a bill –
the Boards of Guardians (Default) Act – giving him authority
to supersede Guardians who 'misused' their powers, by others
appointed by himself. This delivered a crushing blow to certain
areas, particularly Durham and South Wales, where local
government was Labour-controlled. From now on, the strict
letter of the law was to be observed, the Means Test applied in
all its humiliating completeness, and relief granted, in most
cases, only as a loan to be repaid by deductions from future
pay-packets or by some other means. By September, the Guardians, particularly in the mining areas, had been forced drastically
to reduce the scales of the relief payable. From this point on, it
was clear that even the precarious 'safety net' formerly provided
by 'parish relief' was to be withdrawn. In the final analysis, parish
relief as then administered was found to be 'poor law' in every
sense. It was superseded by the reforms introduced into local
government by Neville Chamberlain in 1928.

Meanwhile, with Poor Relief gradually diminishing to almost
vanishing point, the mining communities were being forced
back more and more on their own devices. It was such devices,
more than any outside financial help, Russian or other, that
revealed most characteristically the heart and soul of the 'siege'.

10

The besiegers

Before, during and after the General Strike, 'Mr Baldwin's behaviour had been that of the sporting Englishman whom the middle class are accustomed to reverence'. Mr Kingsley Martin, writing thus in an interesting short book published at the end of 1926,[1] went on to observe that 'By leaving the miners and mine-owners alone to waste the precious month after the publication of the [Samuel] Report, although the Report itself had emphasised the futility of so doing, he had made a conflict inevitable. He won the battle, and in the kindest of speeches forgave the strikers. His plea for an unvindictive settlement was both dignified and popular'.

The Prime Minister was determined to cultivate and hold on to such popularity. On 1 June he professed his willingness to help with negotiations at any moment. He made it clear that, although the former subsidy offer had lapsed, some form of temporary subsidy was essential. In fact, however, no offer was made, at this stage, to the miners which did not threaten a substantial decrease in their standard of living. Every important suggestion made by the Samuel Commission, moreover, had by now been discarded by the Government. The Commission had, as it were, served its purpose during the period of Government mobilisation before the strike, and was now virtually a dead letter.

The Government's only positive contribution to the problem was to advocate an eight-hour day, the one solution explicitly condemned by the Commission. But it was a solution which had attractions for a shrewd Prime Minister who dreaded the appearances of siege by frontal assault against the mining communities. For it could be argued that longer hours down the pit did not, as

such, threaten living standards. And of course the owners would
be delighted, as this was the very proposal they themselves had
made in the first place. 'By certain adjustments,' claimed Lord
Londonderry at this time, 'the rate of the lower paid men could
be maintained at the present figure and probably increased, while
an elasticity in the hours of working could certainly have no
effect in depressing the standard of living.'[2] Baldwin accordingly
acted quickly without attempting any preliminary soundings of
miners' feelings. The Government's programme of legislation,
announced on 15 June, duly confirmed the miners' worst sus-
picions. A bill was to be introduced permitting a lengthening of
the working day to eight hours exclusive of winding times, to be
followed by measures for the reorganisation of the industry. The
decision was bitterly resented in the coalfields, not all of which
were affected in quite the same way by such proposed legislation.
Indeed the owners' long-standing argument that the individual
areas in the country differed so greatly, geologically, economically and socially, that district arrangements as to wages and hours
were preferable to any overall national agreement, was now being
implicitly impugned. For the envisaged Bill sought to impose
uniformity in working hours despite differing local conditions.
The idea of an eight-hour day was particularly disliked in the
North-East, already badly hit by the long-term depression in the
coal export market. The estimated savings in cost-per-ton of
commercially disposable coal by means of an eight-hour day in
Durham would go very little way toward matching the losses
incurred during the previous months. And in this particular
county, the hewers were the most important single group of
workers among the colliers. Their traditional working time
would be seriously disrupted by the adoption of an eight-hour
day. 'Of all the influences which strengthened the Durham miners
in their struggle during the summer of 1926 the threatened eight-
hour day was perhaps the greatest. The adoption of an eight-hour
day for hewers never, in fact occurred but the determination of
the local owners to seek such a change provided the Durham
Miners' Association and its membership with a power of resistance
sufficient to help overcome the distress encountered by the major-

ity of miners and their families.'[3] Thus, all unknowingly, Baldwin was buttressing the defences, in one key area, of those whom he was seeking to besiege by stealth, rather than by blitzkrieg methods.

Less auspiciously, he was countenancing a Government repeal, for the first time for a hundred years, of an important piece of social reform. More ominously for his immediate tactics, it was, to some, 'obvious that the Eight-Hour Bill would prolong the stoppage'.[4] There was a deep, almost superstitious, dread among miners of the addition of a whole extra hour to the working day: the 'last hour' of work, with strain and tiredness at their maximum was notoriously feared for being particularly accident-prone. The owners were fond of producing statistics to disprove this belief; but the belief persisted. Even, however, without taking this last hour to be more dangerous than any other, it could be shown on a simple law of averages that the proposed lengthening of working time would add 28,500 to the year's total of accidents. Dr Charles Myers, a specialist in industrial psychology, meanwhile asserted that longer hours were not conducive to greater output. There was little disagreement in the world of the miners that better organisation was the only real answer. Experiments had already shown that lack of it was responsible for considerable time wasted in the pits, and that improved illumination alone could increase output by ten per cent.[5] The Prime Minister had, by his new proposal, not only brought a settlement no nearer, he made it seem more remote than ever. Jack Lawson, the popular M.P. for Chester-le-Street, spoke for many in declaring that 'So far as this Bill is concerned, terrible as the prospect is before us, our men and women are going through with this thing to the end. They realise that the Government, in this Bill, are not asking or praying for peace. This is a declaration of war.'[6]

A long 'siege' then was inevitable. The Government was resigned to such a fact and had, of course, less to fear than the miners provided resistance fell short of serious rioting and revolutionary action; and provided a minimum level of fuel could somehow be maintained until coal could once more be brought out of the earth. It was in such circumstances that certain key figures among the 'besiegers' were looking beyond the present conflict. They were on the scent of a weapon for dealing a crippling blow to the whole Labour movement for at least a generation to come. And the present conflict provided a most suitable background for the furbishing of such a weapon.

On 22 June there was a meeting of the Conservative Party's Central Committee at which plans were put forward for restricting trade union rights. 'The fate of the draft Illegal Strikes Bill 1926, which the Government had drawn up during the emergency and then been forced to scrap because of pressure from moderates and the King, was clearly very much in the minds of Steel-Maitland, Birkenhead and other cabinet members who wanted to strike a blow against labour.'[7] Birkenhead was the most passionate and skilful advocate of the idea; and it was Birkenhead, the cleverest man in Baldwin's cabinet, who, more than any other individual, gave teeth to a latent Establishment longing to fight back against adverse factors threatening its ascendancy ever since the war. Such factors had been operative in three fields: Ireland, India and the domestic scene within Britain. Birkenhead was a key figure in all three arenas, to which a common denominator could be said to have been the motto of 'divide and conquer' or, at any rate, 'divide'.

The greatest obstacle to Home Rule for Ireland had been Ulster's determination to have no part in any such arrangement. And yet both Houses of Parliament had, before the Great War, voted for such Home Rule for the whole (all thirty-two counties) of an undivided Ireland. This provoked the threat of armed resistance under the banner of Sir Edward Carson and the cry of 'Ulster will fight, and Ulster will be right.' Although such a threat was unconstitutional and amounted to a treasonable willingness to defy the wishes of the Crown in Parliament, it was backed not only by Carson but also by Birkenhead, two of the Crown's most 'respected' law officers and Cabinet ministers. The 'gunrunning' into Ulster and arming of the North were illegal but connived at. Their aim was to frustrate, by force if necessary, any implementation of the Home Rule Bill which was to have come into operation after the war. Their action provoked a rising in Dublin in Easter week, 1916, the execution of some of whose leaders united an Ireland not hitherto fundamentally anti-British in fanatical determination to be completely rid of the British connection if humanly possible. Four Protestant and anti-national-ist counties in the North remained equally determined to stay outside any kind of independent Ireland. The post-war violence, involving the notorious Black and Tans, led to the Anglo-Irish negotiations already mentioned, when the Irish negotiators were pressurised into agreeing to a partition of the country. Birken-head, then Lord Chancellor, had taken a leading part in these negotiations. So had Winston Churchill.

The Irish plenipotentiaries were assured that a Boundary Commission would clear up anomalies arising from the proposed frontier dividing off six counties in the north from the Irish Free State. (Four counties had been considered too few to make a viable entity; thus the Catholic and nationalist counties of Fermanagh and Tyrone had been added.) But the Irish negotiators had been assured that these two counties and the important town of Newry near the border, would be returned to the Free State with which an attenuated 'Northern Ireland' would ultimately have to throw in its lot.[8] Such objects would be accomplished by the Boundary Commission – it was claimed – when the immediate task of assuaging Ulster fears had been accomplished.

It was all, of course, double talk designed to dispose of the centuries-old 'Irish problem', even if by a crude, and possibly only temporary, expedient. The Treaty was duly signed, but the Boundary Commission became a dead letter. Two of the six counties of the North remained in an 'Ulster' of which they wan-ted no part but in which they had no power, because of carefully gerrymandered constituency boundaries, either to influence or escape from by democratic means. Thus were sown the seeds of murderous civil war in Ulster. Such seeds yielded abundant fruit fifty years later.

Birkenhead was soon given the task of overseeing the destinies of India on behalf of Great Britain. Here again there was rising clamour for 'Swaraj', or home rule. Birkenhead, as Secretary of State for India from 1924 to 1928, 'made Indian policy in White-hall. In so doing he was guided by an attitude epitomised in his

pronouncement in the House of Lords in 1929.'[9] In the pronouncement in question he asserted that the idea of the Indian people
being in charge of their destiny in one generation, two generations, or even a hundred years, was unthinkable. 'The legal mind
had no eyes, yet he, with Irwin* ruled India. One touch of Birkenhead made all Indians non-cooperate.'[10] In order to 'spike the
Swarajists' guns'[11] Birkenhead favoured the device of a Royal
Commission to look into Indian affairs. He well knew how
successfully similar Commissions, such as those of Sankey and
Samuel, could be used to divert attention while the Government
got on with what it really wanted to do. He appointed a Royal
Commission for India in 1927, two years ahead of schedule,
since he wished no risks to be taken that its nominations might
be in the hands of a succeeding Labour Government if there was
one. Once more the seeds of disunity were sown, this time among
the forces of nationalism in India, and home rule was successfully
put off. Muslims and Hindus came together, it is true, as a temporary reaction to Birkenhead's extraordinary arrogance and tactless-
ness in dealing with them. But in the last analysis they could not
agree on essentials and the rift got wider and wider with the years.
Independence, when if finally came, had to bring with it all the
tragedies of Partition.

Similar principles inspired Birkenhead's attitude toward the
General Strike and the British miners. Skating, for once, on
extremely thin legal ice, he denounced the former as unconstitutional in language of unusual vehemence.[12] That this was entirely
inconsistent with his own support of unconstitutional action over
Ulster was not due to his having forgotten what he had said and
done on the other occasion. 'So adept was he at self-deception,' as
his son and biographer has pointed out,[13] that such inconsistency
was all too possible. Already, in June 1926, he was envisaging
legislation to curb trade unionism by means and in a manner that
went far beyond the actual needs of the hour.† During the Strike
itself it was the production of his 'formula' that was the most
subtle stroke of the negotiations. Its acceptance by the General

*Lord Irwin (later Lord Halifax); Viceroy of India.
†See Chapter 14.

Council could only produce a cataclysmic split between the miners and the rest of the TUC; its rejection made certain a General Strike which the Government was sure of bringing to a swift and ignominious end. Birkenhead thus played a more decisive role in the pre-Strike negotiations than any other member of the cabinet, including the Prime Minister himself. His participation in the continuing Lock-Out was less active than that of his colleagues; but he had already made a lasting contribution to the success of the siege, chiefly by way of driving so solid a wedge between the miners and their fellow trade unionists at leadership level.

Ironically, however, Birkenhead has been credited with a 'doveish' role in the whole affair. It is perhaps a measure of his success that he managed to make his pistol-to-the-head resemble an olive branch in the eyes of chroniclers. The 'hawks', on the other hand, are generally agreed to have been Churchill, Neville Chamberlain and Joynson-Hicks. These men were prominent leaders of the 'siege'. Churchill was, in the early days, less of a hawk than a plain honest-to-God bully. He revelled in his job of editing the *British Gazette*, not scrupling at what distortions of the news he countenanced in the worthy cause of putting down the 'enemy'. He could not entirely suppress his overgrown schoolboy's enthusiasm for vigorous action even after the Strike ended, and carried it over into the post-Strike period. All the more interesting, as will be seen, was his sudden assumption of the role of peacemaker when the supposed 'change of heart' occurred later in the summer. With typical volatility, he went from one extreme to the other when his experience of the coalowners at close quarters did little to endear them to him. His own change of heart in fact was first visible as early as June; for 'Churchill, who felt considerable sympathy towards the miners now that the Strike had been defeated, argued that the Government could not afford simply to stand aside from what looked like a policy of starvation'.[14]

This was not the sort of approach favoured by Neville Chamberlain, who, as Minister of Health, was responsible for the administration of the Poor Law which soon became, for many, the only tangible means of staving off complete destitution. In his diary on 20 June, however, he noted of the miners and their families that 'they are not within sight of starvation, hardly of under-nutrition . . . they are not living too uncomfortably at the expense of the ratepayer'. This convenient view 'was not echoed by those who visited the South Wales, Durham, and other coal-fields.'[15]

Meanwhile the Home Secretary, Sir William Joynson-Hicks, was well known for his uncanny ability to spy imaginary Reds under non-existent beds. This was the key to his attitude and policy throughout the Lock-Out. His evangelical fervour had something to do with the inquisitorial zeal with which he pursued those whom he solemnly believed to be the State's mortal enemies. The latter included most trade unionists – on his assumption that the unions were dominated by Communists. It had been at his direction that the trial of the twelve Communists had been prosecuted in the October of the previous year. 'This was one of the few occasions in recent English history when men were punished for their opinions, not for acts of practical significance. It bore striking testimony to the anti-bolshevik panic at any rate of some Conservatives; or perhaps it was merely a demonstration by the preposterous "Jix" [the Home Secretary's nickname] that, whereas Sir Patrick Hastings failed to slay his Communist, Jix could slay twelve.'[16] When, during the Lock-Out, the miners received financial help from Russian trade union sources, Joynson-Hicks was a leading figure in the (unsuccessful) attempt to stop such help arriving.

Men like Birkenhead, John Simon and Joynson-Hicks, however were not the only ones whose view of 'the law' was coloured by personal or political feeling. Seeing for himself the suffering in the mining areas which the politicians barely even visited, Robert Smillie,* in the House of Commons,[17] examined some of the effects of the first eighteen weeks of the Lock-Out. He came to the conclusion, though 'loath to say anything that I feel to be untrue or unfair, even against such a thing as a Government,' that 'the passing of the Eight Hours Act was a clear proof that the Government of the country are on the side of the mineowners in this fight'. More significantly, however, he drew attention to the legal anomaly involved in the original posting of the Lock-Out

*Former President of the MFGB, then General Council Member of the TUC.

notices by the owners: 'The workmen were invited to go into the pits on 1 May and to work an eight-hours day as against the seven-hours day provided by law. I feel sure that, had they been ordinary common people like myself – what are called "agitators on the Labour side" – they [the coalowners] would have been prosecuted and sent to prison for inciting people to break the law. That is one reason why I feel that the Government consciously is in league with the employers in the present dispute.'

In point of fact, however, it would have been very difficult for the Government to avoid giving the impression of siding with the owners when it had to assume the whole burden of dealing with the mining industry's problems in this time of travail. The owners, for their part, were able to slip into the background while the Government wrestled with the problems of restoring Britain's normal economic life by having, if not without reluctance, to force the miners into a position of surrender. In washing their hands of the dirty work with which the Government was landed the owners were not, at this stage, any more than in the past, acting in a purely cold-blooded and callous manner. As far as they were concerned the miners' own best hopes lay in an early return to work at the rate of wages being offered. To take any harsher view of the owners – as a group of individuals – would be greatly to exaggerate their collective responsibility. Their very lack of such collective responsibility was one of the charges levelled against them under the head of faulty organisation. It could thus be rightly said at the time that the Mining Association 'does not represent the industry as a whole. It is the single owner multiplied a thousand times.'[18] Average individual owners, bound by the horizon of their own collieries, could honestly see no way out of the deadlock except through longer working hours at lower pay – at least for the time being. Again as individuals, they had no interest in dealing a devastating blow at the working classes as a whole or keeping living standards down. They felt themselves as much victims of economic circumstances as anyone else. To have acted or thought otherwise would have been to deny their faith and their tradition. It was observed at this very period that 'if the owners rarely plead for a higher standard of living among the miners; if they seldom raise their voices against the hideous unsanitary hovels which every visitor to English and Scottish mining towns has seen; if they never paint the hopelessness of childhood, the lack of opportunity for education, the calamity of illness, accident and old age; if they do not focus on these miseries it is not because they are indifferent to human suffering. The explanation lies rather in the fact that the owners believe that private enterprise yields to the workers as large a measure of the good life as is possible in this moment of civilisation. It is in the labourers' advantage that wealth should increase as rapidly as possible; and if they who control industry focus on that problem, they do more for the workers than scores of well-meaning philanthropists.'[19]

The siege of the miners between May and November 1926 was, in other words, primarily of political motivation and in political hands. It was carried through by those who had engineered victory in the General Strike, and of whom it was written while the Lock-Out was still on: 'up to the present, their "victory" is entirely a political victory and not economic. That they will use their increased political power to secure economic advantage is more than likely, but at the moment they are holding back from a general attack pending the settlement of the issue with the miners. That they have increased their political power can hardly be disputed.'[20]

Naturally, the speedy termination of the Lock-Out – if only in view of the vast losses otherwise sustainable by the public purse – was politically desirable. The besiegers, particularly Churchill, Joynson-Hicks and Chamberlain, were united as perhaps never before in a political undertaking. They had little in common as individuals but now shared a single goal.

There was another common denominator between them, and this was their complete ignorance of what life was like in the mining communities at this time: what was being experienced by the four million of the 'besieged'. They were even ignorant that the latter, to begin with, had been enjoying the best holiday they had had for years. They remained largely in ignorance of the reality that followed now that the 'honeymoon' was over.

I I

'Heartbreak Valley' and beyond

July was in many ways the worst month of the Lock-Out as far as the miners were concerned. The physical rigours had far from reached their height; but, in the midst of continuing heat, the cold grip of fear had tightened on the tiny houses of the terraces where the miners slumbered uneasily instead of responding to the colliery caller's loud knock at two, four or six in the morning. 'Weeks and weeks of waiting and hoping merged into more weeks when we just waited.'[1] Thoughts of a quick settlement had vanished. The early, almost carefree, enthusiasm had been forgotten as if it had never really existed. The determination based on fatalistic defiance, if not desperation, had yet to come. The experience of being thrown back so heavily on their own devices was proving to be more onerous to the mining communities now than it had been in 1921. Hundreds of thousands, especially wives and mothers, were fearful that such 'devices' would crack under the strain.

The first week of July, the ninth of the Lock-Out, saw the Government's Bill to lengthen the hours of work in the mines to eight hours pass its Third Reading. Regulations under the Emergency Powers Act were extended for another month, while the General Council of the Trades Union Congress denounced the Eight-Hours Bill and the Government's attitude to the dispute. The General Council called for financial support for the miners and urged the Trade Councils to strengthen their organisation. Such window-dressing, however, had little practical value, and the effort of the Miners' Federation to get the other unions to operate an embargo on imported coal was unsuccessful. Also turned down was their suggestion of a small levy on individual members of trade unions to provide financial help for the mining communities.

The country at large remained safely aloof and largely ignorant of the state of affairs among the miners. The National Society for the Prevention of Cruelty to Children – whose patrons included some prominent recipients of royalties from coal – claimed, after investigating the colliery areas, that no children were in need of food. One of their reports even stated that the children were better off than when their fathers were at work (a rather sad commentary on the adequacy of miners' wages in 'normal' times). The Report was designed to assuage alarm caused by the appeal of British Church leaders to the United States on behalf of miners' children.

Evidence collected at this same time by the *Daily Herald*, however, indicated in most colliery areas a state of affairs completely contrary to that which had been reported by the NSPCC. But such evidence was not taken very seriously. Neville Chamberlain had already testified himself that the position of the miners was not really serious. In his diary for 20 June he had written, 'They are not within sight of starvation, hardly of under-nutrition, so well are they looked after by the guardians. They are not living too uncomfortably at the expense of the ratepayer, while the nation is gradually overcome by creeping paralysis.' Any suggestion that a substantial proportion of the population was faced with starvation conditions struck a sensitive nerve in Government circles. As July began to take its toll, and a Labour delegation left for America to collect funds for the mining areas, even Baldwin was roused from his inertia. He addressed an 'open letter' to the American people before going off on his holiday to France in August, denying that there was any substantial suffering among the miners. In a certain rather horrible sense he was right, as suffering is relative and shortage of food was far from an unprecedented phenomenon in places like the Rhondda, South Wales. H. V. Morton, when *In Search of Wales*, dubbed it, with reference to this period, 'Heartbreak Valley'. It became, as it were, a sign or symbol of numerous other mining valleys where starvation really did begin to threaten hundreds of thousands in the

July of 1926, despite whatever the Prime Minister believed to be the case. Baldwin's tragedy, at this time, was that he had 'lost contact with the ordinary people'. Unlike Emanuel Shinwell, he did not tour or attend meetings in the mining areas and thus gain first-hand knowledge of what was really happening.[2]

The reality of the situation had to be measured against the background operation of the Poor Law as already described. When the figures of relief being doled out are quoted they sound impressive enough. The extra £250,000 a week above normal as distributed to miners and others affected by the stoppage was no inconsiderable sum in the eyes of the ratepayers. Yet, 'it worked out at less than 3d. per head per day special expenditure on account of the lock out'.[3]

During the first twelve weeks of the dispute, moreover, that is until the end of July, £225,000 was spent in poor relief on feeding school children in the mining areas. Assuming 1,700,000 children in these areas, this amounted to 2½d. per week per child, or just under a ha'penny a day. Nevertheless communal kitchens were set up everywhere, and one adequate free meal for children was served every day. In most areas, the adults managed to get at least two or three proper meals a week from the same sources. This feeding of the four million was primarily an achievement of the communities themselves, without outside help. Voluntary associations were formed from the first day and remained active till the end. With the elimination of unnecessary costs and all waste, and by the use of all such food as individuals themselves could contribute, the miracle was made possible.

Palliatives against social ills from the past assumed new significance in this particular crisis. Tales from the hungry forties and fifties of the last century were still well known. They related to days removed only by a long lifetime from the nineteen-twenties. Labourers, driven off the enclosed common and open fields, had had to look elsewhere for scraps of land on which to grow a modicum of food. They had often found these in allotments and potato patches provided by well-disposed squires, parsons and farmers. The allotment movement had, thereafter, grown slowly but surely. Most miners in the twenties worked their own allot-

ments (for half a crown a year paid to the local Council). In the
summer of 1926 they worked them overtime. The Co-Ops and
other traders gave credit and some gifts of food. Every ounce of
ingenuity and housewives' thrift went into the preparation of
childrens' meals. Many mothers went without food for themselves.
Their capacity to exist on tea and crusts of bread was phenomenal
and had been tested already in their lives. Some families kept a
pig or some poultry. The more 'prosperous' – as such families
were considered – had made some money on the side by selling
bacon and eggs. Now they set up 'shops' in their front rooms, but
the food, instead of being sold, was given away. As a salve to
pride, the recipients pledged their credit; but few repayments
were ever made or even expected. The small-holdings for which
some had saved for years with great sacrifice, such as foregoing
drink or tobacco, soon yielded up all they had. Their owners, who
had long dreamed of themselves inheriting the fruits of their wise
husbandry, found themselves queuing up and begging for parish
relief. Almost the only people doing thriving business were the
pawnbrokers; but there was a limit to the amount of miners'
Sunday suits they could find room to store!

An element of the 'survival of the fittest' brought its own form
of unfairness. Parcels of clothes came occasionally to 'Heartbreak
Valley' (from such centres as Friends House, or Toc H in London
and elsewhere) but it was ususally the loudest shouter, not the
most needy, who gained by these. 'The ones who are in real need
do not often go out on the streets to broadcast their poverty; that
is why the superficial observer rarely learns what he sets out to
do.'[4] The same observer gives a graphic description of the actual
procecure followed in his (South Wales) area for benefiting by
the Poor Law, as he took his place in the relief queue. 'Six deep,
it stretched all round the large chapel and along the road. There
was no privacy inside or out – we were on show for everyone to
see, although it did not matter much in this village where ninety
per cent of the men went there. Everyone could hear what was
said inside. Some of the men did not mind, but the more sensitive
ones suffered a great deal. The ones who stammered seemed to
feel it badly, for their nerves were upset by the conditions, and

Arthur Wilson, train derailer of May 1926

there was an impatient officer and an eager crowd waiting for each word. I have often thought this a method that needed alteration at the Labour Exchange as well.'[5]

One day, during just such a ritual, a scene was enacted that had its counterpart, in one form or another, in every section of the mining world. Word was brought that the local colliery was offering pre-stoppage pay in its bid to re-open pits running into disrepair. An additional bonus would be given to every man who went back to work. The temptation to accept was almost overwhelming. When it was refused, the village suffered the indignity of seeing, a week later, lorry loads of miners from other areas, arriving under heavy police escort, ready to work on the terms offered. The blacklegs had to face the silent rows of locked-out miners, lining the streets with caps off and heads bowed, as they came down from work. There was no rioting. The idle miners were in no mood for such a useless form of protest, even had there been no deterrence in the form of ubiquitous squads of imported police.

It marked the beginning, however, of the great war of nerves. Men desperately wanted work. Work was available and was being offered at what was, in some areas, an acceptable wage. How long could such a fight go on for a matter of principle – re-organisation and national agreements? How long could such solidarity bind together all the mining areas, both prosperous and otherwise? If such questions were in the back of many minds, they were not being openly asked as early as July. The whole spirit pointed in a quite different direction, as one mining community after another became no longer a 'community' but a veritable 'commune'.

It is hard to find parallels in modern British history of co-operative living thus springing up in spontaneous fashion on so wide a scale. The communal kitchens (or 'canteens') became more than just the physical centres for providing the daily meal for the miners' children (and for their families as well as many times a week as possible). Being run by the people themselves for each other, they had nothing in common with the charitable soup kitchens set up in other areas and at other times of depression, such as those familiar to East End Londoners. And of course they had still less in common with the emergency feeding centres 'manned' during the General Strike by debs and patronised by undergraduate volunteer workers, which provided an intriguingly different *mise en scène* for social gatherings from the usual drawing-rooms of Eaton Place or Belgrave Square.

In the average soup kitchen of 'Heartbreak Valley' the food was provided from a large variety of sources. Many farmers were generous with their potatoes and turnips. The mean ones often made involuntary contributions, since the beleaguered miners had little compunction in removing six or seven sackfuls of 'tatties' from their fields by night. (Moral theologians would have been hard pressed to disapprove of their actions.) A whole network came into being whereby stolen vegetables, never a vast quantity but potentially a cause of vigorous prosecution and added bitterness, were exchanged as between various needy areas to avoid detection. The system was quickly perfected in Scotland, which had its own 'heartbreak valleys', and often more extensive opportunities for 'poaching' in this specialised and systematic form: 'So we took tatties, and hens, and sometimes lambs out of the parks. But we were not daft, mind you. What was lifted in Stirlingshire went overnight to Fife. They sent theirs to Lanark and Lanark sent theirs to us. It wouldn't do to have the landowner come down with the police to our soup kitchen and find his potato sacks there.'[6]

Ingenuity and co-operative endeavour tapped every conceivable source of food for communal consumption. 'Most of the homes had gardens and everybody tilled them or had a little patch, an allotment, and gave cabbages, turnips and swedes. The farmers gave vegetables and the bakers gave bread. We would fish for trout in the streams and gather blackberries and whinberries. The good weather made a big difference. There were mushrooms everywhere . . . . There was a lot pinched off the railways, but nobody pinched off each other.'[7] Resourcefulness was complemented by good organisation and almost everything was done co-operatively.

Peoples' hobbies were turned to good account and full use was made of the extra time available in the absence of regular work. No one wanted for boot-repairing, clothes-mending, carpentry and almost every imaginable kind of odd job. Amongst themselves, the miners were ashamed of none of the favours they asked and knew they would not be refused. Nothing like it was known in Britain again until the blitz, which exhibited the same good humour in the midst of privation and fear. The soup kitchen was the centre of the 'commune'. A meal was not just a meal but an occasion for singing, carnival band competitions or a meeting to discuss progress and strategy. The fact that the women were brought into the deliberations, because of their work in preparing the meals, made an enormous difference. This element greatly added to the solidarity, there being no question of the men being off spending their strike money in the pubs, and the women longing for a general return to work. There was no strike money to spend. There was not even a strike. The women felt as much locked out – or cut off – from ordinary life as their menfolk.

The crisis inevitably exposed human nature at its worst as well as at its best. Long-standing rivalries and inter-union disputes came to the fore and such newspapers as the *Western Mail* – Berry-owned and dominant in South Wales – played up the divisions. As early as this very July there was talk of a split among the miners. Even in the communal kitchens, there was confrontation between different kinds of workmen. Some worked in the pits as carpenters, electricians, safety men, or at other specialised jobs, rather than as colliers. Many belonged to 'craft' unions rather than the Miners' Federation. Some of them alleged 'federation tyranny' in Rhondda, and even that craftsmen were being refused food in the soup kitchens, unless they agreed to throw their lot in with the Federation. Craftsmen retaliated here and there by setting up their own kitchens.

Misunderstanding of the miners' position was not confined to traditionally inimical quarters. An American of Welsh origins, Mr William Lloyd-Williams from Pittsburgh, attacked the Welsh workers in his Welsh-American periodical, *Druid*. He called the miners 'men who do not want to work as long as they can get the dole', a remark showing extraordinarily limited comprehension of the position in 1926. Even the weather let the miners down in the second week in July when the heat was re-placed by a freakish cold spell and snow and hail fell freely. A. J. Cook was still active, but often found himself pushed on to the defensive and having to spend a lot of time denying peace moves and splits in the ranks. On 13 July he had second thoughts about an earlier scheme for calling the safety men out of the pits. This would have meant nobody to man such essential functions as pumping, and widespread flooding would have occurred. Safety men were not always members of the Miners' Federation, and the decision by Cook was regarded by some as a craft union victory.

The 'churches', however, were generally behind the miners both at local and, later, at national level. Lloyd-Williams lamen-ted the emptiness of some Welsh chapels; but the non-Con-formist tradition of social justice was something on which the miners had leaned heavily for so many years. There was to some extent a conflict of interest between attendance at chapel and attendance at trade union meetings in the transitional circum-stances of the twenties. The Lock-Out proved to be an important testing period. Its tensions were to some extent personified by men like Aneurin Bevan who respected the idealism of chapel thinking and the stress laid on family unity. He also saw that the harsh facts of economic reality often dictated less cheek-turning attitudes.

A family that stuck together during the Lock-Out often risked suffering one of the unhappiest by-products of the Poor Law and Means Test. If one member was earning anything, the others could get either no relief or only very little. The earning member inevitably had to go and live somewhere else. This form of break-up became more and more widespread in the depression days afterwards; and when the solidarity called for by the Lock-Out slackened off in the anti-climax that followed, the eventual loss of united family and community life was one of the saddest legacies of the whole dismal affair.

While the fight was still on, however, solidarity included the active participation of religious bodies in most areas, especially South Wales. The Christian Industrial Fellowship and the Society of Friends gave concrete expression to their long-standing concern with the problems of the coalfields. The Rhondda Quakers supplemented their familiar social service activities with more ambitious schemes. In one area they took over a large house with extensive front and rear gardens where they built outhouses in which to conduct various academic courses. The philosophy section was run by a young man called Henry Brooks, a future Conservative Home Secretary, who had then just come down from Balliol. They started weaving rooms where fleeces were carded, spun, woven and even treated with vegetable dyes. The products were of high quality and fetched good prices. They also set up cobbling shops.

Such encouragement of new skills had lasting effects, and there was even a salutary short-term provision, if only on a tiny scale, of acceptable alternative employment. The Quaker lead was followed elsewhere, and other and varied new skills were studied. The St John's Ambulance Association arranged lectures; doctors gave free tuition, musicians were willing to devote time to the developing of hitherto hidden talents. Many an enthusiastic autodidact made the Great Lock-Out the departure point for a new phase in his life. 1926 was looked back on by some as a sort of sabbatical year. It was all part of a quiet revolution, a new phase in social history, at all stages much more than a mere perverted strike. It was more even than a simple struggle for higher wages. It was the last offensive of its kind aimed at a complete new deal for miners. It brought victory of a kind only to the generation after the next.

When, at the time, Lord Thomson, greatly daring, attempted to put the case for the miners in the House of Lords, he found his audience to be disconcertingly composed of 'an inert mass of lethargic indolence, the desperately effective weapon of the thoroughly comfortable'.[8]

12

North-East frontier

In 1926 the decision was made not to hold the most famous annual gathering of its kind, the Durham Miners' Gala. It was no doubt a prudent decision by the leadership in view of the high emotion engendered at the Gala even in 'normal' times. In the heat and fervour of the end of July 1926 the nearest thing Britain had even got to an attempted peaceful revolution might well have been buried in bloody riots. There was nevertheless widespread disappointment at this particular cancellation of the 'Big Meeting' at which, each year, 'every sensitive participant' felt 'a realisation of being part of something deeply moving, something continuous, steeped in the significance of recorded time. This is due in no small measure to the symbolic messages of the banners, which remind the onlookers of our declared hope for the future.'[1] In consequence of the cancellation 'Unprecedented scenes' were reported 'in the colliery village of Burnhope, which for a few hours had a population of about 35,000. The occasion was the miners' gala, organised by the Burnhope Colliery Lodge, as substitute for the Durham Miners' Gala. . . . There were over 50 colliery lodges represented, and the bands and banners made a brave display.'[2]

These colourful, often gawdy and, to some, strange-looking banners are more than a mere picturesque sidelight to the saga of the miners during their years of struggle – particularly in the North-East of England. Their heyday has passed, having served its purpose, a purpose that was largely symbolic – but something else besides – in the 1900s, and, in many areas, even as late as the 1920s. The visual impact of the banners was functional as well as spectacular. In the days when few could read the banner took the place of written words. Imaginative designs and pictures, representative often of folk art and always of highly skilful manufacture, spoke volumes, and also made individual lodges instantly recognisable at the Gala, as equally at local rallies. It was on such occasions that, 'throughout the years of depression the miners remained steadfastly loyal to their tradition of demonstrating their solidarity and determination to better their condition. . . . In many parts of the Durham, Northumberland and South Wales coalfields the need for something to break the dullness associated with prolonged inactivity and privation proved hardly less urgent than the need for material relief.'[3]

This bracketing together of the coalfields of the North-East and of South Wales is of constant occurrence. These were the areas that, through the years, suffered most and were, in consequence, the most militant. In most respects the north-eastern area of Northumberland and Durham and what is now the county of Tyne and Wear was the most important of all the principal coalfields. Like South Wales, however, its prosperity depended very largely on the notoriously changeable export market. The constant uncertainty of this market inhibited even the most far-seeing and humane of owners from expending vast sums on working conditions and housing. These two areas thus became particularly associated with the worst evils of the pre-nationalisation years with few of such compensating factors as brought some relief to the more prosperous areas notably the Midlands. The relentless pursuit of more and more coal nevertheless went on. As late as 1888 – the year in which the Miners' Federation was formed – the North-East was still producing more coal than any other district. When its vast output was finally outpaced – in 1914 – it was by South Wales.

Apart from its extensive commercial importance, the North-East was also the oldest of all the country's coalfields. The reason for not sending 'coals to Newcastle' was because the traffic had all been in the opposite direction ever since the thirteenth century.

The coal trade was in operation three hundred years before border warfare ceased. When the Corporation eventually claimed the royalty, minerals and surface of the great Town Moor, the people raised objection. Seeing their entire city about to be dug up, they made a case and won a Charter granting the Freemen 'for ever' the free use of the Town Moor, and certain other precincts that would remain untouched. 'The voice of the people is the voice of God' ran an inscription on gifts presented to the men who fought and won the case. It is primarily to the North-East that one instinctively turns today to listen to that same *vox populi* when trying to illustrate from all-too-real life the vicissitudes of the last fifty years.★

As for the border warfare, this gave a permanent sensation of background 'siege' to the earliest efforts in searching for coal. Even before that the North-East had become a veritable 'frontier', a status it has retained in one sense or another – military, social, dynastic, industrial – right up to the present day. For Newcastle, situated literally on the strategic equator dividing England from Scotland, took the brunt of most of the ancient conflict. From the holocaust of Saxon paganism, it became the centre of early Christian activity; out of the violence of the Norman era, it rose to become a City and County in its own right. Still, however, suffering border strife when other places lived in peace, Newcastle was the war front, the centre of news, England's northern army base, maintaining its prestige even against the competitive threats of the twentieth century. From the fifth century until the Union with Scotland in 1603, England's national life, cultural development and security itself depended on this Tyneside bastion.

Mining brought its conflicts from the earliest days. The usual cause was greed in one form or another. In the early sixteenth century the Newcastle merchants demanded that Durham coal be sold to them at their own price rather than prices fixed arbitrarily at the place of origin. They were roundly abused by Cardinal Wolsey, who was then Bishop of Durham and the recipient of that ecclesiastical See's not insubstantial temporalities. In such trade disputes little quarter was given or expected, and the magistrates charged with adjudicating as between contending parties went about their business only under the shadow of heavily armed bodyguards.

A century later, some of the merchants encountered opposition

★See Chapter 15.

of a different and unexpected origin. For, during the period of the Commonwealth, an amazing industrial experiment occurred at Winlaton when a steel works was established by workers who formed themselves into a 'crew'. They formulated and contrived to operate their own laws, anticipating by four centuries the 'worker-control' experiments of today. If market prices went beyond what they considered the optimum figure, they took matters into their own hands, successfully defying not only the would-be manipulators of the market but also the militia.

More than in most areas, the getting of coal in the North-East was primarily a vocation, never just a job. It came to be in and of the blood, which flowed strongly through a group of human beings by no means all of local origin. The opening of new pits and the ebb and flow of working potential produced constant migration and intake from outside. The Northumbrian of today numbers among his forebears the men of Lancashire, Cumberland, Yorkshire, Staffordshire, Cornwall, Ireland, Scotland and Wales. They came primarily because they knew there was coal to be dug; but they were slow to lose their former identities and ways of speech, and a form of clan warfare was long carried on in rough and ready fashion. To the idiom common to all colliers – the famous 'pitmadic' – were added the lacings of that distinctive 'Geordie' dialect which itself drew on so many diverse linguistic elements. But through it all the unions and mining officials had a different and far more difficult job than in other coalfields; and the polyglot communities among whom they worked were peculiarly vulnerable during periods of depression. The complex and fortified blend of their make-up, nevertheless, gave them greater strength and solidarity in times of adversity. Such qualities had never been more urgently needed than in the summer of 1926.

The North-East fought back with particular vehemence during the lock-out months. Improvisation, however, was often more determined than decisive; more desperate than effective. Only those with wealth or power can actually prepare for a siege; the North-East produced the strongest political contribution to the General Strike, largely in reaction to the physical rigours of the years before. The accumulation of such very rigours, however, made the miners of this area less well equipped even than South Wales to cope adequately with the hungry months that followed. 'Local schemes of self-help could not prevent many families from being solely dependent upon the Boards of Guardians nor could sporadic aid from outside sources even begin to substantially ease the situation.'[4] The Guardians, however, could give help only after the usual rigorous and degrading means testing. Where they lent money, it was repayable at interest as soon as the Lock-Out was over. A burden that assumed a doleful air of apparent permanence was thus inherited; years after the dispute had ended, miners, unblissfully ignorant of accountancy methods, were paying debts to the Guardians, usually in the form of deductions from their weekly pay-packets.

The special difficulties of the North-East served at least to intensify the communal and co-operative efforts made during 1926. The local communities went immediately into a routine made familiar from previous stoppages as to the organising of soup kitchens and the distribution of such gifts of food and clothing as became available. In this area the feeding of many of the children was undertaken by the local education authorities by virtue of the 1921 Education Act. Between the beginning of May and Boxing Day 1926 nearly twenty million meals were provided at 309 feeding centres for children by the Durham County Education Authority; the total cost was £238,781.[5] Quickly worsening privation prompted generous help from outside bodies. Free loaves of bread for South Shields, Sunderland and Durham came at the rate of 1,000 per week from Hunter's Bakers at Gateshead; and at the end of May the famous firm of J. S. Fry agreed, all the way from Bristol, to distribute 7,500 tins of cocoa to Durham mining families.[6] The Co-Operative Societies duplicated their familiar roles in other areas and arranged credit with local mining lodges. Such efforts, however, were inadequate to fill such a colossal need; and help from parish and local government sources was pitifully meagre in relation to the numbers being deprived of any form of livelihood. The Durham Miners' Association brought a test case to the courts, submitting that miners locked out by their employers were entitled to unemployment benefit. The Court's ruling was unfavourable. In law, if not in equity, men refusing to accept terms offered by the owners had entered into a 'trade dispute' which disqualified them from relief.[7] The sting of the Board of Guardians (Default) Act of 15 July was felt with particular acuteness in the North-East. The majority of the Guardians were already acting in strict accord with the severe limitations put on them by the Ministry of Health's 5 May Circular. At Chester-le-Street, however, the majority of the Guardians represented Labour, and continued to make adequate relief payments despite warnings from the Ministry. The Board's elected representatives were accordingly suspended on 30 August and their powers were transferred to a Ministry Inspector. From then on relief was drastically reduced. That the fight was not given up is shown by a pathetically heroic stand made in a plea to those entitled to vote when a by-election was pending for the Gateshead Board of Guardians. The particular parish involved awakened memories of the same village that had made history in the time of Cromwell. It was none other than Winlaton, of the one-time worker-management steel plant. Within days of the collapse of the Lock-Out, a manifesto was issued on behalf of Labour Candidate George Ollier. It stated that,

Unlike other Boards controlled by 'Moderate' elements, we are not using the Poor Law as a weapon of starvation to help the Mine-Owner, but are giving the maximum amount in relief allowed by the Minister of Health to locked out miners' wives and children.

We have also wiped out a debt of many thousands of pounds paid in 1921 by the previous Board which they were endeavouring to recover by intimidation.

It is not our policy to ask for the direct repayment of relief granted in this stoppage of 1926. We have also distributed on an easy payment system thousands of pairs of boots to miners' children. . . .

We claim that in dealing with individuals we have not been guilty of submitting them to a third degree examination but have treated them as human beings. . . .

The staggering blow that has been delivered to the Government in the recent Municipal Elections resulting in 150 seats to
our party, shows that Mr. Baldwin has not got the confidence nor the backing of the country in his attack upon your
wages – we therefore urge upon you to follow the lead and
give another knock-out blow to reaction.[8]

It was a brave effort but coming as it did in mid-November,
a futile one. The Lock-Out was all over within a few days. And
the emotive language about Mr Baldwin's Government – in
keeping with the exaggerated phraseology of such appeals to
electors – could not conceal the fact that it was far from 'staggering' under any adverse electoral blows. That such blows were
nevertheless being delivered is of interest to the historian in view
of a too ready assumption that the General Strike and ensuing
Lock-Out were looked at wholly with disfavour by the general
public. The latter, though rightly adamant that revolutionary
action was impermissible – in fact no revolutionary action had at
any stage been attempted – were far from unsympathetic toward
the several million people who were suffering for what they
believed to be basic justice.

An important test of opinion took place just after the Durham
miners had been gathering at Burnhope for the substitute Gala.
On this occasion the irrepressible Arthur Cook had, in the course
of yet another impassioned speech, referred to the pending by-
election at Wallsend. To the voters of this Tyneside constituency
– a key barometer to feeling in the North-East – the Prime
Minister had written, 'I beg the electors of Wallsend not to believe
that I or any other Minister have the least intention of any general
attack on hours or wages as is so often falsely stated.' Cook
claimed that this statement ill accorded with the Eight-Hours Act
that had been so recently passed. The truth, however, was that
even Mr Baldwin himself was unaware of the intense depths of
bitterness that the passing of this Act had had on the entire mining
community. As for the public's verdict at Wallsend, it was more
than mildly sensational. The Labour candidate was someone
whose life story 'is almost unconsciously the story of the rise of

the working-woman to industrial and political emancipation'.[9]
She was Margaret Grace Bondfield, the first woman to be appointed (in 1923) to a Ministerial position in any British Government.
She lost her seat at Northampton in the 1924 'Zinoviev' election
and was adopted as candidate for Wallsend when Sir Patrick
Hastings announced his intention of relinquishing the constituency. It was a marginal seat which the former Attorney General
had won only narrowly in 1924. Margaret Bondfield increased
the Labour vote, while that of her Conservative opponent was
cut by nearly half.

A tremor of renewed hope stirred along the North-East frontier; and the local pickets increased their vigilance in the direction
of blacklegging and 'subversion' of the cause. Though the left-
wing tractarians would have us believe that all such pickets were
heroes, such a judgement is not uniformly true. Legitimate
activity was supplemented by indefensible intimidation here and
there. A band of pickets might turn up at the house of a miner
suspected of being 'black' and threaten to beat up his wife and
children should he attempt to return to work. These incidents
were the ugly but inevitable symptoms of the brutalising effect of
the siege on desperate people; and such intimidation was one of
the pretexts for the passing of the Trade Disputes Act of 1927.
The North-East frontiersmen and their like, however, knew real
life better than most of those who legislated for them. They knew
that legislation does not change human nature and were able to
laugh off or otherwise mitigate any supposed 'injustice' arising
from picketing that was not always 'peaceful'. They were amused
by ill-informed middle-class moralisings on such subjects. They
realised, after all, that the locked-out miners were as fanatical
about solidarity as were the owners themselves. A small gap in
the defences could quickly widen, in which case the besieged
communities would soon be swamped. One young man in
County Durham was coming home from work one day during
the Lock-Out looking extremely dirty. He had once been a
collier; he was now a cobbler. His appearance suggested that he
had been working a coalface, and he was promptly surrounded by
pickets. The truth, when it emerged, enabled him to escape un-

harmed but duly warned. In future he carefully avoided any roaming bands of pickets until he could get home and wash.[10]

The Wallsend result – or rather the general trend of feeling that it presupposed in most parts of the North-East – had other more positive and humane effects. There was an upsurge of morale accompanied by stepped-up communal efforts toward greater self-sufficiency. While the miners' wives took turns in the soup kitchens the men made door-to-door collections of all such food as could possibly be spared or wheedled from the usually amenable shopkeepers. There was, ironically, less privation at this time for some of the children and old people as far as food was concerned, though much less available for those in between. A moot point arose in this connection for the Guardians of the North-East, and, for that matter, other areas as well. Relief was not payable for any 'able-bodied' man locked out of work (officially 'on strike') unless – according to an ingenious suggestion now made – lack of food rendered him no longer 'able-bodied' and therefore unable to work. The idea came in a report to the Guardians of Easington (County Durham) conscious of the terrible dilemma posed by local hardship and the Guardians' duty to conform to the letter of the law if humanly possible. 'What I suggest,' he wrote[11] 'is that provided the Relieving Officer is satisfied that any single man has been without food for 24 hours and has no means to obtain food, it may be assumed that he is no longer able-bodied and may be relieved in *kind and on loan*, to the value of a day's ration. Thus to keep him from actual starvation, he would receive one day's ration every alternate day.

'This may be stretching the law, but I think it may be assumed that although a man may not have reached the point of actual starvation on 3 days' rations a week, he cannot be said to be able-bodied for work on such a limited quantity of food.

'This can only of course be applied in *genuine* cases of *urgent necessity*, each one of which must be closely and *separately* investigated by the Relieving Officer, as the Minister definitely refused to allow us to act on any general automatic rule.'

This memorandum proved to be of some help to such Guardians as realised that the full rigours of official policy could produce intolerable hardship in certain given cases. A degree of flexibility resulted until the Board of Guardians (Default) Act cast its shadow over the whole process. Relief was usually half in kind, and where children were given meals at school an appropriate amount was deducted from the relief provided. The tragedy was in the burden imposed of paying the debts to the Guardians, and that such debts were not written off in all areas as they were in some. 'As late as September, 1931 there was still £44,756 2s. 8d. outstanding to the Easington Board from 1,962 cases.'[12] The mining areas, particularly of the North East and South Wales, can still remember the years of 'depression' as having a special meaning for them; and the indirect effects of the greatest of all industrial lock-outs in our history had dismally long-term effects. Even in 1926 Durham ranked as the county with the highest percentage of working-class families overcrowded in the country according to the standards laid down in the 1935 Housing Act. The figure reached ten per cent in the predominantly mining area of the Seaham Harbour Urban District and the Durham and Easington Rural Districts.[13]

One very important by-product of parish relief was the extent to which, by taking at least the worst edges off hunger and other privation, it reduced violence. This is the impression very strongly given by those who talk about the Lock-Out today, fifty years later. Desperation was not the same as despair, and at no time were men and women driven to violence on a large scale. The outbursts were sporadic and limited. For the most part, throughout the North-East, ingenuity in collecting food and otherwise helping oneself and others went hand in hand with constant outdoor activity in the form of organised sport and other communal events. Such a peaceful reaction to the locking out for over six months of a million workers today is hardly imaginable.

The ingenuity referred to took many forms. Margarine instead of butter was of course a normal and axiomatic substitute even in the best of times. But there came even to be a substitute for margarine in the form of a paste made from turnips. The problem of how to get the turnips was solved by nocturnal raids on the land of neighbouring farmers. The turnips had to be taken from the centre of the fields so as to postpone detection for as long as possible, and the excursions were perilous when the moon was full. The farmers eventually realised what was happening. Some turned a blind eye; others were indignant. The raiders spent a large amount of their time diving under the level of the tops of the turnips when they scented investigation. There were some narrow escapes and amusing adventures; but many sackfuls were obtained in this way.

As in South Wales, mutual help combined with the squeezing of every available source of actual nourishment. The rabbit-breeders of the community became key figures, and the allotments responded with almost miraculous yields to more vigorous working than had ever been known before. There was, however, no cutting down on certain revered standards. The miners' bellies may have been empty but their pride was not yet broken. Appearances, as a matter of honour, were not allowed to slip, especially when it came to walking out in one's 'Sunday best': traditional cloth cap at 'correct' (slightly jaunty) angle, showing signs of careful seclusion during the week in a special ring to keep its shape; blue serge suit; well-polished boots; possibly a whippet at the heels when out for a walk. (This was not so much a status symbol as a token of the universal popularity of grey-hounds and dog-racing.)

Apart from the pit-pony contests, another kind of racing now helped to occupy the miners' long hours of enforced idleness. The already popular races known as 'foot handicaps' came into their own. They were basically ordinary running races between the local amateur athletes, in which all could compete with a chance of winning. The handicapping was secured by so much lead fastened to the shoes. 'Heavy pumps' made an average difference of about two yards in every hundred. There was much fancying and small betting, accompanied by lively exchange of information and hot tips. There was more time than ever for street and alley games traditional in many mining areas, such as 'catty and dog', in one or other of its variations, and 'kites' (quoits) played with heavy iron rings thrown to try and straddle the 'hob' about twenty yards away. There was need for improvisation even in the keeping going of sport. Footballs fell to pieces, but were patched over and over again. Old balls would be put inside newer ones till they finally disintegrated. Footwear gave out to be replaced as and however was possible. Footballers would wear a clog on one foot and a boot on the other.

When miners played football against other workers, and all had their shirts off, the former were immediately identifiable by their black backs. For apart from the reasons mentioned earlier for not washing their backs, most colliers had a positive obsession that to do so would weaken them where they most needed strength for the sometimes almost crippling underground work. This work was their life. There was a constant reminder of the fact in the eternal frustrations of idleness, as every day brought a heightened desire to be back in the 'loved-hated' pit, working for a living wage.

Meanwhile as week followed week, with each hopeful glimmer of settlement quickly eclipsed, the same scene was enacted every Friday in some households. They had ten shillings available (from parish relief) for seven days' provisions for the whole family, and the man of the house would cautiously and shrewdly take his time as he sized up the week's 'bargains' in some such emporium as the local Home and Colonial Store. There was the keenest possible buying, with the shopkeepers actually helping customers to get best value for their money. In such transactions there was an abundance of camaraderie in contrast to relationships between proprietor and colliers in many private shops. There, in 'good' times as well as bad the miner invariably had to stand back while the 'quality' customers were being accorded attention. The 'cave-men' came last.

The bitterness and fanaticism against all 'capitalists' was intense in certain localities. The Durham town of Chopwell became famous locally, and even further afield as 'Little Moscow', and, with its strongly left-wing local council, began to sprout new streets with such names as Engels Terrace and Marx Crescent. Though the Communist Party had only limited successes, it had much raw material on which to work in 1926. The wonder was not that there was so prolonged an effort to wring some justice from a 'coalowner-dominated government' backed by the 'dope press', as that there was not in fact a revolution. But revolution is alien to Britishers even in such times of hardship unimagined by, and even unknown to, most people to this day. The opposition to the General Strike – mostly middle-class – sprang, when not prompted by a mere desire for adventure, from the fear, carefully nurtured by official comment, of revolution; there was no such widespread opposition to the actual demands of the miners, where these were known. But there was naturally a feeling of apathy and a realisation by well-wishing onlookers that, as individuals with their own problems, there was little they could do to help.

As the weeks of the Lock-Out dragged out into months, privation deepened and the first symptoms of desperation began to steal into the picture. As the hillsides became denuded of possible fuel in the form of small trees, pickings from drifts, wood and anything burnable, the 'home fires' remained unlit for longer and longer periods. The housewives knew that the long, mostly hot, summer could break with abruptness at any moment, and that reserves were low. During the Second World War, at least, all were roughly in the same boat. In 1926 a deprived few – some, of course, said it was no more than their deserts – had to watch others eating and living well while they themselves faced slow starvation. The scene is hard to conjure up in all its poignancy by those who did not actually live through it. But it is possible to draw on an analogy from the speculations of what might have happened, had the war gone differently in 1940, to all the British Isles, and not just to an unlucky minority, as really did happen in 1926. Happily the Germans never did cross the Channel, but in reflecting what their occupation of the British Isles would have meant one image remains in the mind, recorded in his diary by a Guernsey man in 1943: an old woman in her seventies trudging wearily for miles along a road carrying a heavy can of tar, the only fuel she could now obtain, while requisitioned cars and lorries driven by healthy young Germans roared past choking her with dust. Such scenes would have become a daily commonplace in the lanes of Devon and Yorkshire, of Angus and Inverness, of Carmarthen and Merioneth, had Britain fallen.[13]

13

Change of heart

Gradually the strain of the stoppage came to be felt throughout the country and, as the Lock-Out entered its third month, the Church felt no longer able to keep silent. It might have made some move earlier but for memories of the rebuff administered to its efforts during the General Strike. Churchill had refused to print – in the *British Gazette* – an appeal for peace by the Archbishop of Canterbury until it was too late to be revelant. And pressure had been successfully put on the BBC to stop the proposal from being broadcast. The Archbishop of the day, Dr Randall Davidson, had had the support of the Free Churches and, ostensibly, that of the leading member of the Roman Catholic hierarchy, Cardinal Bourne, Archbishop of Westminster. The most important statement, however, in fact made by the latter was a condemnation of the strike as sinful, being a rebellion against lawful authority, and therefore against God. This statement – made in a sermon preached at Westminster Cathedral – was duly accorded full and immediate prominence in the *British Gazette* and on the BBC.

The statement, however, had scandalised and offended many Roman Catholics and others for the rigidity of its moral theology, which at that time, drew over-heavily on the cold tenets of mere canon law. Unfavourable contrasts were drawn with the redoubtable Cardinal Manning, who had championed working-class rights forty years earlier. (Manning's intervention on behalf of the London dockers in their 1889 strike had become legendary.) Bourne, on the other hand, insisted on the letter of the moral law then interpreted by his Church, and this made obedience to the

State paramount, regardless of social or other injustices. The more liberal view taken by Archbishop Davidson on behalf of the Anglicans was much resented by Churchill and a source of embarrassment to the Government in general. The Churchillian concept of 'unconditional surrender' – which stayed with him to the end of his life – was shared by others at the time of the General Strike. But Dr Davidson condemned the carrying on of the struggle 'to the bitter end'. He defended the right of the workers, which meant the miners in particular, to hold out against the imposition of worse conditions; and he pleaded for 'not only a reasonable but a generous settlement'. 'For the first time in its history,' thought Hamilton Fyfe at the time, 'the Church of England has put itself on the side of the people against the privileged class. The old Archbishop has been splendid.'[1]

The Churches in fact, often accused of wishful thinking and meddling where not wanted, were nearer to reality than the self-interested, and possibly self-deceiving, arbiters of Establishment thought. Dr F. W. Norwood, preaching at the famous City Temple during the Strike, 'reflected public sentiment more accurately than the Deputy Chief Civil Commissioner',[2] when declaring that, 'There is no attack on the constitution. It is impossible to witness the remarkable order on both sides and believe that we are in the grip of reckless revolutionaries. The conviction behind the Strike may be mistaken, but it is honest and sincere.'

The important thing from the Government point of view, however, was that 'Baldwin had managed to prevent the Archbishop of Canterbury from broadcasting his appeal for peace along lines similiar to the Samuel memorandum.'[3] The Church's initiative in the third month of the Lock-Out thus prompted interested speculation as to the welcome it would receive. At the beginning of July, on the Archbishop's initiative ten members of the hierarchy, led by the Bishop of Lichfield, worked out proposals similar to those already mooted in the *New Leader*.[4] They had previously approached the MFGB whose Executive Committee, at the end of June, had agreed to meet them; and on on 15 July the miners decided to recommend to their Delegate Conference the proposals made by the Bishops. These were for an immediate resumption of work on the basis of pre-stoppage wages and hours; a four-month Government subsidy under a scheme prepared by the Samuel Commissioners, pending a national settlement; urgent reforms also supervised by the Commission which would work out its wage proposals in detail. (Attention to the latter subject had so far been seriously neglected.) If agreement were still not reached, it was proposed that a Joint Board should appoint an Independent Chairman whose award should be accepted.

The Church leaders, in view of the backing of the Miners' Federation for their proposals, confidently asked to meet the Prime Minister. This they did on 19 July. Mr Baldwin politely but firmly rejected their proposals on the grounds principally that the Government could give no further subsidy. The arguments in favour of this assertion, however, somehow lacked conviction in view of the large remissions of surtax made over the previous two-year period. The cost to the community, moreover, of a continued stoppage would be greatly in excess of the £10 million estimated to be needed for a four-month subsidy.[5] The money for a subsidy, or at least part of it, could have come from coal royalties, had the Royal Commission's urging of nationalisation of such royalties been adopted. Even without nationalisation, funds could have been raised from the same sources either by way of loan or levy or by utilising royalty income as a security against borrowings. Baldwin, however, was not vastly interested in the practicalities of the matter. He might have done better to refuse a subsidy on principle. He was justified, on the other hand, in wondering what could be realistically expected to happen when the four-month period had come to an end. Many argued that time bought by subsidy would prove valueless.

Much would depend on the extent to which reorganisation could begin to have any real effect. In this connection the Bishops had proposed that the Commissioners should provide raw material for actual Bills incorporating the much needed reorganisation scheme, and that the Government should give assurances for new legislation to reach the Statute Book as soon as possible. If there were a genuine will to reorganise, a way could surely be found to make its influence felt, if only psychologically, even within so short a period as four months. There could be practical advances as well with such reforms as the strongly advocated centralised selling of export coal beginning to bear fruit. The hated Eight-Hours Bill would, into the bargain, be, at the very least, held in abeyance meanwhile. In attempting to protest about the harm-fulness of this particular Bill, however, Lord Arnold was un-ceremoniously closured in the House of Lords. Arthur Ponsonby, M.P., pointed out[6] that this was due to no general ill will on the part of the Government peers, but only to the fact that Lord Salisbury wanted his dinner.

The Government's rejection of the Bishops' proposals was bound to have some effect on the reaction to them of the rank-and-file of miners. The latter, as soon became clear, were sharply divided in their views. The Durham and South Wales Miners' Executives protested vigorously against the acceptance of the proposals by the MFGB without the authority of a Federation Conference.[7] At a Conference in fact held on 30 July there was deadlock and a District ballot was agreed upon. The collecting of the District votes took over a week, and the result was not officially announced until 16 August. It showed a very small majority against the proposals, largely due to the two large block votes of South Wales and Yorkshire. Durham was in favour of the proposals as were fourteen of the other nineteen Districts. The actual voting figures (367,650 against 333,036) are deceptive. It has often been too readily assumed that the Churchmen were rudely rebuffed on all sides, and that their rejection by the miners was outright and decisive. The overall trend of events, however, between mid-July and mid-August tells a very different story.

The Government rejection of the Churchmen's formula had been brusque and almost summary, though Baldwin himself had been courteous and diplomatic. Tactically this was sound as it took the heat quickly off the Cabinet and caught the miners off balance. The Government at the same time knew how the owners' minds were working at this potentially decisive period in the last part of July. The Lock-Out was coming up to its thirteenth week. 'The miners with their families (counting something more than one tenth of the population of Britain and bigger than the total population of some of the lesser European States) were in a difficult position. They were being starved out, they felt, by coal-owners and Government in alliance. Their resources were less, as each day and each week of their endurance went by.'[8] The owners were now arguing that, on the 1921 precedent, the men's resistance should now just about be reaching its limit. Their calculations were confirmed to the extent that a crack in the miners' solidarity had appeared in Warwickshire where some of the men were returning to work. Provided the Government did not lose its nerve, the owners felt confident that a general collapse of the miners' resistance must come in days rather than weeks. Any idea that the siege could last for another four months was unthinkable.

One of the most important elements of the battle from now on became the luring of men back to work in certain areas and the frantic efforts to withdraw them again so as to preserve the solid and united front that alone could make it all worthwhile. Part of the counter-attack was provided by Arthur Cook, who acted as a sort of one-man flying column. He raced from one danger spot to another and, by pouring the concentrated fire of his oratory on the vital area, managed to plug the gaps for the time being. In response to his foray into Warwickshire, where the largest pit had started to work a seven-hour day, the men came out again. It was obvious that he could not keep up this marathon for ever, especially, as happened through August, when the gaps proliferated and, in some areas, began to widen ominously. But in the early days of the running battle the Warwickshire contest was considered crucial. The temptation to bored and hungry men was almost irresistible. They were offered wages not just up to but above the April levels, with a guarantee that these would be maintained for nine months. From a material point of view – looking well ahead – there was every possible incentive to return to work. For therein lay future security and the best possible hedge against victimisation. They were bombarded by propaganda from the owners' side, which, unlike Cook's case, had no need to rely on largely abstract arguments. Cook countered as best he could by pointing to the unfairness of pressure being brought on the miners by local house-owners, shopkeepers and even police.

What were such miners to do? Should they be prudent and return to the role of 'respectable' citizens, no longer turned away from lodgings by landlords, or refused credit by unsympathetic tradespeople? Should they accept the friendly advances of the police whose guarantees of complete protection against irate pickets they knew would be honoured to the full? Even the lure of the comparatively lush life at three and four pounds a week – compared to a pitiful few shillings – was not as great as the psychological pressures. The miners in the 'prosperous' areas were beginning to earn the opprobrium not only of the middle classes but of their own class as well. The TUC General Council had, after all, stated in an interim Report that the General Strike had been terminated 'for one sufficient reason only – namely, that in view of the attitude of the Miners' Federation, its continuance would have rendered its purpose futile.' The Council had gone on to regret that 'so great a demonstration of loyalty by the Trade Union Movement found so little practical appreciation or response on the part of those for whom the sacrifice was made.'[9] The view taken by the majority of the miners that they had been cynically let down by a cowardly TUC leadership who had been outmanoeuvred by the Government was not so widely propagated in working-class circles as a whole.

Though solidarity was so far unshakable in such areas as South Wales, where blacklegs were treated like outcasts, the feeling was very different in the Midlands. And for many a miner the greatest conflict was played out in his home. A desperate wife and mother was little impressed by slogans. Where was the next meal coming from if her man continued to be obstinate? His first loyalty should be to her and his family. The dilemma implicit in all this provided the background to the reaction by both the Government and the miners in the Districts to what came to be known as the 'Bishops' Memorandum'. The Government was in a quandary. It became arguable that their original rejection of a negotiable formula, as derivable from so unimpeachable a source as a representative Church body, may have been to hasty. The July estimates of both the *Economist* and the Board of Trade showed that more was being lost in national income each week than the £10 million needed for the once-for-all subsidy. Almost more important was the fact that increased export demands had pushed coal prices up by forty per cent since March (the date of the Samuel Commission findings). Such steep rises nullified former arguments that no wage increases were possible.

Baldwin, however, failed to make any bold or decisive move. He was content, and even then only under pressure, to manoeuvre from day to day according to circumstance. The Selling Agency idea (advocated in March to rationalise sales and exports) remained ignored; the promised Commission of Enquiry was convened only in July, and would take a leisurely three months to produce its findings. It was thus none other than the Warwickshire scene that indirectly raised hopes that the Government might reconsider its former decision. This, in turn, had been influenced by the beginnings of a return to work and the confidence that this would continue in all areas. The Warwickshire 'breakaway' had seen between 5,000 and 7,000 men going back to the pits. By the end of the first week in August, however, only 1,000 were at work. At this point there was no weakening elsewhere. This led to optimism that the Government would, after all, accept the Bishops' scheme in some form even if only with a subsidy limited to £3 million. It was estimated that this amount might be sufficient if, on re-commencement of work generally, such abuses as over-production in certain areas could (with the help of a central Selling Agency) be eliminated.[10] Baldwin, however, for all his apparent inertia, never lost sight of the long-term objectives of power as retained by himself and his friends. It was for these that he had worked, planned and gambled from the early twenties onwards. The Carlton Club meeting, the 1923 Election, the reuniting of the Conservatives, the determination to outmanoeuvre MacDonald: all these were now at risk. Having emerged triumphantly from the General Strike, he dreaded the loss by default of the fruits of his ingenuity. He felt he could not afford to be seen making concessions to labour. On the other hand, prolonged industrial unrest would tantalisingly delay the potential economic boom of which he would be a principal beneficiary. The July–August period of 1926 thus became another keen test of his gambling instincts. He fully realised, even if the general public were mercifully distracted in other directions, the importance of winning the game against the miners. The owners were no less anxiously privy to the political poker session that developed at the time of the Bishops' move, while the miners, though on the defensive, were making bold use of such cards as they held.

The scene of the potentially crucial struggle was set in the Cannock-Dudley colafields of South Staffordshire sprawling in a roughly shaped crescent to the north-west of Birmingham. This area was, for a short time, a battleground on which many eyes were focussed. Unprecedentedly generous terms were offered. And, since an eight-hour day was being insisted on, care was taken to recruit potential new workers from those considered least 'politically troublesome', while owners told their regular men that their places would be filled unless they returned. Land-lords and shopkeepers felt it right, here as elsewhere, to ally themselves with their owners, their principal tactics with the miners being threats of eviction and refusal of credit. Pooley Hall became the first pit in the country with a full complement of men (just over 5,000) back at work. The Miners' Federation was gravely apprehensive as it eyed the vulnerable areas at a time when the Guardians were drastically slashing the rates of relief. Apart from those of Bolton, the Guardians of Lichfield, in the peculiarly sensitive locality of South Staffordshire, were achieving the greatest notoriety for callousness. Despite this, the Pooley Hall contingent of scab workers rapidly came down to 600, and the MFGB breathed again – for the time being. They remained on the defensive, however, and distinctly divided on the advis-ability of suing for peace.

Baldwin himself, though he never lost sight of his long-term objectives, acted in good faith toward the miners as far as his limited knowledge of their lives allowed him to. Recording his comment on the Lock-Out as of mid-July – 'Leave it alone – we are all so tired' – his most distinguished biographers add that 'no one, except Steel-Maitland, had done more to worry out a solution nor to hold the delicate balance between social justice and economic reality. He had failed, although both sides had scars as well as salves to remember him by.'[11] It is ironical to recall that during the very period when Baldwin had been bemused by the coal conundrum he had solved the problem posed by the need for reorganising the coal industry. A report was produced in March 1925, with the necessary legislation coming in the following May. 'At one blow, 438 separate generating stations, all with surplus capacity, individual frequencies and different voltages, were to be unified, not merely in a monopoly, but a State monopoly financed half by Government guaranteed stock and half by local undertakings. . . . The electricity legislation was quite possibly the most important single Act passed between the wars. . . . It was the living proof to a sceptical generation of what reorganisation could do. But the rest of industry was slow to learn from the example and Baldwin's political philosophy did not permit the application of such a solution to a staple industry like coal.'[12]

Baldwin, in fact, exhausted himself during the summer of 1926 in trying to solve the coal problem with inadequate remedies which were divorced from human reality. A political philosophy circumscribed by invincible vested interests precluded the one solution that could have worked.

More realistic was the 'well-meaning interference'[13] of the Bishops, whose terms proved, come August, to be acceptable to Cook, Smith and the Miners' Executive. The majority of the actual miners, however, seemed to be reasoning that as the proposals had already been turned down by the Government it was pointless for them to accept them. What they did not realise was that they were thus putting themselves at unnecessary risk; that the Government was probably not so adamant as it made out; that the owners, with rising export prices, could be made more amenable on wages if the Government gave a strong enough lead; and that, by lukewarmness toward the Bishops' Memorandum, they were losing a valuable opportunity of further winning over public opinion to their side. There was the added risk that the 'weak' districts of the South Midlands would not so easily rally after a breach of the defences on future occasions. It was thus that the Executive decided not to take as final the five per cent margin against the Memorandum as recorded in the Districts (not all of which voted anyway) by differing and unreliable methods. Ultimate authority, in any event, lay with a Delegate Conference. Such a Conference met at Kingsway Hall in London on 16–17 August. One of its first actions recorded the depth of shock aroused by Baldwin's message to the U.S.A. – on the eve of the departure of a fund-raising mission on the miners' behalf – assuring the Americans that there was no hardship among the mining communities. It resolved:

> That this conference emphatically protests against the action of the Prime Minister in sending an untrue communication to the American Press, timed to reach America when the Miners' Federation delegation landed in that country. This was done obviously with the object of preventing so far as he possibly could the American trade unionist and general public from subscribing to the fund for the relief of the wives and children of the British miners who are the principal sufferers through the lock-out of the miners by the mine-owners.

Ironically Baldwin was probably right in asserting that 'in many areas' the miners' children were being better fed now than in 'normal' times. The psychology behind his message, however, could hardly fail to have been hurtful to adults who were themselves suffering grievously. The Prime Minister even put R. C. Wallend, the M.P. for Merthyr, in mind of Browning's Fra Lippo Lippi, trying to convert a starving youngster to the priesthood with the lash of hunger. 'Had Mr Baldwin seen the South Wales valleys for himself, where practically the sole industry is coal mining, he dared not have sent such a message. . . . I say there is privation, there is starvation, infinitely greater than there was before the stoppage. . . . I have never seen anything to approach the present state of affairs.'[14] The Merthyr M.P. also reminded his readers of something that was true in almost all areas, namely that the mining stoppage had brought to an end all subsidiary employment. Practically everyone, down to the most recently employed young girl, was out of work. He reported, nevertheless, that the spirit was astonishingly buoyant, and this was reflected universally in the wake of the victory at Wallsend. There, as the famous 'Clydesider', John Wheatley, put it, 'the standing army of labour' had put up an 'historic fight'. There was strong gut reaction against tampering with the seven-hour day, which miners felt to be the optimum working period as far as productivity was concerned. And there was a feeling at just this juncture that by standing firm the miners stood a good chance – now or never as far as the middle generation was concerned – of making their long-awaited breakthrough. The District vote on the Bishops' proposals thus came as a surprise only to those who had never understood the miners.

The 16–17 August Conference consisted of delegates chosen from all the coalfields. They had the chance to review all the relevant facts, and the power to override the district vote. This in fact they did by a small majority. The Executive thereby obtained the power to negotiate. It was not even tied down to the terms of the Bishops' Memorandum, though this was thought to contain the best available guidelines for an ending of the mutually destructive poker game, and a laying of cards on the table. The moment for a settlement, with honour saved all round, seemed to be at hand. The miners met the owners, not, indeed, cloth cap in hand, but with high hopes that a bridge had been erected between their positions. They met with total rebuff, the owners now making it clear that they would accept no 'settlement' short of unconditional surrender. They disclaimed having any central negotiating body of their own, and could deal with the Mining Association only district by district. The truth was that they now felt sure of getting everything they wanted. Baldwin, having decided to let events take their course, come what may, had left for his annual holiday in France. More and more miners were believing the press reports, however exaggerated, of large returns to work. The owners were more confident of total victory than at any time since the Lock-Out had begun. Asked about the reasons for such confidence, one owner replied,[15] 'Empty stomachs. They are licked. Twenty Cooks cannot keep them out any longer.'

Nevertheless, on 26 August the miners' leaders went hopefully to Downing Street, Baldwin having left for a three- or four-week break in France a few days before. The MFGB met the Chancellor of the Exchequer (Winston Churchill) along with Sir Arthur Steel-Maitland, the Minister of Labour, and Colonel G. R. Lane-Fox, the Secretary for Mines. 'We are asking,' said Herbert Smith, the Miners' President, 'if there is any good service you can render to bring about negotiations to see if a settlement can be arrived at and as to what amount of help can be given by the Government not only in negotiations but financially for a period.' Churchill felt at this stage that he must stay within the strict limits of Government policy as hitherto laid down, and replied that 'the question of giving any financial help to the industry has long passed out of the sphere of practical politics.' He had hoped, he said, for new and definite suggestions. 'There is something pathetically dignified about Herbert Smith's reply':[16]

After your statement I do not think we need detain you long. You seem to me to be of the same mind as the employers. I am not here to make a petition. If that is what you think I am here for you are mistaken. I am here to get an honourable settlement. I have never yet burked the position. I made a statement when we first met that I am prepared to take that book [the Samuel Report] and examine it page by page and accept its findings, but I was not prepared to come into a conference and agree to a reduction in wages before that inquiry took place. You people have shammed to accept this Commission's Report.

First when you write to me on the 30 April and say the owners are prepared to come to a settlement on that Report with a reduction of $13\frac{1}{3}$ per cent and an hour's extension. That is not in the Report. That is the first thing you do. If what you say represents the view of your colleagues I do not think we need go any further into the question. We can carry this fight on a bit further yet. We have got to do it if you can force us to do it.

We have been trying to avoid it. We have been doing all
we possibly could to avoid any pit flooding, but after that
speech we have to fight on; we are forced to fight on; you
force us to do it, because we are not prepared to extend the
hours.

The remark about 'pit flooding' was a reference to the possibility of withdrawing the safety men who remained at work
throughout the Lock-Out. This would have meant, among other
things, that the pumping would be stopped and the ensuing
flooding might damage many pits beyond repair. Had this
happened there would have been grim truth and not mere bald
rhetoric in a famous two-edged compliment flung in the direction
of the miners. This was done by the Labour Party's Chairman,
Robert Williams, at the annual conference on 11 October, when
he declared: 'The miners' decision to continue the dispute is
heroic. They may be likened to the sightless Samson feeling for
a grip of the pillar of the Temple, the crashing of which may en-
gulf this thing we call British civilisation.'

As a result of their visit to Downing Street the MFGB Executive could do little more than issue a statement, bravely styled as
a 'manifesto'. It set out the Federation's refusal of terms which
would break up their national organisation or deprive them of
the seven-hour day, but offered to negotiate on wages.

September began with a critical week which might have been
decisive but ended in frustration. Though there were obvious
beginnings of a significant change of heart on the part of the
miners' leaders, it soon became clear that agreement all round
would, apart from anything else, be a race against time. On 31
August the House of Commons, which the day before had extended the 'state of emergency' for another month, was due to
rise for the summer. Incredibly, a ten-week recess was being
contemplated with complacence. The Opposition argued that the
adjournment should be for one week only, and that during that
time determined efforts should be made on all sides to reach
agreement; but their plea was rejected. The best that could be
arranged was a debate on the Motion for the Adjournment

devoted to the mining situation. Churchill, in the course thereof, made it clear that the Government would take no further steps. The onus of making new proposals was placed solely on the Miners' Federation, who, as it happened, had just heard disquieting news from another Midland coalfield. The Nottingham Miners' Association asked to be released from their obligation to refuse a settlement if the Federation as a whole should fail to restart negotiations during the week. In Parliament, however, M.P.s representing the owners' interests stressed the fact that the Mining Association would no longer negotiate nationally. At the same time the M.P.s in question spoke in the bitterest terms of the miners' leaders, particularly Cook, Herbert Smith, and Robert Smillie. Throughout the debate, however, Churchill showed sensitivity toward any charge – implicit in certain gibes from Lloyd George – that the Government was not acting independently and in the interest of the whole nation:

Mr Evan Williams is quoted by the Leader of the Opposition as saying:
'We have exerted all our influence on the Government to secure the Eight Hours Bill.'
Mr Evan Williams can say exactly what he likes, and I take no responsibility for what he says, but this I do know, that no influence except that of argument, and no influence except that which should be exerted through the legitimate status of one of the parties to a great dispute, has weighed in the least with the Government.

'It was left to the stalwart old miner, Robert Smillie,' as R. Page Arnot puts it,[17] 'to voice the feeling of the men and women in the coalfields':

In this fight we have everything against us. The fight is absolutely unequal. It is not of our seeking. There will be no hunger in the homes of any colliery owners, their children will be fed and clothed, housed and educated just as usual, no matter how long the stoppage continues. On our side, there is privation,

Outside the Labour Exchange

Miners wait to go down the pit

Miners going back to work

Ex-servicemen become buskers

Help from the famous

there is hunger and there is untimely death caused by this dispute. Therefore, we are not on equal terms.

I want, even in face of the speech delivered by the Chancellor of the Exchequer, to say that there is another force against us besides the employers. The Government of the country is on the side of the mine-owners and against the miners in this dispute. I am loath to say anything that I feel to be untrue or unfair, even against such a thing as a Government, but I feel sure that the history of the past eighteen weeks is a clear proof, and the passing of the Eight Hours Act was a clear proof that the Government of the country are on the side of the mine-owners in this fight. Then, we have the Press practically unanimous against us. Nothing is too filthy for them to say, not merely about the leaders of the miners, but of the miners as such.

The urbanity of Ministers was scarcely disturbed by this outburst, accurately reflecting though it did the feelings of miners, irrespective of arguable matters of objective fact. The House having risen, Churchill saw the President and Secretary of the Mining Association, who confirmed the claim that they had no power to negotiate nationally. This effectively opened up a huge gap in the platform on which hopes for a settlement had been building up. The miners' leaders now had to face the possibility of increased breakaways by a growing minority of the workers, even though the majority remained solid for a fight to the end.

Churchill was, however, right in maintaining that the Government was acting independently, if only in a negative sense; and he had already taken the opportunity – on 24 August – of re-emphasising official repugnance to any form of subsidy. The miners could see, at the same time, the direction in which Churchill's own change of heart was taking him. The disappointing factor, despite his generally milder tone, was non-advertence to the cardinal fact of the owners' refusal to envisage a national settlement.

The owners, in fact, had now put themselves out of step both with Government thinking and public opinion, but were confident that they could sustain such a position in the absence of decisive Government action. E. F. Wise probably reflected the man-in-the-street's feelings more accurately than he realised when, in the pages of the *New Leader*,[18] he challenged the Government to 'Govern or Go!' But he must have known how meaningless are such admonitions. No Government goes of its own accord, even when it has no intention of governing. Besides, the Prime Minister, still on holiday in Aix-les-Bains, showed no noticeable signs of perturbation. If, however, he had chosen this moment to come back from the Continent with a show of energy and determination, a solution would have been within his grasp. The miners' attitude on wages had been considerably modified. The Executive's acceptance of the Bishops' proposal for determining wages – in the last resort – through an independent chairman had represented a substantial concession. It was a major advance over the position taken up the previous May. But the opportunity was allowed to slip by.

Surrender

On 1 September the two Labour M.P.s for Rhondda (Glamorgan) attended with others a meeting of the Board of Guardians at Pontypridd to appeal for assistance in the provision of boots and clothes for children of those in distress. Colonel Dai Watts Morgan (Rhondda East) said that the dispute showed no signs of ending soon and reminded the Guardians of the approach of the winter. Mr Will John (Rhondda West) stated that he knew of women carrying their children to the communal canteens for food because the children had no shoes. Elsewhere children were going without food. As and where possible, however, the children were the first to be fed, since parents would, as a rule, themselves go without if necessary. The struggle was already eighteen weeks old and the financial resources of parents had become so low that they had been unable to replace the boots, shoes and clothes which they had worn in the earlier days. They all had to consider the health of the children. Small bands of people had gone from house to house collecting articles of clothing and footwear. Mr Ifor Thomas, the chairman, answered that the Board was limited by the Ministry of Health to a total expenditure of £20,000. The Board had its overdrafts.[1] From now on, in other words, the people were largely on their own. Actual starvation was envisaged by many.

Such was the picture (in this case taken from 'Heartbreak Valley') to be discovered by examining almost any of the 'besieged' mining areas among those remaining 'solid' at this juncture. Such areas still outnumbered those that were weakening, though the latter worried the leaders more than ever now that the August attempt at a compromise solution lay in ruins. It was in these circumstances that yet another Miners' Delegate Conference met on 2 September. The owners' refusal to allow national agreement to be the objective of negotiations blunted the otherwise sensationally auspicious initiative emerging from the Conference. A resolution, passed by 557,000 votes to 225,000, authorised the Executive to negotiate subject to the principle of a national agreement. More importantly, '*a reduction of labour costs*' was now, for the first time, envisaged by the miners themselves. The phrase appeared in the letter sent to Churchill by Cook. The former promptly declared that an adequate basis existed for renewed general negotiations. As Chairman of the Cabinet Coal Committee in Baldwin's absence, he was in principal charge of all such developments. It suddenly seemed as if he might emerge dramatically as the man of the hour. With confidence, he summoned the owners to 10 Downing Street. With equal confidence, the owners, that is the Mining Association, reiterated their claim to have no bindingly national negotiating power.

A full dress conference nevertheless followed, Churchill sitting with four other Cabinet Ministers, and supported by leading civil servants. The Mining Association was represented by twelve coalowners headed by Evan Williams. Churchill's blood was up now that he had at last got the measure of the owners and could act in this sphere, if only temporarily, as the Government's number one man. He reproached the Association's representatives for departing from the principle of a national agreement which they had accepted as part of the price for the Eight-Hours Act. In vain, however, did he remind them of their obligations to play the game as part of 'the basis of understanding' that had all along subsisted between the owners and the Government. In vain did he bring out the best of his fighting spirit against this hardline corps of supposed representatives of all the coalowners. Several home truths came out in the course of the confrontation. 'It was a very serious thing,' Churchill asserted, 'for His Majesty's Government to introduce a measure facilitating the lengthening of hours in coal-mines. It undoubtedly is a step which is greatly resented by large masses of the industrial population, a step which was bound to be represented as part of a regular scheme and a policy for lengthening hours.' His conclusion was clear: 'We, as Ministers of the Crown, were justified in our belief that at the time we introduced the Eight Hours' Bill there was no question of departing from the negotiation of a national agreement.'

A change, however, *had* been made by the owners. They had not only turned their back on any national agreement but were now unwilling to meet the men's representatives nationally, even with the Government present. This was the most disappointing setback of all for Churchill, for 'It is on the point of your relations with the Government,' as he put it, 'that I earnestly ask you to consider very carefully what your attitude should be in regard to our formal, deliberate request that you should come with us and meet the men in an open, unprejudiced discussion.' Evan Williams cunningly revealed, in his rebuttal of Churchill's plea, that the Government had urged the owners to offer relatively high terms in certain Districts in order to get what a national settlement could not bring about, namely 'a breakaway piecemeal, district by district'. He held that this common strategy of the Government and the owners ruled out any possible national agreement; and that there had not been, on the part of the owners, any departure from the understanding they had with the Government.[2] He was, in other words, subtly agreeing with Churchill that there was indeed an understanding and a special relationship between the owners and the Government, but that this very understanding had more far-reaching implications than Churchill either admitted or realised. He was virtually saying that they were mutually compromised by their own collusion.

The Mining Association meanwhile confirmed its aversion to any national negotiations, but agreed to refer the matter to the District Colliery Associations. What could have been the reason for this reference back when the mineowners' central committee had so emphatically endorsed Evan Williams's refusal to budge on the matter? 'The reason doubtless,' commented the *New Leader*,[3] 'is that any delay will increase the pressure of the other power with which the owners have an understanding – the power of starvation.' Pending a final decision on the matter, Churchill, on 8 September, wrote to Evan Williams setting out the gist of the problem in terms so statesmanlike that one would have wished that he, Churchill, could have been in sole charge of negotiations from then on. The hated bully of the General Strike days had started to show in a different direction some of the bull-dog approach for which he eventually went down in history. He had, at last, identified the true 'enemy'. Such at least was the language in which Churchill could not help thinking. And he now clearly perceived the quarter from which was emanating unreasonable obstructiveness to a settlement.

'Dear Mr Evan Williams,' he wrote:

I have to thank you on behalf of His Majesty's Government for having deferred to our earnestly expressed wish that the Mining Association should consult its constituents upon the question of resuming national negotiations for a settlement of the coal dispute. I take this opportunity of explaining the kind of three-party conference that the Government have in view and the scope of its work.

Hitherto, national settlements have prescribed the way in which the percentages payable from time to time in the districts shall be determined, viz. the ratio of division, the intervals of ascertainment, the principles of recoupment, the definition of "other costs", and the minimum percentage pay-able. They have set up a National Board of the industry. They have laid down the principle of subsistence wages to be deter-mined in the districts. They have defined the various districts and made provision for their alteration by local agreement.

It is obviously quite impossible in the present circum-stances for any conference sitting in London to do more in the first instance than to lay down certain broad principles and recommend the practical steps necessary to secure an early and universal resumption of work.

We believe that with such national guidance the task of negotiating agreements on wages, hours and other conditions could be undertaken in each district with the assent of both parties under favourable conditions and without any further delay. We cannot afford any further delay or long ceremonial procedure. At least 1,700,000 families affected by the dispute are looking for the opportunity of regaining their weekly wages. Our procedure must be planned to bring about this as quickly as possible on fair and sound terms.

District settlements concluded in conformity with the agreed general principle should form a basis on which work would be immediately resumed. In so far as they dealt with matters which by custom are settled nationally they would require to be referred to the central body for confirmation or where necessary for reference back to the district. It ought not then to be difficult to conclude a national agreement governing many, if not all, of the points that have hitherto been dealt with on a national basis. One point of difficulty, no doubt, will be how the national character of the minimum can be reconciled with the inevitable allowance for district conditions. We ought not to assume that this is insoluble with goodwill once the parties are together.

After prolonged thought, His Majesty's Government believe that this is about the best and shortest path than can be found to reach the vital object in view, namely, a businesslike and honourable settlement for a good long time.

Yours sincerely, WINSTON S. CHURCHILL.

Williams took nearly a week to reply to Churchill, during which time the Trade Union Congress had been held in Bournemouth with results that were demoralising and damaging for the cause of the miners. The TUC was chiefly concerned to justify its own actions over the General Strike. The miners' representatives came away realising that they could expect no help from outside their own ranks if they wanted to continue to hold out against the siege of the Lock-Out, whose intensity was mounting daily. As expected, Churchill was turned down flat by the mineowners, who refused to attend three-cornered discussions. On 15 September the Prime Minister was back in London. It soon became evident that he was unwilling to put any pressure on the owners to induce them to fall in with the Government's wishes. On 17 September new and altogether different terms were put to the miners in a Memorandum annexed to a letter from Baldwin to which a detailed reply was sent by the Miners' Federation. The tone of the Prime Minister's letter was sadly signalled by its very first sentence: 'It is evidently not within the power of His Majesty's Government to bring about a conference.' Churchill's policy, in other words, was abandoned; the coalowners had won.

A special brief return of Parliament was arranged for 27 September so that an announcement could be made. This was preceded by a week of frenzied Government effort to get the coalowners to change their minds and attend tripartite negotiations. Baldwin, however, 'received a letter from the National Confederation of Employers' Organisations which, in effect, advised the Government to desist. . . . The final decision was to do nothing but insist on the letter of the 17th. This represented the Government's withdrawal. Two days later Churchill and Baldwin explained the position in the House of Commons. . . . Steadily the Government's announcements hardened. It is not difficult to sense irritation at the apparent immobility of the miners' leaders while their armies were withering away. Perhaps Baldwin never fully understood the nature of their innermost feelings. The pattern of miners' strikes was always different from that of other industries, owing something to the fiercely independent, corporate nature of mining communities and a tradition of self-help going back into the eighteenth century. In their despair, like a regiment surrounded, they would form a square and fight it out to the end.'[4]

This they now proceeded to do, in a bloody, fighting surrender lasting seven more weeks. It was almost incredible that the fight could have gone on so long; and there was never, even then, a rank-and-file majority vote in favour of returning to work. The principal areas in which the 'armies' were 'withering away' were Nottinghamshire and Derbyshire, where the hated 'non-political' union of George Spencer had been encouraging a breakaway and had given cause to the owners to press for the harshest of terms elsewhere. The traditionally hard-hit areas, notably South Wales and the North-East, reacted with corresponding ferocity to the prospect of being reduced to 'coolie level'. For they knew this was what would happen if each area was left to the mercies of the District owners. Their object thus remained that of getting the whole mining industry treated as a single entity.

Nationalisation would, at the proverbial stroke, have solved this vital problem which formed the inner core of the whole dispute. For it would have provided a single budget for the whole industry. In deference, however to Baldwin's allergy to national-isation – despite what he had already done with the electricity industry – the miners were willing to discuss alternative ideas at tripartite talks. One was that a trust provided it covered the whole country, might have achieved the same objects as national-isation; while yet another alternative suggestion was that of a properly organised selling agency. The latter would regulate output, fix quantities to be produced by each pit and district, completely exclude pits that were hopelessly uneconomic, and fix prices at a level capable of yielding a living wage.

Such points, however, were now little more than academic, though ironically, the press had, at this eleventh hour, largely swung against the owners. The acute suffering of the miners became properly known to millions of ordinary citizens for the first time. 'After the forgetfulness of summer holidays the British public realised suddenly and uncomfortably that the struggle of attrition had gone relentlessly on.'[5] Though 'the opinion of many responsible newspapers was on their side',[6] it was too late for the miners to profit in any way therefrom. At one time they had been alone, though not beaten. Now they were beaten, even if no longer alone. The General Strike might have been seven centuries rather than just seven months earlier for all the relevance it had to what was happening in the real industrial struggle of 1926. Leading a bedraggled army the majority of whom still wanted to fight on, the Miners' delegates, meeting in Special Conference, nevertheless realised, by mid-November, that to do so would be useless, and cause needless and senseless suffering. The Govern-ment's detailed Memorandum of Settlement of 12 November was recommended for acceptance, but rejected by the men in the coalfields by 460,806 to 313,200. It was less than a two-thirds majority, and the Delegates accordingly passed a further, more decisive, recommendation that the Districts should open negotiations. This meant that, whatever weakening there had been earlier in the outer ramparts, the inner citadel had not, until that moment, fallen to the besiegers. Now it was forced to capitulate humiliatingly. The principle of national unity was abandoned. The Districts were left to their individual fates. Everything that had been fought for not only during the Great Lock-Out of 1926 but, in evolving stages, ever since 1888, had been lost. District settlements had won the day, and the miners went back to work at longer hours and lower wages than before 1 May, faced with a 'settlement' containing an ominous portent for the future.

The 'settlement' enabled the owners to ensure that wages could be kept down permanently through a large pool of unemployed miners; for, as accurately forecast by the Samuel Commission when originally opposing longer hours, their effect would be to produce cut-throat competition between the European coal-producing countries. All the Conference delegates could now do was to provide the trappings for a 'fighting retreat' by instructing the Executive to draw up guidelines for the Districts as they, in turn, struggled on their own for such terms as they could get. Thereafter they retired from the lists, shattered and totally defeated.

Some of them, the Executive Committee and the county leaders, came together again to formulate an apologia for the stand they had taken as of the very beginning. It took the form of an official statement to the Trade Union Congress which met on 20 January 1927, and 'can be accepted as the miners' epilogue to the great drama of 1926'.[7]

True community spirit and ready camaraderie were smashed for ever in the long aftermath of the Lock-Out. If one expression occurs almost inevitably in conversations with those who remember the twenties, it is 'life was never the same again'. The whole fabric of existence was broken up, and individual personalities were altered as profoundly as overall patterns. In many localities about a third of the young men joined the army as there seemed no hope of ever working again in the pits. Compared to many of their mates, they thus became 'well off', with their keep provided for, plus 2s. 2d. per day. Those who went off in June got their first leave in September. They returned to their homes to be appalled by the haggard faces and hollow cheeks around them. They were the object of wistful glances if not downright evny; their smart appearance was a cruelly ironic comment on the whole scene. Later it became more and more difficult to join up than for those who, in 1926, signed on for, in most cases, twelve years. They went immediately on reserve in 1938, were the first to be called up in 1939, and many were the first to die in the war. In the years of depression, they had been looked upon as the 'lucky ones'.

The breakup of the old unities and loyalties had other causes, notably the new form of migration, and mobility in finding work. Work was found for many in areas not infected with the blight that had descended on the mining communities. Former colliers found themselves suddenly 'rich' after being supplied with work in such places as the London docks. Weekly pay was about £3.3.0d. – 3s. more than the average for miners. But the price to be paid was the enmity of the Cockneys, who had not all got work themselves. The working classes, for want of work, were in some cases driven into ever-hardening attitudes of internecine rivalry – in some cases hatred. Even so, in the twenties and thirties, for all its hardship, there was greater warmth in the collective struggle against want than in the modern competitive struggle toward ever-increasing prosperity.

In the wake of the miners' actual surrender in November 1926 the various forms of backlash were not long in coming. At colliery offices all over the country the queues formed of men anxious to sign on for work again. Thousands were turned away. If 'your face didn't fit' you weren't wanted. And so, for many, the hardship went on, despite the dole; and of course the solidarity of mutual hardship disappeared to some extent. It often had to be every man for himself. Those, and there were many, whose places in the pits were filled because they had been 'active' during the Lock-Out found it almost impossible to get work elsewhere. Some never worked again.

In general, 'the defeat of the miners in their lock-out led to a serious demoralisation in the working-class movement. Despair replaced hope; the spirit went out of all activities. From the leadership, both on the political and industrial sides, came no encouraging word. . . .'[8] The leadership, in fact, seemed almost to welcome the pervading apathy in order to trim their sails very considerably. The TUC began conversations with the Federation of British Industries with the object of facilitating collaboration. These were known as the Mond-Turner talks, after Sir Alfred Mond and Mr (afterwards Sir) Ben Turner, Chairman of the TUC General Council. Such collaboration might have been more successful had it not been for the psychological effect of a particularly vindictive piece of legislation which was guillotined through the House of Commons in the summer of 1927. This was the the Trade Disputes and Trade Union Act which outlawed general and sympathetic strikes. At the same time, the protection of trade union funds from claims for damages over strikes (given by the Liberal Government in 1906 to the eternal fury of Birkenhead) was removed; picketing was made more difficult. Unions were no longer allowed to levy political funds under the system whereby objectors had to 'contract out', though it was a system whose fairness lay in the concept that as all workers in an industry enjoyed the support of the union they should normally be expected to contribute to its funds. In future, by contrast, those wishing to pay had specifically to 'contract in'. This struck a hard financial blow (as it was meant to do) at the Labour Party, and the Act was repealed in 1946. Ironically, however, the Act strengthened the unions and the Labour Party in an unexpected way and made their eventual return to power sooner and more certain than it might have otherwise been. For the Government's Bill convinced the unions that the alliance with the Parliamentary Labour Party had to be made to work and to endure. Fortunately for him, however, Birkenhead did not live to see the boomerang effect of an Act which delighted him and others at the time, and whose passage marked the greatest single capitulation by Baldwin to the hard-liners of his right wing.

The trade union movement was meanwhile already in retreat, its membership ultimately falling back almost to the 1915 level of 4.3 millions. The Miners' Federation Secretary, Arthur Cook, got together with the universally popular Jimmy Maxton of the ILP to issue a manifesto calling for a return to more fundamental socialism. But it fell on largely stony ground. This was partly because there was a limit to the extent of idealistic stamina in the face of financial embarrassment. In 1927, the accumulated funds of all trade unions dropped from £12.5 million to £8.5 million, the latter sum being set aside for benefits and thus available for supporting strikes. There was neither the heart not the money for striking when, as was soon the case, three million people were out of work.

As for the cost to the nation, economically, of the Lock-Out, this was put at £400 million in terms of lost trade.[9] 'The real loss, in terms of the bitterness which the strike created, is incalculable.'[10] An inkling of what it has meant in practice comes from realisation of the extent to which the Lock-Out had a delayed-action result. For the generation of miners coming immediately afterwards defeat seemed total and all-embracing. All fight had gone out of them. For the generation after that, however, all was different, for they lived in the entirely different world of nationalised mines. They lived on second-hand memories and were determined that *their* world would never resemble the nightmarish one of their grandparents. In their imaginations the injustices of nearly fifty years ago were even worse than they were, and, continued to demand redress. The pattern for such thought began to be formulated after the Second World War: 'When talking to the miners one is continually struck by the fact that the past is deeply ingrained in their minds. Whenever you start a conversation with the miner on the pits, he invariably begins by telling you about the Coal Strike in 1926. The Coal Strike is vividly impressed on their minds, like an event which happened only yesterday. . . . Twenty years in the miner's life is probably like a year for others.'[11]

That an apparently strong and popular Government should fall from power and grace (in 1974) is inexplicable without reference, in part, to 1926. And even before 1926 there was an apocalyptic realisation that 'Whatever is thoughtful and farsighted and faithful in the miners' movement cries out "We want education and art and culture and a finer way of living. We don't know very exactly what it's all like, and we suppose it's too late for us as individuals and we all drink too much beer, and bet too much, and all that, but we want what we don't understand, and perhaps wouldn't recognise, for our children's children". . . .'[12]

It is thus that any assessment of 1926 and its consequences should really begin and end with the thoughts of those most intimately concerned with what was, and is, involved. It is not easy to make a selection of passages from numerous conversations with miners and others; but an attempt must be made to let the 'voice of the people' have the last word.

PART III

THE LEGACY

15

Vox Populi

To sit today round the fire in the house of a retired miner* or the widow of a miner, and hear the piecing together of fifty years of memories has a humbling effect. It is more educational and enlightening than reading a hundred books. It produces, after the experience has been repeated often enough, a constant recurrence of similar themes, but with endless variety of actual detail. Men who never met, and worked hundreds of miles from one another – one perhaps in Durham and the other in Glamorgan – might sometimes be talking about one and the same pit, so uncannily alike are some of their experiences. If there are few other denominators between South Wales, the Midlands, and Northumbria, the collier's life has imposed striking unity in the midst of diversity. As a community within the community that of the miners was unique in this respect.

The memories of half a century ago, and reflections on the years between, tend to flow freely after initial hesitations. The bitterness that often comes to the surface has become more passive with the passing of time. A man talking about himself somehow becomes, at times, the observer of another life, another world; a world in which, for example, food was for sharing and the property of everyone when hunger stalked the miners' terraces:

I was 20 during the 1926 strike. There were five of us children in the family. My father was a pitman, I went down the pit at

*This chapter reproduces parts of a selected number of the large amount of conversations with former miners, miners' widows, and many others – at home or in such places as pubs, or Working Men's Clubs – about the period of the Lock-Out and the years that followed.

14, having worked a year at the top. I had no training. I was given a book, sent down, and had to walk 2½ miles underground, picking up report notes, then another mile and a half to go up and deliver them. At that time I did an 8-hour day. After four months, I was put on the tubs and ponies. I used to come home soaking wet, my clothes all 'clarts'. I remember my mother playing war about it.

I was afraid. We all were. But for my Dad being ahead of me I wouldn't have gone down, the courage it took. Strikes in those days never did the men any good. They didn't get any satisfaction. Today they do. Nowadays coal in most places isn't touched by the human hand. Them days it was skin off you all over to get your hands on it. In the twenties I was 'driving' till I was 16. We had a great spirit though. It was one for all and all for one. If a mother was ill, the man didn't lose work. He went to another home for his meals, what he needed, and baths. Somebody went into his house to do the woman's work. Nobody was friendless, or lonely. That community spirit is gone now.

I was earning 21/– a week at 14. There was a strike in 1921 for higher wages. My mother moved and sent me to another pit. We moved around; each one was a world in itself and we went where we could get work; where we'd be better off. If I was to tell you the real, true story of pit-life your hair would stand on end. You never told your father what you were up against. He gave me the nerve to go down, and he went ahead. After that you kept your mouth shut. Talk about Colditz. Tunnels under the wire were nothing on the 18″ spaces we had to work in. Visitors see the beautiful entrances, with arched girders. Away from the shaft you see the reality. I was still taking visitors down till a few years back. They used to look at the section where the coal comes from, and say, 'I'd want £20 a day to come down here, let alone work.'

It's plain sailing now. The older men then used to look after the lads. They'd protect them, going ahead of them, and working in a bad place. An experienced miner can read sounds in a pit; he knows the weakest point where a roof caves in. He knows when disaster is coming. In 1926 when the owners refused extra wages, we just saw red. There was the threat of even longer hours. We had no strike pay. We just managed by sharing and pooling everything where we lived. The young ones used to fetch and carry. My father had horses; used them to do odd delivery jobs and earn a bit extra. Most miners could do something else on the side; they had to. My father was ill during the 1926 Lock-Out, so we used the horses. We got together and went around collecting meat ends and bones from butchers' shops. We set up a soup kitchen in the village, taking in any poor children standing around, even though they weren't pit-folk. Nearly all of us grew vegetables. Since our village was almost all miners, nobody suffered starvation.

The church folk all got organised. They walked with food as far as they could, to people cut off. But it was all private and voluntary.

Bulletins, supposed to bring us news during the General Strike itself, were so few that they were tattered by the time they reached the majority of men. It was chaos. Then just as we seemed to get organised, it stopped.[1]

Women are often more outspoken than men. They are less likely to romanticise over suffering. At the same time they are able to distinguish the shafts of genuine happiness that managed to break through the gloom during the years after the Great Lock-Out had collapsed. For many this moment was not the end but the beginning. It signalled the long attempt to climb back from the depths. The attempt was finally interrupted by yet another war:

Of course, the effects of that Strike went on until 1939. I was only 6 when the Strike was on, but my relatives went on talking about it all their lives. My father and uncles and all their friends had fought in the 1914 War. Many of them had been wounded, or badly gassed. After that, all they wanted was to work, and keep their families in peace. Instead of that, all they got was the dole and the means test, tramping the streets trying to find work. They weren't fit for it a lot of them. They had fought for their country, then they were not wanted any more; they could go on the scrap heap. It was the ingratitude, and the injustice dried them up.

In spite of that, I knew great happiness and lots of fun. The family and our own faith saved us. We all dug the ground and grew food. Men learned to repair shoes and do haircuts. Poverty brings out both initiative and resources. I think the English race has a spirit for survival. What people don't realise is that the protracted ill-health of so many elderly people later was the legacy of those days. The same ones who were stricken by the Strike, are now on Social Security, eking out an existence alone with prices rising way out of their pockets. It is an utter betrayal of the poor, who never had a chance. Religion was all we had, to give us hope and consolation. That was our anchor, and our strength. Take that away, and people have nothing.

Life was just beginning to get a bit better when the Second World War came.[2]

Ten years after the Lock-Out, with material conditions beginning to improve slightly, there was a different source of discontent in the mining areas. It was strongly felt that the so-called 'National Government' was far from uniformly representative of popular opinion. But the threat of another war inhibited the calling of a much-needed General Election. Men and women with long memories had to make do with palliatives in the absence of an overall effort to stamp out the most glaring social anomalies. For, though life had gone on in the mining areas with a semblance of contentment, none of the basic grievances had been redressed. Proper reorganisation had still to be tackled. Psychological ills abounded. Unemployment had been the lot of those not driven from home in a process that had broken up the old communities and changed their character for ever. The legacy of the Lock-Out seemed endless. An added irritant was the extent to which so many people were apparently oblivious to what the Lock-Out had meant, and went on meaning, for millions. When the 'new deal' for coal finally came after the war, was it too late to heal some of the wounds inflicted on human nature? And had the forgotten by-products of 1926 set up so deep a *malaise* that every new improvement would now only add to the paradox of discontent in the midst of plenty?

It was the '26 Lock-Out that started the rot. Nothing changed things afterwards for us so much as that. We wouldn't have held out so long if we hadn't been desperate. We could have gone longer if the papers hadn't told so many lies about people streaming back to work. Of course the papers supported the coalowners. They were all in it together.

A few owners were quite decent, but they had to toe the line of the Association. I suppose you could say they had their 'union' too. Now people only remember the General Strike. They don't know what you mean when you talk about the Lock-Out. But that was what really counted. The hunger was bad all right, but there was a great spirit about. The spirit wasn't so good when it came to paying back all our debts, like to the Co-Op, and some of the other stores. By that time the depression had got everybody down. It took us nearly nine years to pay £72.

My brother was ill with the dust. Pneumoconiosis. But it didn't rank as an industrial disease then. You just worked on. The pit doctor passed you as fit, like or not. Of course he was paid by the owners. But we were happy when there *was* work. After the war we were mucked about with promises. Nationalisation came too late to do much good. And we weren't united any more. It was every family for themselves. Many pits closed. My brothers had gone to Slough. They looked down on me for sticking in the pit. . . .[3]

There are many variations and paraphrases of the above, succinct, account of a saga of fall, rise and decline that has spanned half a century. One comes from another part of Glamorgan. As often the story jumps about, though the familiar landmarks are recognisable:

Relief? We got no relief. My father owned our house. That made us not eligible. Most didn't own their own houses around here. Only about 10%. My father handed over the deeds of the house to the Co-Op as security for credit. Everything was on tick. It got paid back by deductions from the dividends.

I was 15 at the time of the Lock-Out. June, 1926 was the time of my life. We were all out and about everywhere all day. Games, and Football. Catty and Dog was the favourite game. We went picking coal in the drifts. The police turned a blind eye. But it was all gone by the end of the month. We looked out everywhere for scraps of food. All the odds and ends counted.

Can't remember when it was ever so hot again for so many months. We were bathing at night in October, after picking mushrooms all day. We lived well. But the mothers suffered more than what anyone did in the war. My mother never forgot it. It killed her in the end. Yes, her and a lot more besides.

But they didn't starve us back to work. It was the papers that said everyone was going back. Then came the old insults. Yes, mining was a dirty job all right, but not too dirty for 'scum' like us. Yes . . . that's what we were . . . 'scum'.

At the end of the Lock-Out we lost hope and lost faith. Pity there was no war then, not later. More got killed, I reckon, from our part, in the pit than ever by bullets. The war came when things were better. Then they got worse again.

The mines were nationalised in 1947. We had 12 months' heyday. Then the old ways were back. It was like having new bosses, but the same if you know what I mean. About 1950 a lot of pits were closed; about half. Most round here went to work in transport. It was chaos. Never knew where you were. We could have been happy forty, fifty years ago only for being so looked down on. We were happy in ourselves, and with ourselves, except when the worry got too much. After the Lock-Out was worst, what with intimidation and being afraid to lose your job. The bosses knew which men they wanted and which they would never have back. They treated us like pigs. The best unionists didn't get back. The cripples got the sack too. Only those that wouldn't make trouble stood a chance. It got so you were afraid to pay your dues to the union. A lot of times the women paid them on the quiet.

And of course we had to go on paying *our* debts, even though the others didn't have to. What I mean is the colliery companies. They could even avoid paying the men in the bad times by getting liquidated. A penny in the pound was paid and that was that. Then the same pits would start up again with a different name, but run by the same people.

We always heard they couldn't pay us higher wages. But we knew they made much more than what they said. They kept two sets of books. That was common knowledge. Why do you think all the records got destroyed when nationalisation came?[4]

Whatever the miseries of the 'bad' old days, there were those, one's workmates, on whom reliance was never misplaced. To sink to the depths as a community makes the fight for the welfare state more vehement, but its very achievement brings – has brought – an inevitable reaction. A new generation has been reared on harrowing tales, but has itself inherited a world unrecognisably different. The consumer society has moved in to soak up the fruits of full employment or, alternatively, of the increased rates of unemployment benefit. Demand is constantly titillated; materialism makes its own rules. 'They' were once the untouchable rich. Now everyone has got as much right as 'they' have to whatever is going. Rich and poor thus have something new in common: boredom. The sons of the former may sometimes alleviate it with drugs; the sons of the latter, in the communities with a colliery background, bear with it for the sake of the good life, while the golden rule – for many – is 'never, but never, go down the pit'. The pit was all there once was, and it was hell. And yet . . .

The atmosphere is not as happy now. I've seen the change. Men won't let their sons go down the pit because of the danger.

I reckon it's because the old protection of each other is gone. You're on your own. There are 'bad points' in a pit. In the old days, one pitman would step forward and volunteer to take the risk because he had more experience. They *cared* for one another. Machinery has taken the strain now. Vocational respect has gone. There is much professional insult. Old 'family' pits have been closed down, and the spirit with them.

Miners are putting their sons off the family tradition, because they want them to have a life and education better than they had themselves. If I'd known what I know now, I wouldn't have been a pitman. You can get more money and better conditions outside. Men are lazy now, and selfish. They waste what is provided. There's waste of man-power, setting aside of wise instincts. The picture is very grave. When men do not work as a team, in love of the job and each other, for someone they respect, even if it's only the public, they are just animals. Money gets to be a disease. They don't see it as a means to an end, but an end in itself. They'll do *anything* for money.

A real miner will give all he's got, if he gets justice, and a good, satisfying return for his labour. It has been found that rise in output corresponds with wage increases. But the mining percentage has shrunk in the North East. Profits and personal gains seem all that matter.

I started at 13 and was very happy as a pitman, but came to realise what I had missed. Contentment *within* the profession is necessary. The great thing nowadays is that there is full employment. If a pitman is out of work today it's his own fault or choice. He's paid when he's ill, and he doesn't have to lie in damp or wet, crippled with rheumatism, in a terror of being laid up. The men need to remember that when they grouse.[5]

Had there actually been a plot to divide the working classes and thus clip their wings for a generation or more – rather than a merely instinctive defensive move by men of property against apparent erosion of privilege – it could hardly have been more successful than what happened anyway in many areas. The misery of the miners rubbed off on other workers; but the latter felt that it might not have been nearly so bad but for the futile exhausting struggle symbolised by the Great Lock-Out and all that it represented. The point cropped up in different ways in numerous conversations. The most unlikely jobs were affected, and the whole period often marked a permanently sad turning point for the future fortunes of an entire family:

My husband was a scene-shifter in a local theatre. We had a family of five, little in the way of savings. Looking after the children and a man was as much as I could do. When the big strike came, he was paid off. He was good at his job but there was nothing else he could do. I wondered why, when all the trouble was nothing to do with him, just miners and shipyard workers. I had to go out to work. It broke my heart, and my spirit. I had to scrub the big houses, and watch my own home getting in a state, the children neglected. We had to eat. For them I swallowed my pride. My, but it was hard. I was paid ten shillings a week for scrubbing a huge house from top to bottom. When I got home at night I just cried. Life finished for us. It was years before he got work again in any way that was regular. Then he got a very bad illness. I nursed him till he died. I still feel angry, that our lives had to be ruined; the times I was wrenched away from my own children, when they needed me, just to get a bit of money a man was willing and able to earn. It was wicked. Just wicked.[6]

Words alone do not always tell the full story. The facial expressions of those using the words are often more eloquent. They change subtly as memories begin to probe deeper into the past. The pint may be brimming or the fire comfortably stoked, but there is something of past battles still in the air when certain incidents come to life. For some, even amidst peace and plenty,

. . . the fight is still going on. We can't forget '26 and what it brought. But today's youngsters, mind, well they've got it all haven't they? But it still doesn't need much to cause a fight. And it's in the blood to support the union. What else would you expect after what went on? Big strong men cried like babies for sheer want and frustration. The women didn't cry. They suffered in silence. But what silence! It cut through a man sometimes. As if it was all his fault there were only a few coppers to show for a miserable few days of 'piece work'. The pay packets got better later on, but always there were deductions for this and that. And of course the amount to be paid back long after relief was given. And how we hated that relief! If we hadn't been desperate nothing could have made us crawl to the parish. But we were proud to be colliers even if others weren't so proud of us. Oh no! There was some of the lasses didn't go for miners! They might go out with us once or twice, and then usually they were done with us.

But thank God for the women during the Lock-Out. That is the older ones. They had sense. And they were clever! They could put you up a meal out of nothing, and make it look smashing. Dumplings made from water and flour. Some turnips – stolen like as not – round a good bit of fish someone had got out of a stream. No questions asked where. Some even had too much for that day. So the neighbours got it. You got on with each other and nothing was too much trouble. You always helped another bloke if he was in trouble, unless he was a gaffer or a scab. Now its frustration everywhere, even with all your smart offices. The Labour politicians? As bad as Ramsay MacDonald ever was, most. They don't like it if *we* make a fuss. They'll squeeze and freeze us if they have to. So we have to stand on our own. We even fight when we don't need the money. Yes, the fight's still on.[7]

The women, thinking back, remember different things, have different impressions. Sensitive to surroundings, they have nostalgia for a life that was 'clean' even though surrounded by shabbiness and dirt; for laughter that was real – and free:

I was in industry; it was slave labour. I can just remember the twenties when I was a little girl, when the depression was on. Everyone wore patched and darned clothes, and we *never* had enough to eat: but people were kind and tried to share what little they had with each other. Although we were poor, I can remember simple, ordinary pleasures. Walking in the country, picnics consisting of jam and bread, helping my dad and uncle with their allotment, going to the library for books, and always in spite of the pinching and scraping and poverty and my dad's ill-health, there was a feeling of love and security. There wasn't the mental illness, the crime and the sordid shops we have today. It was *clean* poverty, lots of laughter and fun and a great love of God. We had the great gift of family, and we were happy.[8]

Older women still, bent in fact with age, and with features nobly wrinkled, may say, when asked, they have forgotten what really happened. But as the kettle boils, some memories stir. Then too many memories come all at once. Lock-Out? Almost a laugh. *Which* Lock-Out? There were lots you know. Or at least, there always seemed to be trouble of some kind. Then, the tea made, the particular events of 1926 may come out into some kind of perspective. . . .

Yes, that *was* different. The weather for one thing. Hot nearly all the summer. Worse than 1921? I just don't remember. . . . I expect it was. My husband was what they call a gaffer. He'd worked his way up, and studied at nights. He became a manager. But he kept in with his friends. Tried to do right by them. He stayed at work all through the Strike . . . Lock-Out if you like . . . He had to have the police to protect him more than once. We had people in and out the house all the time. They had meetings, and the men were for ever talking. Lots of them enjoyed it I expect. . . . No, I can't say as I remember 1926 being much worse than other years. Not just because my husband had got on. We were really all in the same boat. And times were bad all over for everyone remember. . . . They went on bad for a long time afterwards. There was no work only in the pits where we were, and lots never got back. No, not till their dying day. . . .[9]

The note of irrevocable change, almost always for the worse, is echoed again and again. Thousands and thousands of women, prematurely widowed as the wives of miners so often were, live alone with their memories. They seem bright and cheerful. They are invariably hospitable to a perfect stranger coming, with but informal introduction, into their homes presuming to jog their memories of 1926 and its aftermath. But underneath, the waters, when stirred, are disturbingly black. No amount of pensions and rising standards of living can seem to erase the stain once so deeply made on life. No amount of material compensation can counterbalance a legacy of total collapse, since there was, in many cases, nothing left on which to rebuild a future based on inner peace. The actual shell of reconstruction is often counterfeit. The 'brightness' is of someone who has got over the worst pains of bereavement, but nurses a dull ache deep down, and will go on doing so for ever:

> My husband retired, from ill-health, contracted at the pit in 1926. We'd worked hard, brought up a family, and invested all our savings in a business of our own. We had fine hopes, and a good family strain. We had dignity and privacy. We were cast into poverty, reduced to begging from relatives better placed and had to move away from our own home town, where all our roots were. All at a time of life when people are hoping for something else and the chance to relax. It killed my husband. It broke all our hearts. It put a hard streak in all the family – a normal reaction to cruelty I suppose. It broke us up, as a family. I'll never forget.[10]

Sometimes good came out of all the evil, but only by a hard road. There was deep humiliation as well as financial ruin in losing everything you had built up. One day, as a shopkeeper, you were serving villages with groceries, making a modest profit and building up some capital. Then suddenly you were faced with a harsh dilemma. To refuse to supply such food as you could on credit seemed tantamount to condemning others to starve.

Naturally there was only one possible choice; but to make it could change life in strange ways:

> We were in business in Newbiggin. It was a general, useful store, bakery, sweets and vegetables. The strike ruined us. It finished my mother; she never recovered. She had a heart attack as a result of the struggle to live, and the disgrace of losing everything. All the money we had was lost because of that strike. People couldn't buy the goods, or pay back what they owed. Trade fell down and drove us out of the running. We sold up and couldn't get the price it was worth. It was the biggest disappointment of our lives. Decent people brought down for life, with no chance to pull out.
>
> All the sons left home, at a time when my parents needed and deserved some financial return. They went to the forces, or to London, where there was better opportunity. That took away my parents' future.
>
> My husband had a good apprenticeship with a shoemaker. At 21 he was dismissed from the only employment he had; a craftsman without work. Our local shops all suffered. People didn't either buy shoes or have them repaired. They went into wooden clogs, or had to manage. It was a country place; no wealthy business. It was because of the injustice and hardship he became a lay preacher, identified with the tragic conditions of the time. He did turn the disaster to good, but many couldn't.[11]

The very familiarity of poverty in the twenties made some people such as the locked-out miners with so little to lose quite reckless as to taking actions that could render their plight 'worse'. Such values were relative, as was poverty itself. Some felt themselves 'rich' in the midst of almost total privation. The very lack of modern refinements – and all the acquisitiveness which these have inevitably brought – was the breeding-ground for this sort of resourcefulness that saved many during the hungry days of the Lock-Out, and its aftermath. People had become used to using their wits. They knew, for example, that without refrigeration butchers and other food-suppliers could not risk keeping perishable stocks over the weekend. Rock-bottom prices were obtainable before closing time on a Saturday, sometimes very late in the evening. An 'auction' might be held, and joints, good for a week, could be got for 1/6. Such things were, in fact commonplace.

The psychology behind a combination of thrift and certain rigid rules seemed to give enormous strength to the besieged households of the Lock-Out period, and the long years of lowered living standards that followed. The women were seldom as easily disheartened as the men. The ritual of cleaning and polishing, scraping and saving, made the concept of 'no surrender' to a crisis quite obvious, not necessarily 'heroic'. The built-in stamina of semi-starving people in the twenties seems astonishing when compared with what might be expected today. It is less so when measured against the criteria imposed by daily life at that time. One lady, the wife of an elderly miner, who barely spoke while her husband talked of his younger days, afterwards, of her own accord, most kindly sent me, through a mutual friend, an account of such daily life, written out in beautiful copperplate handwriting:

> During the Lock-Out there were the soup kitchens where one went for a bowl of soup every day. Keeping the home fires burning was rather tricky. Coal was got from drifts. In most cases the village bobby would turn a blind eye. Most miners passed the time away playing quoits. If they had a copper to spare, they would go into the nearby woods and play pitch and toss. It was of course illegal. If they could afford it, they also had pigeons; the love a tough miner has for those birds is wonderful to see.
>
> Also, a mention of the village midwife. In the twenties and thirties: she was just a neighbour, probably untrained, who brought most of the babies into the world. Nothing was a trouble to her; when a woman's time was near, she was in and out of that house like a yoyo. A miner going to work day or night seeing the midwife around would know someone had

died or someone was born, as she also had the job of laying out
the dead. Also in our mining village in those years if anyone
died a man would go round the colliery rows with a public
announcement, telling everyone the day of the funeral and the
time. The coffin would be brought out and placed on two
chairs in the street awaiting the hearse which was an elegant
glass vehicle drawn by a beautifully groomed black horse. If
you could afford it, there would be two horses. One paid a
penny a week insurance, maybe twopence.

Before the funeral a man would stand at the colliery offices
and ask the men for a copper collection for the bereaved family
– help toward the wreath, etc. Of course afterwards was the
funeral spread, ham and tongue. Needless to say there were the
usual gatecrashers at these feasts for a good feed. The tears shed
with the family then the rush for the first sitting down. One
old neighbour was notorious. She never missed a funeral tea.
Some of the miners' cottages had a front room which always
had a damp smell as the small fires were hardly ever lit – only
if friends or relations called on a Sunday. I would think the
first suites in those rooms would be made of horse hair. There
were the usual aspidistra plants with the polished leaves, the
lovely old oil lamps. This furniture now is worth a fortune.
If you could afford a front room like that in those days, which
would cost only a few shillings, you were very posh indeed.

Of course each mining village had a different type of cottage;
some had yards; some had two bedrooms – if you could call
one a room; hardly bigger than a box, the stairs up to the rooms
were really just glorified ladders. At the cottages down where
I lived, the back doors opened out onto the earth road. Across
the road was the earth lavatory with the wooden seat which was
lifted up to put the ashes down when the fire was cleaned out
and lit every morning. Every Friday morning the kitchen
range would be blackleaded until it shone; fire irons, poker,
etc., cleaned and put by.

A steel fender one could sit on was also used to put the bread
to rise; it would then be powdered. Under the fire where the
ashes fell was kept whitewashed, as was also the inside of the

oven. The big cast iron kettle was kept blackleaded and never off the bar or simmering on a hook over the fire. The brass candlesticks on the high mantelpiece were regularly cleaned. These mantelpieces had a frill round from any kind of pretty material. . . .

There followed a detailed description of other domestic objects and daily household routine:

Then we had the Miners' Gala held in Durham City on a Saturday once a year; on Friday evening the colliery band would parade the village starting from Eshwood Hall, the home of the mine owner, Cochrane. Of course the public houses did a great trade. Always on the bar were clay pipes and boxes of matches in those days. They were free to anyone who wanted them and here and there on the floor were the spittoons with sawdust in. The morning of the Gala there was great excitement, getting the children ready and the families racing down the old clay bank to catch the train to Durham. Those days it was a wonderful sight in the city. . . .

Going back to Cochranes, they were very strict regarding the houses on the main road where they passed up and down in their horse-drawn carriage. Those front door steps had to be always white as snow. They were cleaned with scoury stone. Rag and bone men came round with their horse carts trading jam jars and old rags for the scouries.

Getting back to the miners. They had a great feeling of understanding and loyalty towards each other. They had to. Working in the pit, danger to their own lives was forgotten if their marras, as they call them round here, were hurt or trapped. And regarding village life, the friendly atmosphere of those bygone days in the colliery rows will never be found on a council estate.[12]

In the wake of the Great Lock-Out a new heterogeneity came over the whole of British society and its make up. Men took to the roads on foot, with nothing more than what they could carry,

Locked-out miners scratch for coal

Unemployed, late thirties

like refugees from a war. A poetic friend of mine, a walking
encyclopaedia on the vicissitudes of the Rhondda Valley, has
watched the passing parade of two generations in the course of
his own work and travels. He was not one of those who left the
valley behind him when it had seemed to become petrified by the
depression. Like many others, his native tongue alone would have
held him back. This tongue he heard far and wide among those
who had been scattered after surviving the Lock-Out and then
being turned away from the pithead when they tried to get back
to work afterwards. Many thousands suffered this fate:

By far the most serious consequence of the 1926 General
Strike and the Miners' Lock-Out was the creation of a high
mobility of labour. Margaret Attlee in her pamphlet, *Mobility
of Labour* shows something of what this meant for Wales: 'I
myself in my journeys by road between London and the
Rhondda (usually on my bicycle) met many miners trudging
their way to the newly opened Kent coalfield. Others I met
at that time on Victoria Embankment. I spoke to many who
came from the Rhondda and neighbouring valleys.'
More serious still was the migration of adolescents to the
comparatively prosperous south-east of England where industry was coming to the great estates being built on the western
and northern sides of London. Large numbers of girls went nur-
sing in England and many young men sought work of almost
any kind away from home. There is a quite special reason why
this depopulation was so serious. It is that the 'valleys' contained
certain communities bound together by something like a religious culture. Moreover, one valley's substantial form was different from that of another. When migration begins, it is often
likely to become a habit. There is, moreover, a fatal fascination
about the megalopolis. People, especially the young, seem
drawn to it as by a magnet. It is true that many miners and
others from 'the valleys' had gone in former days, some to the
U.S.A. and others to Canada. A hilly part of Porth is still
colloquially called America Fach (Little America) because so
many went thence and because so many returned.

Other parts of Wales have known great migrations; but here there was a difference. The migration to the southern Argentine of whole groups made up of families created a genuine enclave where a 'little Wales' existed and still exists. There were similar enclaves in the U.S.A. (Here is a difference between Welsh and Irish migrations in the near past.) The new migration from the Glamorgan and Monmouthshire valleys was amorphous. One illustration comes to my mind. A young man from the Gwynfi valley, Welsh speaking, came to live near Clapham Junction. We became friendly and he told me that, when he went to the Welsh chapel at Clapham Junction, he felt alienated from the other worshippers because they came mainly from west and north Wales and formed a social group into which he was not admitted. Alas, they were middle class; he was a formerly unemployed miner, who by the way was an accomplished violinist. There was one sign of solidarity, but it was one which sharply distinguished the new migrants from the older ones. It could be seen in many a main London street in the late twenties and early thirties, the spectacle of a dozen men forming a busking male voice choir. We could be certain that they came from south-east Wales with perhaps one or two from the anthracite region of eastern Carmarthen.[13]

The acute legacy of suffering that fell to the miners of a whole generation – more than compensated in the post-nationalisation era of the generation that followed – is well known to be responsible for another kind of legacy: that of an unforgiving spirit obtaining even when life has changed out of all recognition. Few are more conscious of this by-product of the lean years than those innocent men and women whose legacy may have been even harder to bear. For they themselves were not all miners:

We had been married a year to the day when my husband was paid off from the Hotel in Sunderland where he worked as 2nd man; the highest paid barman in the firm. He had been with them 7 years, and had been employed 13 years without a break; but the Strike and Lock-Out hit the bars hard. There

was no money to spare, and all credit stopped. He being the
highest paid was the first to be sacked. What an anniversary
present. From £4–10–0 a week from him, I was reduced to
23/– a week dole. I got down with pencil and paper to see what
we could manage without. We were lucky we had no debt,
weekly payments or such. I had always saved by baking my
own bread and doing his shirts myself, instead of the laundry.
It wasn't so bad at first, but I was worried about my mother,
as all my brothers were in the pits. There was no coal, and they
used to go beach-combing for pebbly coal; shale we call it.
My brother would walk all the way from Seaham to Sunderland to bring me a bag. The stone in it crackled and jumped
out, so we had to keep the blazer up. It gave heat, but no
pleasure.

People were starving; it was terrible to watch. Not only
mines but places of business of every kind closed down; and the
people who had worked in them were never seen again. I was
pleased my father wasn't alive; he was Secretary of the Miners'
relief fund, and would have had no peace. There just wasn't
the money to go round. Lots of people sold up their homes and
emigrated; in the end the government took over the mines. By
that time many had been brought to their knees and were no
better off.

My father died in 1924. He was also a Secretary for the
Union and Insurance. He had a wage of 23/– a week before he
died and that was to keep ten on. Before I married I worked at
the schools, helping a caretaker, for 7/6 a week. My young
brother worked at the pits on top, for 7/6 a week. There wasn't
much going into the house.

It was pitiful to see houses that were cosy and comfortable
reduced to bare necessities, and the painfully thin faces of the
people.

Thank God people are not so badly off now. The miners'
work was hard and dangerous, but people lost sympathy for
them because they suffered so much *through* them. Now look
at them. They live like lords and rule the world, yet have less
to do; it's all machinery now. They go to work dressed and

change at the pit-head They have baths and a meal in the canteen, then go to a show. Pit yards are full of cars belonging to the workers. They couldn't afford a bicycle then.

Yet we go on suffering. For me the Strike spoiled my life. I was successful in making ends meet, still managing to keep a good table, clean home, and a respectable look, but it ruined my health, and it made my husband lazy. He slept all day in bed, because he had no work to go to. When the baby was born, I used to push him up to the park with two-pennyworth of biscuits and a bottle of milk. We stayed out from 8.30 a.m. to 4.30 p.m. I used to bring vegetables in and bits of lap from the butcher on the way, then make a big pan of hash. The smell used to wake the man up, he ate his fill, and then sat the the rest of the night listening to the gramophone.

It killed him, as a man. He was never the same. The shock of being sacked in his prime. He was $4\frac{1}{2}$ years out of work and by then didn't care if he worked or not. He was always afraid it would happen again. That killed any feeling I had for him. I took odd jobs to see the baby well cared for. Often when he was *offered* a job he wouldn't take it, unless I went with him as stewardess. It broke him, that Lock-Out. If it hadn't been for that we could have been happy.[14]

Notes and sources

Unless otherwise stated, the page numbers refer to the original edition

PART I
Chapter 1

1. Tawney, R. H., 'Reorganising the Mines', The Manchester Guardian Weekly, 11 June, 1926.
2. Trotsky, Leon, *Collected Writings and Speeches on Britain*, Vol. II, p. 15.
3. Lubin, I., and Everett, Helen, *The British Coal Dilemma*, p. 116.
4. New Leader (editorial), 16 July, 1926.
5. Durham Chronicle, 3 June, 1932.
6. Coal Industry Commission (Report) 1919, II, Q. 20, 745.
7. Lawson, J., *A Man's Life*, p. 30.
8. Garside, W. R., *The Durham Miners, 1919–1960*, p. 286.
9. Webb, Sidney, *The Story of the Durham Miners, 1662–1921*, p. 130.
10. Garside, *op. cit.*, p. 288; and Webb, S., *op. cit.*, p. 131.
11. Durham Chronicle, 11 November, 1921. (The Report was that of (T. Eustace Hill, Medical Officer of Health in Durham.)
12. Cf. in particular Page Arnot, R., *The Miners: Years of Struggle*.
13. Bryant, Arthur, *English Saga*, p. 73.
14. *Ibid.*, p. 74.
15. Page Arnot, R., *op. cit.*, p. 50.
16. *Ibid.*, p. 300.

Chapter 2

1. Farman, C., *The General Strike*, p. 52.
2. Middlemas, R. K., *The Clydesiders*, p. 14.
3. Author of *Progress and Poverty* and pioneer campaigner for taxing land values.

4. Renshaw, P., *The General Strike*, pp. 75–6.
5. Fifth Marquess of Bute whose wife was Augusta Bellingham. (The latter's mother was the author's great aunt.)
6. *Royal Commission on the Coal Industry (Samuel) Report, 1925.*
7. Court, W. H. B., *Coal*, p. 5.
8. Royal Commission Report, *op. cit.*, p. 47.
9. Williams, D. J., *Capitalist Combination*, p. 14.
10. Bryant, A., *op. cit.*, pp. 307–8.
11. Jones, T., Whitehall Diary, Vol. II, p. 3.
12. Williams, W. H., *The Miners' Two Bob*, p. 27. (This work contains an interesting section – 'The Capitalist Organisation of the Coal Industry' – found particularly helpful in this chapter.)
13. See: Slater, M., *Stay-Down Miner*.
14. The Economist, 2 May, 1925.
15. Williams, W. H., *op. cit.*, p. 12.
16. Daily Telegraph Special Supplement: 'The Coal Mining Industry' (1930), p. 48.
17. Garside, W. R., *op. cit.*, p. 152.
18. Gainford, Lord, 'The Coal Problem', Contemporary Review, 119, June, 1921, p. 726.
19. Newsom, J., *Out of the Pit*, p. xiv.
20. Interview in Tonypandy, March, 1975.
21. Lubin, I., and Everett, H. *op. cit.*, p. 185.

Chapter 3
1. Turner, H. A., *Trade Union Growth and Structure*, p. 190.
2. Hobsbawn, E. J., *Industry and Empire*, pp. 16, 30.
3. Raynes, J. R., *Coal and its Conflicts*, pp. 71–2.
4. Nearing, S., *The British General Strike*, pp. 7–9.
5. Williams, W. H., (ed.), *op. cit.*, p. 82.
6. Page Arnot, R., *op. cit.*, p. 84.
7. Williams, W. H., *op. cit.*, p. 84.
8. Conversation with Sir William Lawther, Cullercoats, Newcastle-upon-Tyne, March 1975.
9. Hodges, F., *Nationalisation of the Mines*, pp. 56–7.
10. *Ibid.*, pp. 57, 78.
11. A sensational pamphlet written by Noah Ablett and others and published in South Wales.
12. Page Arnot, R., *op. cit.*, p. 117.
13. Garside, W. R., *op. cit.*, p. 97.

14. Symonds, J., *The General Strike*, p. 3.
15. James, R. R., *Memoirs of a Conservative*, p. 49.
16. Hodges, F., *op. cit.*, p. 102.
17. Garside, W. R., *op. cit.*, p. 102.
18. Farman, C., *op. cit.*, p. 16.
19. Renshaw, P., *op. cit.*, p. 83.
20. See: Bevan, A., *Why Not Trust the Tories?* pp. 14–24; Page Arnot, R., *op. cit.*, p. 392.
21. Wilson, J. H., *New Deal for Coal*, p. 15.
22. Raynes, J. R., *op. cit.*, p. 187.
23. Hodges, Frank, *My Adventures as a Labour Leader*, p. 33.

Chapter 4

1. Middlemas, K., etc. *Baldwin*, p. 212.
2. Mowat, C. L., *Britain Between the Wars*, p. 166.
3. Taylor, A. J. P., *English History, 1914–1945*, p. 206.
4. See in particular: Hutt A., *The Post-War History of the Working Class*, Chapter IV.
5. Hutt, A., *op. cit.*, p. 76.
6. Taylor, A. J. P., *op. cit.*, p. 205.
7. Hutt, A., *op. cit.*, pp. 77–8.
8. Van Thal, H. (ed.), *The Prime Ministers*, Vol. II, p. 250.
9. Van Thal, *op. cit.*, p. 229.
10. Mowat, C. L., *op. cit.*, p. 140.
11. *Ibid.*, p. 142.
12. Taylor, A. J. P., *op. cit.*, p. 195.
13. *Ibid.*, p. 257.
14. Dobrée, B., *English Revolts*, p. 168.
15. Renshaw, P., *op. cit.*, p. 74.
16. James, R. R., *op. cit.*, p. 178.
17. *Ibid.*, p. 179.
18. MacFarlane, L. J., *The British Communist Party*. Its Origin and Development until 1929, p. 78.
19. *Ibid.*, p. 82.
20. James, R. R., *op. cit.*, p. 177.
21. *Ibid.*, p. 180.
22. Quoted by John Murray in *The General Strike of 1926*, p. 199.

Chapter 5

1. Wilson, J. H., *op. cit.*, pp. 15–16.

2. Farman, C., *op. cit.*, p. 18.
3. Young, G. M., *Stanley Baldwin*, p. 199.
4. Lee, W. A., *Thirty Years in Coal*, pp. 13, 52.
5. Murphy, J. T., *Political Meaning of the General Strike*, p. 38.
6. Forster, Eric, *The Story of the Montagu Pit Disaster*, Newcastle Evening Chronicle, 24/25 & 26 March, 1975.
7. Hodges, *Nationalisation of the Mines*, pp. 28–9.
8. Renshaw, P., *op. cit.*, p. 127.
9. Page Arnot, R., *The General Strike*, p. 50.
10. The Times, 1 October, 1925.
11. Farman, C., *op. cit.*, p. 116.
12. *Ibid.*, p. 37.
13. Clynes, J. R., *Memoirs*, p. 73.
14. Tracey, Herbert. (ed.), *The Book of the Labour Party*, Vol. III, p. 142.
15. Taylor, A. J. P., *op. cit.*, p. 194.
16. MacNeill Weir, *The Tragedy of Ramsay MacDonald*, p. 209.
17. Page Arnot, R., *op. cit.*, p. 93.
18. Page Arnot, R., *The Miners: Years of Struggle*, p. 421.
19. John Murray, *op. cit.*, p. 91.

Chapter 6
1. Page Arnot, *op. cit.*, p. 416.
2. Farman, C., *op. cit.*, p. 101.
3. Citrine, Lord, *Men and Work*, Chapter 10.
4. The British Worker, 11 May, 1926.
5. Citrine, Lord, *op. cit.*, p. 172.
6. Debrée, B., *op. cit.*, p. 185.
7. Cooper, Duff, *Old Men Forget*, p. 145.
8. Citrine, Lord., *op. cit.*, p. 176.
9. Murphy, J. T., *The Political Meaning of the General Strike*, p. 87.
10. The Nation, 16 June, 1926, p. 663.
11. Brailsford, N. H., New Leader, 21 May, 1926.
12. Middlemas, R. K. *The Clydesiders*, *op. cit.*, pp. 196–7.
13. Leeson, R. A., *Strike, A Live History*, p. 87 (Quoting George Hodgkinson, Coventry Labour Leader and shop steward).
14. Report of Trade Union Executives' Special Conference, January, 1927, p. 45.
15. Debrée, B., *op. cit.*, p. 44.
16. In conversation with the author, March, 1975.

17. Westminster Worker, 12 May, 1926.
18. Moran, Lord, *Winston Churchill, The Struggle for Survival*, p. 247.
19. See: Mason, A., *The General Strike in the North East*, p. 69.
20. For full accounts of the incident, arrests and subsequent trial, see: Northern Echo, 11 May, 1926; Newcastle Chronicle, 11 May and 1 July, 1926; Daily Herald, 15 June, 1 July and 2 July, 1926.
21. Conversation with the author, May, 1975.
22. Forster, Eric, Evening Chronicle (Newcastle), 31 January, 1973.
23. Mason, A., *op. cit.*, p. 70.
24. E.g., by Oswald Mosley in the House of Commons in March 1921. (See: *Mosley*, by Robert Skidlesky, 1975.)

PART II
Chapter 7
1. Edwards, H. W. J., *The Good Patch*, pp. 219–20.
2. Foot, M., *Aneurin Bevan*, pp. 72–3.
3. Great Newspapers Reprinted, No. 31: Daily Sketch for 19 August, 1926, London, Peter Way, 1975.
4. Coombes, B. L., *These Poor Hands*, p. 176.
5. *Ibid.*, p. 177.
6. Renshaw, P., *op. cit.*, p. 236.
7. Mowat, C. L., *op. cit.*, pp. 323–4.
8. Nicolson, H., *George V*, p. 419.
9. Murray, *op. cit.*, p. 170.
10. Page Arnot, R., *op. cit.*, p. 300.
11. *Ibid.*, p. 464.
12. Garside, *op. cit.*, p. 204.
13. Page Arnot, R., *op. cit.*, p. 463
14. By-Election Results: 1924–1927. The Labour Year Book, 1927, pp. 30–1.
15. Daily Herald, 25 May, 1926.
16. Cole, G. D. H., *History of the Labour Party*, p. 193.

Chapter 8
1. Zweig, F., *Men in the Pits*, p. 39.
2. Lubin, I., etc., *op. cit.*, p. 192.
3. Webb, S., *Story of the Durham Miners*, p. 72.
4. Boyd, N., *Coal, Pits and Pitmen*, p. 25.
5. Dataller, R., *From a Pitman's Notebook*, p. 86.

6. Carter, Paul and Carol, *The Miners of Kilsyth in the 1926 General Strike and Lock-Out*, p. 9.
7. Conversation with ex-miner, Tondee, Glamorgan, March, 1975.
8. Western Mail, 13 June, 1926.
9. Cook, A. J., *The Nine Days*, p. 24.
10. Western Mail, 10 June, 1926.
11. Conversation in Coalville, Leicestershire, Working Men's Club, June, 1975.
12. Punch, 19 May, 1926.
13. Sharp, Evelyn, 'Diary of the General Strike', New Leader, 21 May, 1926.
14. Boothby, B. J., 'The How and Why of the Strike', New Leader, 21 May, 1926.
15. Nevinson, H. W., 'Mr. Churchill has his day', New Leader, 21 May, 1926.

Chapter 9

1. Middlemas, R. K., *The Clydesiders*, p. 202.
2. Brockway, F., *Inside the Left*, p. 145.
3. Stalin, J. V., *The General Strike, 1926,* Labour Monthly, April, 1953.
4. *Red Money*, p. 27.
5. Page Arnot, R., *The Miners: Years of Struggle*, p. 49.
6. Renshaw, P., *op. cit.*, p. 237.
7. Bosanquet, Helen, *The Poor Law Report of 1909*, p. 1.
8. Trevelyan, G. M., *English Social History*: Vol. IV, p. 77.
9. Public Records Office: MH57/115/X/J:766 7
10. The Times, 6 June, 1926.
11. Letter of 9 September, 1926: PRO: MH57/115/X/J:766 7
12. Ministry of Health Statistics: Labour Year Book, 1927, p. 431.

Chapter 10

1. Martin, Kingsley, *The British Public and the General Strike*, p. 119.
2. Letter (written before 15 June) to Colliery Guardian, 18 June, 1926.
3. Garside, W. R., *op. cit.*, p. 208.
4. Brailsford, N. H., 'An Armistice in the Mines', New Leader, 2 July, 1926.
5. New Leader, 2 July, 1926.
6. House of Commons Debate, 197. 5s., 938.
7. Renshaw, P., *op. cit.*, p. 241.
8. O'Brien, W., *The Irish Revolution*, p. 144.

9. Fischer, L., *The Life of Mahatma Gandhi*, p. 274.
10. *Ibid.*, p. 275.
11. Nanda, B. R., *Mahatma Gandhi*, p. 274.
12. Birkenhead, Earl of, *Last Essays*, Chapter VIII, 'The General Strike'.
13. Birkenhead, Second Earl of, *F. E.*, p. 544.
14. Farman, C., *op. cit.*, p. 248.
15. Symons, J., *op. cit.*, p. 233.
16. Taylor, A. J. P., *op. cit.*, p. 242.
17. 31 August, 1926.
18. Page Arnot, R., 'The Miners Struggle in Mid-Summer 1926', The Labour Monthly, July, 1926, p. 402.
19. Lubin, I., etc., *op. cit.*, p. 178.
20. Murphy, J. T., *The Political Meaning of the General Strike*, p. 122.

Chapter 11

1. Coombes, B. L., *op. cit.*, p. 177.
2. Shinwell, E., *Conflict Without Malice*, p. 99.
3. Labour Year Book, 1927, p. 272.
4. Coombes, B. L., *op. cit.*, p. 177.
5. *Ibid.*, pp. 178–80.
6. Leeson, R. A., *Strike*, p. 106.
7. *Ibid.*, p. 107.
8. Ponsonby, Arthur, M.P., 'The Government for the Mineowners' New Leader, 9 July, 1926.

Chapter 12

1. Moyes, W. A., *The Banner Book*, p. 69.
2. Journal and North Star, 19 July, 1926.
3. Garside, W. R., *op. cit.*, p. 297.
4. *Ibid.*, p. 205.
5. Mason, A., *The Government and the General Strike*, pp. 392–3.
6. DMA, 19 May and 27 May, 1926.
7. Newcastle Daily Journal, 5 May, 1926.
8. PRO: MH57/115/X/J:766 7; 15 November, 1926.
9. Tracey, H. (ed.), *op. cit.*, Vol. III, p. 259.
10. Conversation at Ushaw Moor, Co. Durham, January, 1975.
11. Clarke, J. F., and Leonard, J. W., *The General Strike*, 1926; Archive Teaching Unit No. 7., Document 27.
12. *Ibid.*, Handbook, p. 25.
13. Longmate, N., *If Britain Had Fallen*, p. 185.

Chapter 13

1. Fyfe, H., *Behind the Scenes of the Great Strike*, p. 59.
2. Farman, C., *op. cit.*, p. 148.
3. Renshaw, P., *op. cit.*, p. 214.
4. New Leader, 23 July, 1926.
5. Wise, E. F., M.P., 'The End to Coal Peace', New Leader, 23 July, 1926.
6. New Leader, 23 July, 1926.
7. Page Arnot, R., *op. cit.*, p. 461.
8. *Ibid.*, p. 471–2.
9. TUC General Council Report, July, 1926.
10. One of the best summaries of this whole episode of the Lock-Out is contained in 'The Story of the Warwickshire Struggle', by Sydney B. M. Potter in the New Leader, 6 August, 1926.
11. Middlemas, K., and Barnes, J., *op. cit.*, p. 432.
12. *Ibid.*, pp. 393–4.
13. *Ibid.*, p. 433.
14. 'South Wales Sees it Through', New Leader, 20 August, 1926.
15. Daily Chronicle, 23 August, 1926.
16. Symons, J., *op. cit.*, p. 224.
17. Page Arnot, R., *op. cit.*, p. 476.
18. 3 September, 1926.

Chapter 14

1. Western Mail, 2 September, 1926.
2. Page Arnot, R., *op. cit.*, p. 482.
3. 10 September, 1926.
4. Middlemas, K., and Barnes, J., *op. cit.*, pp. 437–8
5. *Ibid.*, p. 440.
6. Symons, J., *op. cit.*, p. 224.
7. Page Arnot, R., *op. cit.*, p. 507.
8. Brockway, F., *op. cit.*, p. 194.
9. The Economist, 21 November, 1926.
10. Renshaw, *op. cit.*, p. 239.
11. Zweig, F., *op. cit.*, p. 10.
12. Butts, Frank, 'The Nation and the Athenaeum', 30 July, 1921.

PART III
Chapter 15
1. Retired pitman, still active in social work. Tyne and Wear.
2. Woman in fifties who had recently lost an aged, invalid parent. Northumberland.
3. Retired collier, Pontypridd, Glam.
4. Union official and one time miner. Tonyrefail, Glam.
5. Retired miner who had done 51 years underground. Newcastle-upon-Tyne.
6. Newcastle-upon-Tyne widow.
7. Veteran collier. Coalville, Leicestershire.
8. Retired seamstress and nurse. Near Newcastle-upon-Tyne.
9. Miner's widow. Langley Park, County Durham.
10. Pensioner whose late husband had been a pit manager. Northumberland.
11. Newcastle widow (aged 76) whose husband had become a Methoodist minister.
12. Veteran miner's second wife. Ushaw Moor, County Durham.
13. Retired Civil Servant. Trealaw, Rhondda Valley, Glam.
14. Widow of former barman, now 77. Sunderland.

Bibliography

APPLETON, W. A., *What We Want and What We Are* (London: Hodder & Stoughton 1921)

BADGER, ALFRED B., *Man in Employment* (London: Arthur Baker 1958)

BARNES, GEORGE N., *Industrial Conflict: The Way Out* (London: Pitman 1924)

BAYLISS, F. J., *British Wages Councils*: (Oxford: Basil Blackwell 1962)

BEVAN, ANEURIN, M.P., *Why Not Trust the Tories?* (London: Victor Gollancz 1944)

BIRKENHEAD, Earl of, *Last Essays* (London: Cassel 1930)

BIRKENHEAD, Second Earl of, *F. E.* (London: Eyre & Spottiswoode 1960)

BLACK, CLEMENTINA, *Sweated Industry and the Minimum Wage* (London: Duckworth 1907)

BLOOMFIELD, MEYER, *The New Labour Movement in Britain* (London: T. Fisher Unwin Ltd. 1922)

BOSANQUET, HELEN, *The Poor Law Report of 1909* (London: Macmillan 1911)

BOYD, NELSON, *Coal, Pits and Pitmen* (London: Whitaker 1892)

BROCKWAY, FENNER, *Inside the Left* (London: George Allen & Unwin 1942)

BROWN, TOM, *The British General Strike* (London: Freedom Press 1943)

BRYANT, ARTHUR, *English Saga 1840–1940* (London: Collins 1943)

CARTER, PAUL & CAROL, *The Miners of Kilsyth in the 1926 General Strike and Lock-Out* (History Group Pamphlet 58: London 1974)

CITRINE, Lord, *Men and Work* (London: Hutchinson 1944)

CLARKE, J. F. and LEONARD, J. W., *The General Strike* (Newcastle-upon-Tyne, Education Dept.)

CLYNES, J. R., *Memoirs* (London: Hutchinson 1937)

Coal Industry (Sankey) Commission, Report, 1919. (Cmd. 359)

COATES, KEN, *Democracy in the Mines* (London: Spokesman Books 1974)

COLE, G. D. H., *A History of the Labour Party from 1914* (London: Routledge & Kegan Paul 1948)

COLE, G. D. H., *A Short History of the Working Class Movement 1789–1927* (London: George Allen & Unwin 1927)

Communist Party of Great Britain, *The General Strike in the North East*. (Historian's Group No. 22 1961)

COOK, A. J., *The Nine Days* (London: Co-Operative Printing Society 1926)

COOMBES, B. L., *These Poor Hands*. The Autobiography of a Miner in South Wales (London: Victor Gollancz 1936)

COOPER, DUFF, *Old Men Forget* (London: Rupert Hart-Davis 1955)

COURT, W. H. B., *Coal* (London: H.M. Stationery Office and Longmans Green 1951)

DATALLER, ROGER, *From a Pitman's Note Book* (London: Jonathan Cape 1925)

DEMANT, V. A., *The Miner's Distress and the Coal Problem* (London: SCM 1929)

DOBRÉE, BONAMY, *English Revolts* (London: Herbert Joseph 1937)

Durham Miners' Association (DMA) Minutes of Council and Executive Committee Meetings, 1913–1960 (Durham: National Union of Miners)

EDWARDS, H. W. J., *The Good Patch* (London: National Book Association & Jonathan Cape)

FARMAN, CHRISTOPHER, *The General Strike, May 1926* (London: Rupert Hart-Davis 1972)

FISCHER, LOUIS, *The Life of Mahatma Gandhi* (London: Jonathan Cape 1951)

FOOT, MICHAEL, *Aneurin Bevan*, Vol. I (London Macgibbon & Kee 1963)

FURNEAUX, ROBERT, *William Wilberforce* (London: Hamish Hamilton 1974)

FYFE, HAMILTON, *Behind the Scenes of the Great Strike* (London: Labour Publishing Company 1926)

GARSIDE, W. R., *The Durham Miners 1919–1960* (London: George Allen & Unwin 1971)

HANNINGTON, WAL, *Unemployed Struggles 1919–1936* (London: Lawrence & Wishart 1936)

HOBSBAWN, E. J., *Industry and Empire* (London: Weidenfeld & Nicolson 1968)

HODGES, FRANK, *My Adventures as a Labour Leader* (London: Newnes 1925)

HODGES, FRANK, *Nationalisation of the Mines* (London: Leonard Parsons)

HUTT, ALLEN, *The Post-War History of the British Working Class* (London: Victor Gollancz 1937)

JAMES, R. R., *Memoirs of a Conservative* (Weidenfeld & Nicolson 1969)

JONES, TOM, *Whitehall Diary* (ed. R. K. Middlemas) Vol. II (London: Oxford University Press 1969)

LAWSON, JACK, (Lord Lawson of Beamish) *A Man's Life* (London: Hodder & Stoughton 1944)

LEESON, R. A., *Strike, A Live History* (London: George Allen & Unwin 1973)

LONGMATE, NORMAN, *If Britain Had Fallen* (London: BBC and Arrow Books 1975)

LUBIN, ISADOR and EVERETT, HELEN, *The British Coal Dilemma* (London: George Allen & Unwin 1927)

MACFARLANE, L. J., *The British Communist Party* (London: Macgibbon & Kee 1966)

MACNEILL WEIR, L., *The Tragedy of Ramsay MacDonald* (London: Secker & Warburg 1938)

MARTIN, KINGSLEY, *The British Public and the General Strike* (London: Hogarth Press 1926)

MASON, ANTHONY, *The General Strike in the North East* (Hull: University of Hull Publications 1970)

MASON, ANTHONY, *The Government and the General Strike, 1926* (International Review of History, XIV 1969)

MASON, ANTHONY, *The Local Press and the General Strike:* An Example from the North East (Durham: Durham University Journal, June, 1969)

Men Without Work. A Report made to the Pilgrim Trust Introduction by the Archbishop of York (London: Cambridge University Press 1938)

MIDDLEMAS, KEITH and BARNES, JOHN, *Baldwin* (London: Weidenfeld & Nicolson 1969)

MIDDLEMAS, R. K., *The Clydesiders* (London: Hutchinson 1965)

MOORE, ROBERT, *Pit-Men, Preachers and Politics*: The Effects of Methodism in a Durham Mining Community (London: Cambridge University Press 1974)

MORAN, Lord, *Winston Churchill, The Struggle for Survival* (London: Constable 1966)

MOWAT, C. L., *Britain Between the Wars, 1918–1940* (London: Methuen 1955)

MOWAT, C. L., *The General Strike, 1926* (Archives Series) (London: Edward Arnold 1969)

MOYES, WILLIAM A., *The Banner Book* (Newcastle-upon-Tyne: Frank Graham 1974)

MURRAY, JOHN, *The General Strike of 1926* (London: Lawrence & Wishart 1951)

MURPHY, J. T., *The Political Meaning of the General Strike* (London: Communist Party of Great Britain 1926)

NANDA, B. R., *Mahatma Gandhi* (London: George Allen & Unwin 1958)

NEARING, SCOTT, *The British General Strike.* An Economic Interpretation of its Background and Significance (New York: Vanguard Press 1926)

NEWSOM, J., *Out of the Pit.* A Challenge to the Comfortable (Oxford: Basil Blackwell 1935)

NICOLSON, HAROLD, *King George V* (London: Constable 1952)

PAGE ARNOT, R., *The General Strike* (London: Labour Research Department 1926)

PAGE ARNOT, R., *The Miners: Years of Struggle* (London: George Allen & Unwin 1953)

PALME DUTT, R., *The Meaning of the General Strike* (London: Communist Party of Great Britain 1926)

RAYNES, J. R., *Coal and Its Conflicts* (London: Benn 1928)

Red Money: A Statement of the Facts relating to the Money raised in Russia during the General Strike and Mining Lock-Out in Britain. Prepared by the All-Russian Council of Trade Unions. Translated by Eden and Cedar Paul. (London: Labour Research Department 1926)

REITH, J. C. W., *Into the Wind* (London: Hodder & Stoughton 1949)

RENSHAW, PATRICK, *The General Strike* (London: Eyre Methuen 1975)

Royal Commission on the Coal Industry (Samuel) Report (Cmd. 2600) 1925

SHINWELL, EMANUEL, *Conflict Without Malice* (London: Victor Gollancz 1955)

SLATER, MONTAGUE, *Stay-Down Miner* (London: Martin Lawrence 1936)

STRACHEY, JOHN (ed.), The Socialist Review New Series No. 5 (London: The Socialist Review, June 1926)

SYMONS, JULIAN, *The General Strike.* An Historical Portrait (London: Cresset Press 1957)

TAYLOR, A. J. P., *English History 1914–1945* (London: Oxford University Press 1965)

TRACEY, HERBERT (ed.), *The Book of the Labour Party* (London: Caxton Publishing Company)

TREVELYAN, G. M., *English Social History*, Vol. IV (London: Longmans 1952)

TRORY, ERNIE, *The Sacred Band.* A Contribution to the Social History of Brighton (Brighton: Crabtree Press 1946)

TROTSKY, LEON, *Collected Writings and Speeches on Britain*, ed., R.

Chappell and Alan Clinton (London: New Park Publications 1974)

TRUEMAN, Sir ARTHUR, (ed.), *The Coalfields of Great Britain* (London: Edward Arnold 1954)

TURNER, H. A., *Trade Union Growth, Structure and Policy* (London: George Allen & Unwin 1962)

VAN THAL, H. (ed.), *The Prime Ministers,* Vol. II, (London: George Allen & Unwin 1975)

WEBB, SIDNEY, *The Story of the Durham Miners, 1662–1920* (London: Fabian Society 1921)

WHITE, JOHN W., and SIMPSON, ROBERT, *Jubilee History of West Stanley Co-Operative Society Limited,* 1876–1926 (Pelaw-on-Tyne: Co-Operative Wholesale Society 1926)

WILLIAMS, D. J., *Capitalist Combination of the Coal Industry* (London: Labour Publishing Co. Ltd. 1924)

WILLIAMS, W. H., *The Miners' Two Bob* (London: Martin Lawrence 1936)

WILSON, J. HAROLD, *New Deal for Coal* (London: Contact 1945)

YOUNG, G. M., *Stanley Baldwin* (London: Hart-Davis 1952)

ZWEIG, F., *Men in the Pits* (London: Victor Gollancz 1948)

Principal Newspapers and Periodicals consulted:

British Gazette
British Worker
Daily Chronicle
Daily Herald
Daily Mail
Daily Telegraph
Durham Chronicle
Economist
Evening Chronicle (Newcastle-upon-Tyne)
Journal and North Star
Labour Monthly
Leicester Mercury
Manchester Guardian
Morning Post
New Leader
Northern Voice
Sunday Worker
The Times
Western Mail (Cardiff)
Westminster Worker

Index